Islamic Finance in Western Higher Education

IE Business Publishing

IE Business Publishing and Palgrave Macmillan have launched a collection of high-quality books in the areas of Business and Management, Economics and Finance. This important series is characterized by innovative ideas and theories, entrepreneurial perspectives, academic rigor and practical approaches which will make these books invaluable to the business professional, scholar and student alike.

IE Business School is one of the world's leading institutions dedicated to educating business leaders. Palgrave Macmillan, part of Macmillan Group, has been serving the learning and professional sector for more than 160 years.

The series, put together by these eminent international partners, will enable executives, students, management scholars and professionals worldwide to have access to the most valuable information and critical new arguments and theories in the fields of Business and Management, Economics and Finance from the leading experts at IE Business School.

Titles include:

ISLAMIC FINANCE IN WESTERN HIGHER EDUCATION
Ahmed Belouafi, Abderrazak Belabes and Cristina Trullols (*editors*)

ISLAMIC ECONOMICS AND FINANCE
Jonathan Langton, Cristina Trullols and Abdullah Q. Turkistani (*editors*)

BEYOND TRIBALISM
Celia de Anca

SIMPLY SEVEN
Erik Schlie, Jörg Rheinboldt and Niko Waesche

THE LONG CONVERSATION
Peter Kawalek, Boumediene Ramdani, Gastón González and Oswaldo Lorenzo

THE LEARNING CURVE
Santiago Iñiguez de Onzoño

IE Business Publishing Series
Series Standing Order ISBN: 978–0–230–29248–2

You can receive future titles in this series as they are published by placing a standing order. Please contact your bookseller or, in case of difficulty, write to us at the address below with your name and address, the title of the series and the ISBN quoted above.

Customer Services Department, Macmillan Distribution Ltd, Houndmills, Basingstoke, Hampshire RG21 6XS, England

Islamic Finance in Western Higher Education

Developments and Prospects

Edited by

Ahmed Belouafi
Islamic Economics Institute (IEI), King Abdulaziz University, Saudi Arabia

Abderrazak Belabes
Islamic Economics Institute (IEI), King Abdulaziz University, Saudi Arabia

and

Cristina Trullols
IE Business School, Spain

palgrave
macmillan

First published 2012 by
PALGRAVE MACMILLAN

Palgrave Macmillan in the UK is an imprint of Macmillan Publishers Limited,
registered in England, company number 785998, of Houndmills, Basingstoke,
Hampshire RG21 6XS.

Palgrave Macmillan in the US is a division of St Martin's Press LLC,
175 Fifth Avenue, New York, NY 10010.

Palgrave Macmillan is the global academic imprint of the above companies
and has companies and representatives throughout the world.

Palgrave® and Macmillan® are registered trademarks in the United States,
the United Kingdom, Europe and other countries.

ISBN 978–1–137–26368–1

This book is printed on paper suitable for recycling and made from fully
managed and sustained forest sources. Logging, pulping and manufacturing
processes are expected to conform to the environmental regulations of the
country of origin.

A catalogue record for this book is available from the British Library.

A catalog record for this book is available from the Library of Congress.

10 9 8 7 6 5 4 3 2 1
21 20 19 18 17 16 15 14 13 12

Printed and bound in the United States of America

Contents

Part II Islamic Finance Higher Education in the West: Cases and Experiments

Part III Islamic Finance Higher Education in the West: Research and Other Initiatives

List of Figures and Tables

Figures

Tables

Notes on Contributors

Editors

Ahmed Belouafi is a researcher at the Islamic Economics Institute (IEI), King Abdulaziz University. He holds a Master's in Money Banking and Finance and a Ph.D. in Economics from Sheffield University, UK. Before joining the IEI he taught Islamic Financial Contracts and Institutions at the University of Birmingham and London Open College. He has published and participated in various national and international academic and professional activities relating to Islamic economics and finance. He mainly researches Islamic finance education and curricula at higher-education level, Islamic finance in Europe, Islamic finance and responsible financing, Islamic economics and finance literature by non-Muslims, and Islamic finance and financial stability.

Abderrazak Belabes is a researcher at the Islamic Economics Institute, King Abdulaziz University. He holds an MSc in Electronic Engineering, an MSc in Mathematical Economics and Econometrics, and a Ph.D. in Analysis and Policy in Economics from the School of Higher Studies in Social Sciences, Paris. He teaches Islamic Finance from a geo-economic perspective at the University of Strasbourg and Ethical Finance at the International Institute of Islamic Thought, Paris. He mainly researches economic methodology, ethical finance, computational finance, Islamic finance education and the regulatory framework for the Islamic finance industry.

Cristina Trullols is an associate professor of Microfinance at the Saudi-Spanish Centre for Islamic Economics and Finance (SCIEF), IE Business School. She holds a Master's degree from the Executive Financial Management Programme at the IE Business School, with an MBA from the University of Quebec and a BA in Economics and International Relations from Boston College. She worked as a manager in financial control at Citigroup, and as a financial analyst supervisor in the Superintendence of Banks in the Dominican Republic. Her main interests are microfinance, economic development, alternative finance (including Islamic microfinance) and the regulatory framework of financial institutions.

Contributors

Adel Ahmed is Accounting and Islamic Finance award director, senior lecturer at Liverpool Hope University, Hope Business School. He is involved with career planning development to enhance graduate employability. Adel obtained his BSc and MSc in Accounting from the University of Alexandria, Egypt and his Ph.D. from Liverpool Business School. He has taught accounting and finance courses at various higher education institutions, including Alexandria University and Leeds Metropolitan University. He researches financial accounting, Islamic finance and analysis of Islamic financial institutions. He has published papers and made conference presentations on these subjects. He is a member of the British Accounting Association and Islamic Banking and Finance Group. He is a reviewer for a number of journals and is a member of the editorial advisory board of *International Journal of Islamic and Middle Eastern Finance and Management*. He is an external examiner for a number of universities and business practitioner accreditation bodies.

Abdul Karim Aldohni is a lecturer at Newcastle Law School, Newcastle University, UK, where he teaches the core Islamic finance modules on the Business School MSc programmes. He obtained his Ph.D. in Banking and Financial Regulation at Leeds University. He is a specialist in commercial law and financial regulation with special reference to Islamic banking and finance. His research focuses primarily on the legal and regulatory aspects of Islamic finance.

Celia de Anca is currently director of the Centre for Diversity in Global Management at IE Business School. She was previously the director of corporate programmes at the Euro-Arab Management School (EAMS), Granada. She has also worked for the Fundación Cooperación Internacional y Promoción Ibero-América Europa (CIPIE) and at the International Division of Banco de Santander. She has a Master's degree from the Fletcher School of Law and Diplomacy (Boston), and from the Universidad Politécnica de Madrid. She holds a degree and Ph.D. from the Universidad Autónoma de Madrid, with a comparative thesis on Islamic, ethical/ecological investment funds and on the London Market. She is the co-author of *Managing Diversity in the Global Organization* (2007). She has had articles published in academic journals, in addition to regular articles in the press. She is a member of the Ethics Committee of InverCaixa's Ethics Fund, Spain and a member of the International Scientific Committee of the University Euromed in Marseille, France and a member of the Scientific and Academic Advisory Council of the Gender Equality Project. She is also a member of the Executive Committee at IE Business School. In 2008 she received the award of Woman Executive of the Year from the Business Women Association of Madrid (ASEME). She is fluent in Spanish, English, French and Arabic.

Simon Archer is a visiting professor at the ICMA Centre, Henley Business School, University of Reading, UK, with particular responsibility for Islamic Finance. He is also adjunct professor at INCEIF, Kuala Lumpur. Previously, he was professor of Financial Management at the University of Surrey, after being Midland Bank professor of Financial Sector Accounting at the University of Wales, Bangor. After studying PPE at Oxford University he qualified as a chartered accountant with Arthur Andersen in London and then moved to Price Waterhouse in Paris, where he became partner in charge of management consultancy services. He has undertaken numerous consultancy assignments, including acting as consultant to the Accounting and Auditing Organization for Islamic Financial Institutions (AAOIFI) and the Islamic Financial Services Board (IFSB). He has been a visiting professor at a number of universities and business schools, including IIUM in Malaysia, Bordeaux, Metz, Paris-Dauphine, HEC and EAP-ESCP in France, Copenhagen Business School in Denmark, and Frankfurt and Koblenz in Germany. Professor Archer is the author and coeditor of a considerable number of works and academic papers on international accounting and on issues in Islamic finance, including *Islamic Finance: Innovation and Growth* (2002) with Rifaat Ahmed Abdel Karim, *Islamic Finance: The Regulatory Challenge* (2007) with Rifaat Ahmed Abdel Karim and *Takaful Islamic Insurance: Concepts and Regulatory Issues* (2009) with Rifaat Ahmed Abdel Karim and Volker Nienhaus. In 2010 he received an award from the Central Bank of Bahrain and Kuwait Finance House, Bahrain for his 'outstanding contribution to the Islamic Financial Services Industry'.

Toseef Azid taught for more than 25 years at various universities in Pakistan. From 2005 to 2007 he was a visiting professor at Markfield Institute of Higher Education, UK. In 2006, he was scholar in residence at Los Angeles, USA. From 2008 to 2011, he taught at Taibah University, Madinah, Saudi Arabia and University Islam Sultan Sharif Ali, Brunei. He obtained his Ph.D. from the University of Wales, Aberystwyth, UK. He has published articles and presented papers at international conferences held in Australia, Canada, Saudi Arabia, Malaysia, Bahrain, Iran, Brunei, Indonesia, Qatar and Turkey. He mainly researches Islamic economics, labour economics and input–output analysis.

Abdelhafid Benamraoui is senior lecturer in Finance at the University of Westminster Business School. In 2003 he completed his Ph.D. in the area of banking and stock markets from the University of Greenwich. He started his academic career in 2000 teaching various undergraduate, postgraduate and professional courses. His research has been published in a number of refereed academic journals and the proceedings of national and international conferences. His expertise covers a wide range of areas, including conventional finance, banking, stock markets and Islamic finance.

Ishaq Bhatti is the founding director of the Islamic Banking and Finance Programme at La Trobe University (LTU), the first in Australasia. He is a member of LTU's academic board and previously taught at Monash, Griffith, and the University of Alberta. He has also visited Rider, Magberg, Hitotsubahi, Auckland and Middle Eastern Universities. He is the author of three books and more than 80 articles. He is a member of the editorial boards of various journals. His major areas of research, scholarship and teaching are in quantitative finance, Islamic finance and applied econometrics. He is a winner of the national ALTC award 2010, LTU curriculum award 2010 and postgraduate teaching award 2009. He was a member of the team that won AusTrade project, Victorian Department of Education ESL financial modelling project and Australian Research Council Discovery Grant jointly with Suren Basov. He is involved with multifaith activities at LTU's Centre for Dialogue, Melbourne city circle, Australian Intercultural Society. He is also involved with the Islamic council of Victoria's NILS (no interest loan scheme) in conjunction with National Australia Bank.

Ghassen Bouslama is professor of Finance at Reims Management School and an associate member of the 'Regrads' research centre at the University of Reims. He is the coordinator of Islamic Finance courses at Reims Management School and responsible for the Islamic Banking and Finance Certificate. He is the author of several academic and managerial articles and book chapters on banking and finance. He mainly researches in the field of Islamic finance, bank mergers and acquisitions, bank–SME relationship lending and organizational architecture.

Valentino Cattelan is a lecturer at the University of Rome Tor Vergata, Italy. He researches legal and financial pluralism, law and economics, Islamic law of finance, comparative law, European law and legal education. He qualified as a lawyer in the EU and actively contributes to seminars, workshops and conferences in Islamic law and finance. The

European Commission has awarded him a grant for a teaching module titled 'Integrating Islamic finance in the EU market' (September 2010–August 2013). He is the editor of *Integration through Legal Education: The Role of EU Legal Studies in Shaping the EU* (2012) and of the volume *Islamic Finance in Europe: Towards a Plural Financial System* (forthcoming, Edward Elgar).

Ibrahim Zeyyad Cekici is a Ph.D. candidate at Strasbourg University. His topic is the 'French Legal Framework of Islamic Credit Operation'. He is also a teacher and lecturer on Islamic finance. He has written papers on the legal aspect of Islamic finance. He was among the first to acquire a Master's degree in Islamic Finance from Strasbourg University.

Mohamed Daoudi is an assistant professor at the Department of Geography and GIS, Faculty of Arts and Humanities, King Abdulaziz University. He holds an MSc in Physical Geography, an MSc in Regional Planning and a Ph.D. in Geography from the University of Liege, Belgium. His research focuses mainly on physical geography, teledetection and geographic information systems.

Abul Hassan is a lecturer in Finance, Markfield Institute of Higher Education, UK. He obtained his MSc in International Banking and Finance from Loughborough University, UK and his Ph.D. in Finance from the University of Durham, UK. His teaching and research interests include corporate finance, Islamic portfolio management, security investment analysis, corporate governance; financial reporting and development economics. He is also a visiting lecturer of the postgraduate programme (MSc) in Islamic Economics and Finance at Trishakti University, Jakarta, Indonesia. He has attended international academic conferences in Europe and Asia and published papers in academic journals. His forthcoming book is titled *Contemporary Issues on Islamic Banking*.

Reza Zain Jaufeerally is a specialist researcher in Islamic and Ethical Finance at the Centre for Economics and Ethics at the University of Leuven. A barrister by training (Middle Temple), he holds a triple LLM (International Business, Intellectual Property and ICT law specializations) from the University of Leuven. His research focus is the synergies between Islamic finance, ethical finance and socially responsible investment and entrepreneurship. He has acted as an expert on Islamic finance for Bain & Company in their recent study of Islamic finance in France. He is currently involved in the creation of ethical and *Shari'ah*-compliant financial instruments.

Kader Merbouh has a Master's in Market Finance from the University of Toulouse. He also has a Banking and Finance Master's from the Paris XII University. He is the coordinator of the Islamic finance branch (Executive Master and conferences) of Paris Dauphine University. He is often invited to advise on ethical finance in universities, training centres and French local authorities. He has published several papers and articles on equitable finance in general and Islamic finance in particular. He was one of the founders of the first training courses in Islamic finance in France and coorganized the first education and business trip in Malaysia in collaboration with the Association of Ethics and Islamic Finance (Dauphine University). He is the founder and president of Finequity, dedicated to research and communication on ethical finance, banking, micro-finance and communication between professionals. His research themes are micro-finance, Islamic finance, socially responsible investment (SRI), social banking (Web 2.0 finance) and the convergence between Islamic and ethical finance and education.

Philip Molyneux is professor in Banking and Finance and head of the College of Business, Social Science and Law. He has published widely in the banking and financial services area, including articles in *European Economic Review, Journal of Banking and Finance, Journal of Money, Credit and Banking, Economics Letters* and *Economica*. Between 2002 and 2005 he acted as a member of the ECON Financial Services expert panel for the European Parliament. His most recent coauthored texts include *Thirty Years of Islamic Banking* (2005), *Shareholder Value in Banking* (2006), *Introduction to Banking* (2006) and *Introduction to Global Financial Markets* (2010). He recently coedited (with Berger and Wilson) the *Oxford Handbook of Banking* (2010). His research focuses mainly on the structural features of banking systems, modelling bank performance, Islamic banking and wealth management. He has recently held visiting professorships at Bocconi University (Milan), Erasmus University (Rotterdam), Bolzano Free University (Italy) and the University of Limoges. He has acted as a consultant to the New York Federal Reserve Bank, World Bank, European Commission, UK Treasury, Citibank Private Bank, Bermuda Commercial Bank, McKinsey's, Credit Suisse and various other international banks and consulting firms. In July 2010 he was invited by HM Treasury/Government Office for Science to act as an expert on a Foresight Project on technological advances and the implications for financial markets.

Volker Nienhaus received his Ph.D. in Economics from the University of Bochum. He was full professor of Economics at the German universities of Trier (1989–90) and Bochum (1990–2004) and president of the University of Marburg (2004–10). He holds an honorary professorship at the University of Bochum. He became visiting professor at the ICMA Centre, Henley Business School, University of Reading, UK, in 2010. He was a visiting scholar at the University of Malaya in Kuala Lumpur (2010–11) and visiting professor at the Qatar Faculty of Islamic Studies in Doha (2011). He served as a member of several advisory committees and boards, including the Academic Advisory Council of the German Federal Ministry of Economic Cooperation and Development in Bonn (1998–2008) and the Governing Council of the International Centre for Education in Islamic Finance (INCEIF) in Kuala Lumpur (since 2006) where he also became an adjunct professor in 2012. His current research focuses on service sector economics and Islamic economics and finance.

Pierre-Charles Pradier has a Ph.D. in economics from ENS-Cachan as well as a BA in history from Université Paris 1 Panthéon-Sorbonne. He is now vice-president for education at Paris 1 Panthéon-Sorbonne and president of the Conference of the Deans of Economics and Management Departments. He served as dean of the Economics department of Université Paris 1 Panthéon-Sorbonne from 2004 to 2011. He researches insurance, risk theory (his book *La notion de risque en économie* was awarded the Risques-Les Echos Prize in 2007) as well as alternative financial systems. He is a founding member of the Laboratoire d'Excellence RéFi (on FInancial REgulation) and runs, together with Abdullah Turkistani, the joint chair for Ethics and Financial Norms at King Abdulaziz University of Jeddah.

Tariq Saeed graduated from the International Islamic University, Islamabad. After completing his Ph.D. he worked for Halala Mutual Investment Company, the first *Shari'ah*-compliant mutual fund in Europe. He researches quantitative financial methods, computer-based simulation models, Islamic financial instruments and teaching methodologies and approaches. He works at Guthlaxton College, Leicester and is a visiting lecturer at Markfield Institute of Higher Education.

Ignacio de la Torre is the academic director of the Master's in Finance Programmes at IE Business School and partner of Arcano (equity capital markets). With 14 years of experience in diverse fields of investment banking (corporate finance, equity research, specialist sales of media stocks, generalist sales of European equities at UBS and Deutsche Bank), he has been involved as a professor at IE for the last seven years, teaching creative accounting, macroeconomics, finance and valuation courses. He is also founder and vice-president of 'Financieros sin Fronteras'. His research has been quite diverse. He recently coauthored *El Final de la Crisis,* a book on the interrelations between finance and macroeconomics in the credit crisis, awarded the Everis Prize 2009. In 2008 he published *Creative Accounting Exposed,* a book on creative accounting practices and detection mechanisms. His dissertation involved the banking activities of Templar Knights during the thirteenth century (as a result, he later published in 2004 *Los Templarios y el Origen de la Banca,* praised by Nobel Laureate Sir Aaron Klug as 'a key step in research on the origin of banking'). He has also published a book on the origins of Islamism (*Islamismo: el radicalism desvelado*), commended by Jorge Dezcallar, former head of the Spanish Intelligence service (CNI) as 'an excellent work for understanding the ideological roots of Islamism'.

Olivia Orozco de la Torre coordinates the Socioeconomic and Business Programme of Casa Árabe and the International Institute of Arab and Muslim World Studies, where she is the chief editor of a bimonthly economics and business bulletin. She has edited several books on contemporary economic issues in Arab countries and written numerous articles on Islamic economics and finance. In 1999 she coauthored with Professor Alejandro Lorca the first book in Spanish about Islamic banking. She obtained her Ph.D. in History and Civilization at the European University Institute of Florence. Her thesis compared monetary thought of Islamic and Christian scholars in the late medieval Mediterranean. She obtained an MA in Contemporary Arab Studies at Georgetown University and graduated in Economic Sciences at the Autonóma University of Madrid.

Foreword

Islamic Finance (IF) has caught the attention of students all over the world, especially after the crisis of conventional banking in 2007–8. Muslims and non-Muslims want to learn more about IF and to understand the special qualities of what is often seen as an ethical alternative to greedy capitalism. Many students want to explore IF further and suggest their own research projects – often comparative studies of particular aspects of conventional and Islamic banking. Finally, graduates of Western institutions of higher education hope for attractive careers in the IF industry. Acquiring knowledge (learning), applying knowledge (employment) and enhancing knowledge (research) are probably the main motivations of students who enrol in IF programmes of Western universities, colleges, law schools and business schools.

As documented by this book, there is a vast variety of degree programmes in the West, with different approaches and specializations. Beyond all differences, all programmes may face a similar problem, namely that the realities of IF do not meet the expectations of students:

- The reality of Islamic banks may be less ethical or less commercially distinct from conventional banks than expected.
- The employment opportunities may be less obvious and abundant than expected.
- Access to relevant documents and reliable data for research may be more difficult than expected.

While an unexpected mismatch of expectations and realities can create frustration, a prepared encounter with discrepancies and inconsistencies may be taken by students as an intellectual challenge which can release creative energies.

Islamic finance from two perspectives

The study of IF can start from two very different (if not opposing) points of departure. The first is an abstract model of an ideal Islamic economy with an elaborate set of specific institutions (and behavioural assumptions). IF is embedded in a comprehensive Islamic order which is very different from the existing economic systems of Muslim countries. The

second point of departure is the actual business practice of IF institutions as they have emerged in the secular economies of Muslim countries since the mid-1970s.

1. Islamic Economics (IE) emerged as a new academic discipline in
   some universities of the Muslim world in the mid-1970s. Long before
   that, the idea of an IE order and an IF system took shape in the 1930s
   and 1940s when a political movement called for a separate state for
   the Muslims after the withdrawal of the colonial power from British
   India. When this state – Pakistan – became a reality in 1947, it was
   rather secular in its character. The debate on the appropriate order
   continued, and the IE system was presented as a third way between
   interest-based capitalism and godless communism, based on principles found in the *Qur'an* and the *Sunnah*. It was expected that such
   a system would be different from what had been known until then
   and that it would boost economic development. IF is only one – albeit
   a crucial – element of an IE order. Other elements are, in particular,
   zakat and *waqf,* and more recently *takaful.* The early writings of
   Islamic economists conveyed the message that the fundamental difference between conventional finance and IF is the replacement of
   interest-based loans by profit-and-loss sharing (PLS) modes. The academic literature since the 1970s expounded arguments for the superiority of a comprehensive IE order with a PLS-based financial system
   in terms of stability, efficiency and justice. The macroeconomic
   models of Islamic economists usually neglected permissible non-PLS
   modes (such as mark-up sales or the leasing of assets at fixed rental
   rates): their economic characteristics were far too close to interest-
   based financings and thus of not much relevance for an economic
   system that was supposed to be as distinct from the interest-based
   economy as possible. It took quite a long time (until the late 1980s)
   before Islamic economists conceded that the neglected non-PLS
   modes of finance were not only permissible but the major techniques
   applied by the 'real world' Islamic banks. Students who have studied
   IF in the broader perspective of socio-economic reforms were often
   disappointed by this practice of Islamic banks.
2. Contemporary Islamic banks have come into existence in the Arab
   world since the second half of the 1970s and in Asia since the
   1980s. They were generally (with few exceptions such as the Islamic
   Development Bank in Jeddah) set up as private commercial enterprises. Their shareholders were businessmen who expected to get
   all the financial services so far provided by conventional banks in a

Shari'ah-compliant manner from their new Islamic banks. They did not aim at a change of the economic system, but were content with a different legal (i.e. *Shari'ah*-compliant) underpinning of their actual businesses within the established (capitalist) economic system.

Confusion was caused and misconceptions were created when supporters and representatives of Islamic banks took up Islamic economists' arguments of a systemic superiority of IF in keynote addresses and media appearances. This suggested that the operating Islamic banks were implementing the economists' models, but this was not the case: Islamic banks continued to shy away from PLS modes of financing and applied *Shari'ah*-compliant functional equivalents for interest-bearing loans. The replication of conventional products and techniques was even reinforced during the last decade when Western banks made a substantial contribution to the growth of the IF industry in quantitative terms and with respect to the structuring of products: conventional market players – including global players such as Citibank, Deutsche Bank or PNB Paribas – have set up Islamic windows or subsidiaries or converted the whole business of existing banks into *Shari'ah*-compliant transactions. Conventional banks did not enter into the *Shari'ah*-compliant business for the sake of Islam – particularly not if their shareholders were non-Muslims in foreign countries. They did penetrate the Islamic market because they saw profitable business opportunities or threats to their conventional business due to *Shari'ah* preferences of major clients. Islamic banks are generally not charitable or developmental institutions, but for-profit enterprises. There are many good reasons why the Islamic banking practice falls short of the participatory modes of financing: Islamic banks have to compete with conventional banks in a system dominated by interest-based transactions and be afflicted by information asymmetries and principal agent problems. In such an environment, the *Shari'ah*-compliant replication of conventional products and techniques (via 'reverse engineering') is not a deviation from an ideal but a rational adaptation to the market situation. The problem of students here is that they see too few substantial differences to conventional finance and come to question the authenticity of IF – the long-standing 'form over substance debate'.

Teaching form and substance

Shari'ah scholars often insist that the main difference between Islamic and conventional banks is that IF is closely tied to the real economy.

When Islamic banks apply exchange contracts in their financing business, finance is always linked to the transfer of ownership or usufructs of real assets. This implies that Islamic banks are exposed to various types of market risks which do not burden conventional banks. For example, market prices may change while an Islamic bank owns an asset (which it has purchased upon the request of a customer), or banks are responsible for the maintenance of assets leased to customers (operating lease).

The specific risks are of relevance for the supervision and prudential regulation of Islamic banks. The Islamic Financial Services Board (IFSB) has compiled the specific market risks of the various *Shari'ah*-compliant exchange contracts used by Islamic banks. But the IFSB also lists a wide range of risk mitigation techniques to minimize (if not eliminate) the 'real-economy risks', and all these techniques are regularly applied by Islamic banks. It is important to understand the 'classical' nominate (exchange) contracts of Islamic law, but one must also be aware of contemporary modifications, combinations and additions which ensure that Islamic banks do become trading houses but remain financial institutions. They start 'trading' real assets only upon the specific request of a customer, and the customer is typically not looking at the bank as the physical provider of a required asset but as the financier of a purchase which he has factually arranged and executed by himself – even though he may legally have acted only as the 'agent' of the bank. The use of the legal form of trade and rent contracts for financing purposes creates a number of juristic complications, but the commercial substance of standard products of Islamic banks is hardly any different from that of conventional financing products.

But it would be a mistake to stop here. A comparison of conventional and IF must not only focus on the products and the instruments which are in the toolboxes of Islamic banks, it should also consider products and instruments that do *not* exist in IF. This reveals important differences in substance between the two concepts. For example, several *Shari'ah* prohibitions (such as unreasonable uncertainty and gambling) and principles of Islamic law (such as 'you must not sell what you don't own') have prevented the securitization of debt and the engineering of highly speculative derivatives. The toolboxes of IF institutions are restrained especially with respect to functional equivalents to instruments for financial trading activities within the financial sector. For Islamic economists, this is a major strength of an IF system which implies a superior stability, efficiency and equity. However, for some Islamic bankers (with a rather conventional mindset) this is a competitive disadvantage. They have initiated the structuring of financial instruments that could overcome the limitations and facilitate profitable trading activities within the financial sector. Prototypes have been designed, but they are still highly controversial and far from generally accepted.

While participants in training courses are familiarized with products and instruments which are in actual use, students of IF programmes in Western institutions of higher education should go beyond the practice and also understand major ongoing controversies. They should recognize the *Shari'ah* issues which hinder the structuring of functional equivalents for certain classes of widely used conventional instruments, and they should understand the systemic implications. They have to appreciate the efforts of *Shari'ah* scholars, financial engineers, lawyers and bank managers as well as regulators and economists in the continuous process of adaptation of centuries-old classical *Shari'ah* positions to the fundamentally different commercial conditions of today. This is desirable because controversies such as those on complex structured products or on the lack of appropriate tools for participatory financing (in particular of small- and medium-sized enterprises) shed light on the conceptual dynamism of IF. Tomorrow's *Shari'ah*-compliant financial innovations will emerge from today's controversies, and they will determine the impact of the growing IF industry on the global real economy and the international finance industry.

Besides the internal dynamism, students of IF in the West have to be aware of the external relations of *Shari'ah*-compliant contracts with the national legal system in which they are embedded. Even in countries with a very strong inclination towards Islam – such as Sudan, Saudi Arabia and Iran – the commercial law (in particular the corporate law) had been 'imported' from Europe (e.g. Britain, France, Switzerland), and it has never been replaced. Hence, the legal systems of Muslim countries are based either on common or on civil law, and *Shari'ah*-compliant contracts must be structured in such a way that the intentions of the parties are met and that the application of secular law produces the desired *Shari'ah* results. This is of prime importance for disputes when judges decide on the basis of the secular law. The interdependencies of secular law and *Shari'ah* contracts are of particular interest for students of law schools, but business schools should also include some basics in their IF curricula. The multilayer legal structures became practically relevant when *Shari'ah*-compliant transactions were hit during the recent economic crisis.

Employment perspectives

There is a consensus that IF is a rapidly growing segment in the global finance industry, and it is a widely held opinion that double-digit growth rates of total 'Islamic' assets were recorded for more than a decade and maintained even during the years of global financial meltdown. It looks obvious that such a fast-growing business should offer many employment opportunities. This is probably a correct expectation, but maybe somewhat less straightforward than many people may expect.

To start with, the growth of total assets is not a very reliable predictor for the number of additional jobs in the industry. If the nominal value of assets increases but the number of transactions remains the same, this most probably can be handled by the existing human resources. In addition, technological advancements, process optimization and product standardization may even require less manpower for larger volumes. What is more important than total assets is the number of IF institutions. This number has also grown, but it should be noted that this growth is partially due to the conversion of conventional financial institutions into Islamic banks, investment companies, etc. There will be some layoffs and resignations during a conversion, and this creates job opportunities for new employees. However, converted institutions hardly ever dismiss but usually retain most of their existing staff and provide in-house training on the new products, instruments and processes. This is similar to conventional banks that offer Islamic products or open Islamic windows: the majority of the personnel come from conventional business. The reason for such a practice is that 80 per cent of Islamic banking is commercially and technically nearly the same as that in conventional finance, and only 20 per cent is significantly different. This is due to the fact that most IF products have been developed by 'reverse engineering': they are in their commercial substance functional equivalents for conventional products. The difference in the underlying contracts should be known to all employees of an Islamic bank in principle, but they are not of prime concern for most of the staff in the daily business. Therefore, training of existing staff may be more cost-effective than hiring a completely new team. This is even true for stand-alone Islamic banks: a considerable number of their personnel come from conventional banking. Such recruitment practices should be taken into consideration by faculties and programme directors in the West when they design IF curricula.

Graduates with IF degrees from Western institutions who are looking for employment in IF institutions in Muslim countries will not only compete with people who have a background and practical experience in conventional banking, but also with candidates who hold degrees in IF from Islamic and 'secular' universities, colleges and business schools located in the Muslim world. In addition, there will be candidates with academic and semi-academic degrees and professional qualifications from specialized providers of IF education such as the Islamic Finance Centre of the Bahrain Institute of Banking and Finance (BIBF) and the International Centre for Education in Islamic Finance (INCEIF) in Kuala Lumpur. In such a highly competitive and global environment, Western institutions of higher education have to equip their graduates with particular qualifications which could give them a competitive edge over other candidates. This can include the exploitation of the existing reputation and alumni network of the Western institution, a specific knowledge which is in high demand, or a strategic alliance with regional partners with a strong brand name. An alternative to purely IF degrees is the enrichment of a conventional programme with Islamic contents: an institution with a strong reputation in an area of conventional finance – for example, capital markets or insurance – may add IF modules and offer a degree that prioritizes conventional expertise but indicates a specialization in IF.

While the job creation of IF institutions for IF graduates may be less than the asset growth gave reason to expect, other segments of the IF industry are often overlooked although they absorb a considerable number of candidates. With a growing complexity and globalization of IF transactions (such as syndicated cross-border project financing), banks need support from legal and tax advisors, engineers and logistics experts, but also experts for their retail business expertise in marketing and corporate communication or for financial literacy programmes. More jobs have emerged in the fields of journalism and electronic media, market data analysis and information brokerage, regulation and lobbying, etc. The wide range of diverse ancillary services provided to IF institutions and to their corporate as well as retail customers is continuously growing and absorbing more people with an academic education and IF expertise.

While it is obvious to look at the Muslim world for jobs in IF, graduates of IF may also find employment opportunities in the West. Potential employers are not only IF institutions operating or emerging in Europe and North America. The growing general awareness of *Shari'ah*-compliant financing techniques and products in the Western business community can lead to a substantial demand for people with IF expertise and degrees from Western institutions. Although still in its early stage, Islamic capital market products such as *sukuk* may become an option for corporate (or even public) finance in the West. Islamic investment banks are looking globally for attractive uses of funds from Muslim countries, and the demand for people with *Shari'ah*-compliant structuring skills and an understanding of the needs and sensitivities of Muslim investors and Western markets may increase considerably. The general consultancy industry can become an attractive field for graduates – be it as employees of the Big Four, employees of specialized investment boutiques, or self-employed consultants. Besides emerging opportunities in investment banking, some *Shari'ah*-compliant retail products may find increasing acceptance not only among Muslim minorities but also from non-Muslims in Western countries: *Shari'ah*-compliant home financing schemes and *takaful* arrangement are of particular interest. Such products are not only offered through banks but also through several other distribution channels such as agents, brokers or electronic communication. IF expertise will be required in many areas – from direct sales to the management of distribution networks and back-offices.

There are fundamentals of IF that every graduate should have command of. But in view of the huge variety of employment options and the dynamism of this emerging industry, there is a lot of room for individual specializations and for the development of specific institutional profiles and individual core competencies. This book gives an overview of how Western institutions of higher education have so far positioned themselves, and it becomes apparent that there are still niches for newcomers.

Research and academic careers

IF is increasingly recognized as an area for serious study and research in the West. Initially and up to the 1990s, books and papers on IE and IF were only published by publishing houses and in journals in the Muslim world or by Muslim institutions in the West (such as the Islamic Foundation in the UK). But over the last decade, an increasing number of articles on various aspects of IF were printed in long-established Western mainstream journals. In addition, Western publishers have recently launched a number of specialized journals for IE and IF (such as the *Journal of Islamic Accounting and Business Research* or the *International Journal of Islamic and Middle Eastern Finance and Management*). Finally, recent IF textbooks have been produced not only by publishers in the Muslim world but also by Western global players.

Obviously, the general framework for an academic career in the West by research on IE and IF has improved considerably. But a career in Western universities and colleges requires publications in rated journals, and the editors of many mainstream journals have a strong preference for quantitative papers. There are numerous examples of talented students who chose interesting topics for empirical studies, but did not recognize serious shortcomings of the data they used for the quantitative analysis. The examples further illustrate the strange results of an uninformed and uncritical use of numbers and indicate the importance of a sound knowledge of IF practices – even if one does not look for employment in the industry but aims at an academic career. Many cross-country comparisons of Islamic and conventional banks – for example with respect to efficiency or profitability – use Bankscope data. Unfortunately, this database suffers from a number of misspecifications and gaps with regard to Islamic banks. But even if the data were complete, a researcher can arrive at gross misinterpretations of IF in comparison to conventional finance if he or she does not consider that the same name can have different meanings for different institutions.

In the early years of IF, phenomenal returns on capital and returns on assets were reported for a number of Islamic banks. These figures were much higher than the same ratios for conventional banks. The erroneous conclusion was that Islamic banks outstrip conventional banks by far in terms of profitability. But this was not the case: while customers' funds paid into interest-bearing savings or term accounts are recorded as liabilities in the balance sheets of conventional banks, some Islamic banks treated the funds paid into *Shari'ah*-compliant PLS investment accounts as off-balance sheet items. Therefore the total assets of these Islamic banks (excluding off-balance sheet items) were much smaller than the total assets of the conventional banks. However, the total income generated by the employment of on- and off-balance sheet funds entered into the income statements of all banks. With this, the return on assets of the Islamic banks was calculated with a too small denominator, and the Islamic banks' performance looked much better than the performance of conventional banks (or of other Islamic banks that recorded investment accounts on-balance sheet).

In a more recent paper on Basel II and capital requirements for Islamic banks, Bankscope data were used that covered 14 commercial and investment banks in Bahrain with total assets of $60 billion, out of which seven were Islamic with assets of $2.5 billion. Actually, however, the total number of banks in Bahrain (according to the Bahrain Monetary Authority) was 59, with total assets of $74 billion out of which 20 were Islamic with $2.9 billion on- and $3.1 billion off-balance sheet. Bankscope's omission of the off-balance sheet assets in the IF sector could be the explanation for some strange results in the study: for example, the average total assets of seven Islamic banks in the high-income country Bahrain were smaller than the average total assets of three Islamic banks in the least developed country Bangladesh – which is evidently implausible, but was not even commented on by the authors of the study.

With an increasing general level of knowledge about IF, such mistakes should no longer happen. But the sophistication and complexity of IF also has increased, at least in parallel with the general level of knowledge. Hence, the basic problem still exists: one must not take published data at their face value and rush to generalized conclusions. Before advanced mainstream quantitative methods are applied to data from the IF world, the researcher should look at the micro foundations to make sure that he or she compares only the comparable. This is less trivial than it sounds because national accounting standards in the Muslim world vary considerably among countries (AAOIFI standards in some countries, pure International Financial Reporting Standards in others and national standards approximating IFRS in a third group of countries); and even within the same jurisdiction, individual disclosure practices of IF institutions can vary significantly.

An academic career based on research in IF has the advantage of working in a field where vast areas still wait to be discovered. The flipside is that many ingredients for well-established research recipes are not readily available but require considerable preparatory work. This is not only an issue for quantitative research. Qualitative research suffers from the secretiveness of many *Shari'ah* boards and *Shari'ah* scholars when it comes to their legal opinions (*fatwas*) on particular products and techniques. It is already difficult to get access to the (often very short) text of a *fatwa*, but it is usually impossible to get access to the rationale of the *fatwa*.

Obviously, IE and IF have gained the academic attention of Muslims and non-Muslims during the last couple of years – although neither has yet been included in the JEL Classification Codes or in the EconLit Subject Descriptors. Nevertheless, it has become an option for an academic career in Western universities to specialize in IE and IF. Degree programmes like those presented in this collection can provide a basis for further research in IF.

Volker Nienhaus

Former President of Marburg University, Germany

Preface

It is my pleasure to present *Islamic Finance in Western Higher Education: Developments and Prospects*, edited by Ahmed Belouafi, Abderrazak Belabes and Cristina Trullols, which constitutes the second publication from the Saudi-Spanish Centre for Islamic Economics and Finance (SCIEF) in the Islamic Finance series we are developing together with Palgrave Macmillan.

SCIEF was officially inaugurated last December with the conference 'Islamic Finance in the 21st Century' held in Madrid. We had the honour of welcoming as our guest speaker H.E. Dr Ahmad M. Ali, President of the Islamic Development Bank, Jeddah, Saudi Arabia, who shared his vision of the future of Islamic Finance and its increasing importance in economic development in the world today.

Prior to this inaugural event, SCIEF had already developed a solid ground on which to position and centre itself comprising four main activities: academic, research, international awareness and engaging with the business community. Moreover, during its short life, SCIEF has managed to become a hub in Europe for Islamic Finance, showcasing some of the more exiting academic and business initiatives in the area.

It is important to point out that SCIEF's success is mainly due to the quality and generosity of our collaborators, individual experts and institutions. We are particularly grateful to our main supporters, IE and King Abdulaziz Universities, whose presidents always had the vision and the will to create and support SCIEF. We are in collaboration with many renowned institutions such as Casa Árabe Spain, the Chair for Ethics and Financial Norms, University Paris 1, France and Arcano Group Spain among others. We are always grateful for the support of IDB, NCB and Al-Khabir, Spain Invest and the lawyers from Uría and Menendez who among other partners and friends have made possible the development of our activities.

The experts that have contributed to this new publication come from 22 institutions and universities (among the most prestigious in the world), from Spain, Saudi Arabia, the United Kingdom, France, Germany, the United States, Australia, Italy and Belgium. They have shared very interesting insights regarding the state of the art of teaching Islamic Finance in Western higher education institutions, as Professor Volker Nienhaus has skilfully summarized in his Foreword.

The vocation of SCIEF is to be a hub for academic and business activities of Islamic Finance in the West, and for that reason we are particularly thankful to all the very prestigious experts who have contributed to this publication, which will certainly contribute to making Islamic Finance activities well known in Europe.

I hope you will enjoy reading this unique publication.

Celia de Anca
Director, SCIEF

Acknowledgements

This book comes about as a result of the official inauguration of the Saudi-Spanish Centre for Islamic Economics and Finance (SCIEF) that took place in December 2011 in Madrid with the conference titled 'Islamic Finance in the 21st Century'. The objective of this conference was to present the activities that SCIEF has developed since its beginning and to discuss the role of Islamic Finance in Western higher education, its developments and prospects. This publication is an effort to take advantage of the excellent opportunity that this event offered in bringing together numerous academics from prestigious Western universities that shared the past, present and future role of Islamic Finance in each of their institutions.

The editors would like to extend their gratitude to all the authors who have contributed their information and shared their experience in this book. Thanks to Dr Abdullah Turkistani, Dean of the Islamic Economics Institute, King Abdulaziz University, who has encouraged and supported this project from beginning to end. Special thanks must go to all those contributors from each institution and university, including Professor Volker Nienhaus, Professor Simon Archer, Dr Celia de Anca, Professor Ignacio de la Torre, Mr Ibrahim Cekici, Dr Abdul Hassan, Dr Olivia Orozco, Dr Valentino Cattelan, Mr Reza Zain Jaufeerally, Mr Kader Merbouh, Dr Pierre-Charles Pradier, Professor Philip Molyneux, Dr Karim Aldohni, Dr Ghassen Bouslama, Dr Ishaq Bhatti, Dr Abdelhafid Benamraoui, Dr Nazim Ali, Dr Toseef Azid and Dr Tariq Saeed. Finally, thanks must also go to all of those who have not been mentioned herein, who have contributed their expertise and knowledge to the creation of this book and have made this publication possible.

List of Abbreviations

AAIOFI	Accounting and Auditing Organization for Islamic Financial Institutions
ABI	Associazione Bancaria Italiana (Association of Italian Banks)
ACIFP	Association of Chartered Islamic Finance Professionals
AFMA	Australian Financial Markets Association
ANR	Agence Nationale de la Recherche (French National Research Agency)
ASEAN	Association of Southeast Asian Nations
AusCif	Australian Centre for Islamic Finance
BIBF	Bahrain Institute of Banking and Finance
BRICS	Brazil, Russia, India, China and South Africa
CAE	Conseil d'analyse économique (Council for Economic Analysis)
CBB	Central Bank of Bahrain
CEFN	Chair for Ethics and Financial Norms
CEIS	Centre for Economic and International Studies
CF	Conventional Finance
CIBAFI	General Council for Islamic Banks and Financial Institutions
CIFP	Chartered Islamic Finance Professional
CIPIE	Fondación Cooperación Internacional y Promoción Ibero-América Europa
CMES	Center for Middle Eastern Studies
CNAM	Conservatoire National des Arts et Metiers
CNI	Centro Nacional de Inteligencia
DEFI	Degree d'économie Et de Finance Islamique (Degree in Islamic Economics and Finance)
DU	Diplôme d'Université (University Degree)
EAMS	Euro-Arab Management School
EBEN	European Business Ethics Network

EMS	Ecole de Management de Strasbourg (Strasbourg Business School)
ESA	Ecole Supérieure des Affaires
EU	European Union
GATS	General Agreement on Trade in Services
GCC	Gulf Cooperation Council
GEA	Geo-educational Approach
GREFIE	Groupe de Recherche Economie et *Finance Islamique* en Europe
HBMeU	Hamdan Bin Mohammed e-University
HIFIP	Harvard Islamic Finance Information Program
IAIE	International Association of Islamic Economics
IBA	Italian Banking Association
IE	Islamic Economics
IEBS	Instituto de Impresa Business School
IEF	Islamic Economics and Finance
IEI	Islamic Economics Institute (ex IERC)
IERC	Islamic Economics Research Centre
IGIAD	Iktisadi Girişim ve iş Ahlaki Derneği
IF	Islamic Finance
IFE	Islamic Finance Education
IFESI	Institut Français des Etudes et Sciences Islamiques
IFHE	Islamic Finance Higher Education
IFEP	Islamic Finance Education Programme
IFPD	Islamic Finance Professional Development
IFP	Islamic Finance Project
IFSB	Islamic Financial Services Board
IIIT	International Institute of Islamic Thought
IIUM	International Islamic University Malaysia
INCEIF	International Centre for Education in Islamic Finance
IRTI	Islamic Research and Training Institute
IsDB	Islamic Development Bank

ISRA	International *Shari'ah* Research Academy for Islamic Finance
KAU	King Abdulaziz University
LabEx	Laboratoire d'Excellence sur la régulation financière
MAUSS	Mouvement Anti Utilitariste en Sciences Sociales (Anti-utilitarian Movement in the Social Sciences)
MCCA	Muslim Community Corporation of Australia
MIHE	Markfield Institute of Higher Education
NCB	National Commercial Bank
OIC	Organization of Islamic Cooperation
PPP	Private–Public Partnership
RMS	Reims Management School
SAMA	Saudi Arabia Monetary Agency (Central Bank of Saudi Arabia)
SCIEF	Saudi-Spanish Centre for Islamic Economics and Finance
SEC	Securities and Exchange Commission
UoG	University of Gloucestershire
XIFM	Executive Master's in Islamic Financial Management

Glossary of Select Arabic Terms

Bai-al-einah	Spot sale followed by repurchase by the same party at a higher price on a deferred payment basis
Fatwa	Religious verdict made by an Islamic scholar or by a group of scholars through specific arrangements (e.g. The International *Fiqh* Academy of the OIC)
Fiqh	Islamic jurisprudence
Gharar	Alea or hazardous sale
Hadith	What was transmitted on the authority of the Prophet Muhammad, his deeds, sayings, or tacit approval
Halal	Legitimate or lawful activity under *Shari'ah* law
Haram	Illicit or prohibited under *Shari'ah* law.
Ijarah	Leasing
Ijma'	The consensus of jurists
Ijtijad	Exertion of utmost efforts by scholar(s) or qualified person(s) in *Shari'ah* to derive the rulings of *Shari'ah* in contemporary or unresolved issues
Istisna'a	Sale contract based on periodic advance payments for goods yet to be manufactured and to be delivered in the future (manufacture sale facility)
Maqasid Al-Shari'ah	Ultimate objectives and goals of *Shari'ah* (Islamic law)
Maslaha	Greater benefit or interest
Maysir	Games of chance
Mudarabah	Partnership in which one party provides capital to the other who manages the investment, the profits and losses being shared by both parties

Mudarib	Manager or provider of labour and expertise in a *Mudarabah* contract
Murabahah	Sale contract at an agreed mark-up or profit
Musharakah	a type of partnership in which all partners contribute capital to an enterprise, share profits in a prearranged formula, and Losses are shared on the basis of how much capital has been contributed
Qiyas	Analogical reasoning
Qur'an	The sacred book of Islam
Rab ul-mal	Investor or contributor of capital in a Mudarabah contract
Riba	Charging of interest
Sadaqah	Voluntary charitable giving
Salam	Forward sale, full payment made for the future delivery of goods or service(s)
Shari'ah	Injunctions derived from the basic sources (i.e. Qura'an and Sunnah) of Islam
Sukuk	Certificates of equal value representing undivided shares in the ownership of tangible assets, usufructs and services or (in the ownership of) the assets of particular projects or special investment activity
Sunnah	The way Prophet Muhammad lived his life
Takaful	Form of mutual guarantee used as a form of *Shari'ah*-compliant insurance
Tawarruq	Tripartite sale facility
Tawarruq munazam	Organized tripartite sale facility used by Islamic financial institutions
Wakalah	Agency contract where the agent receives a fee for acting on behalf of the principle
Waqf	Endowment in perpetuity
Zakah	Obligatory annual contribution levied on Muslims of sufficient economic means

1
Introduction

Ahmed Belouafi, Abderrazak Belabes and Cristina Trullols

Over the last few decades, the Islamic Finance (IF) industry has achieved an unprecedented presence on the international financial stage. According to various studies and reports, the rate of growth of the industry has almost doubled from 14 per cent during 1994 and 2002 to 26 per cent between 2003 and 2010, and is expected to maintain a double digit pace in the near future.[1] As a result many associated aspects of the industry are attracting more and more attention from various financial quarters and other specialists in different parts of the world. Much of the literature which has been written about this newly emerging field has tried to explore the rise of this phenomenon from various angles. Nonetheless, the vast majority of the literature has concentrated on certain issues such as basic principles and salient features that distinguish IF from its mainstream counterpart, assets' growth and expansion of the industry, product developments and authenticity, supervision and regulation of the IF industry, risk and liquidity managements. More recently, some deeper and complex matters have been investigated; symposia and other channels of knowledge dissemination have been exploring specific issues in a wider context; efficiency of the IF institutions and instruments, financial stability and the role that IF and/or its principles play in this pressing matter, sustainability and viability of the Islamic financial system vis-à-vis that of its conventional counterpart.

One area has not yet received the due consideration it deserves: Islamic Finance Education (IFE). Though it is widely accepted and acknowledged that IFE should play an important role in the supply of properly qualified and trained human capital resources that the industry needs, the wealth of the literature in this area is not as rich and diverse as it ought to be. However, there are some signs that the situation may

1

change in the coming years. An indication of this can be found in the communiqué issued by the delegates attending the 8th International Conference of Islamic Economics and Finance.[2] The communiqué has made a particular reference to IFE by calling for the revival of the 'International Academic Coordination Committee' to work as a platform for coordinating academic programmes and sharing experiences among Islamic economics and finance education institutions.[3]

To the editors' knowledge, this book is the first of its kind in its approach and coverage.[4] Therefore, one of its prime objectives is to fill a gap in this crucial area by exploring some aspects of the developments and prospects of IFE within Western higher education. It is hoped that the content and analysis included herein will provide useful insights and prospects about the educational programmes and other initiatives that the Western higher education institutions are involved in. It is also hoped that the book will be a useful reference to IF industry and the wider spectrum of parties interested in its growth and development.

From individually dispersed to more institutionally concerted efforts

Dealing with various topics relating to Islamic economics, contracts and finance at Western higher education institutions is not new. A preliminary examination carried out by the editors about one aspect of this phenomenon in one country; the UK, which is playing an important role in the promotion of IF in its territory, gives a clear indication for that. According to this very hasty exercise whose results are displayed in Table 1.1, the first doctoral thesis on Islamic economics can be traced back to the early 1950s,[5] and on Islamic finance, banking and commercial law to the 1980s. Having said that, it must be noted that these initiatives were taken on an individual basis; a student or probably a supervisor picking up a topic in one of the aforementioned areas and the project being carried out thereafter. In such a situation, there were no concerted and planned efforts, from the involved individual/ supervisor or the educational institution, to establish a short-term programme let alone a medium or longer term ones. For this reason, many of these efforts appeared once or twice in some institutions, and ceased afterwards. In some other instances, these individual initiatives have been carried out for a longer period until their transformation into institutional initiatives.[6]

Therefore, the phenomenon that the book is studying is quite recent in its establishment and institutional in its orientation. Though this is

Table 1.1   Preliminary information about theses in some British universities

Entered search phrase	No. of items founded	Some details about the earliest theses found in the theme searched for
Islamic Economics	138 documents	The social and economic development of Islamic Society in North India (1290–1320). Author: Aleem, Muhammad Abdul. Awarding Institution: School of Oriental and African Studies (University of London). Awarded: 1952.
Islamic Finance	68 documents	Islamic budgetary policy: in theory and practice. Author: Tahir, Hailani Muji. Awarding Institution: University of Aberdeen. Awarded: 1988.
Islamic Banking	109 documents	Portfolio management of Islamic banks. Author: Bashir, B.A. Awarding Institution: University of Lancaster. Awarded:1982
Islamic Commercial law	15 documents	Sales and contracts in early Islamic commercial law. Author: A.A.H. Hassan. Awarding Institution: University of Edinburgh. Awarded: 1986.

Source: Editors' compilation.[7]

the case, it should be noticed that the pattern of the individual efforts – in terms of the number of theses awarded in the IFE discipline – has been on the rise at Western higher education institutions since the 1980s. This may be explained by the extraordinary growth and appearance of IF industry on the world stage. But it could also be attributed to the impact of the First International Conference on Islamic Economics, that was organized by King Abdulaziz University and held in Makkah in 1976. This may have been the case for some Muslim students who took their Masters and Ph.D.s at Western Universities in topics related to IFE. However, we must stress that there is no concrete evidence for that; we are only making this presumption so that it can be investigated objectively to spotlight some turning points in the historical developments of IFE as distinct disciplines from other branches of 'Islamic' knowledge.

From financing in Islam to 'Islamic Finance'

Throughout history various communities and civilizations have developed financing regimes to facilitate the smooth exchange of goods and services produced by their economies. When Islam came to Arabia, trade was one of the prime economic activities that most of the Arabs were involved in. In fact, the *Qur'an* mentioned two very famous commercial journeys;[8] one in summer to Syria and the other in winter to Yemen. These two trips contributed significantly to the commercial vitality of Makkah, which became an important connection point on the Yemen–Damascus route, and an important source of necessary commodities for Arabia. Thus, before the arrival of Islam, people were conducting trade and arranging for the financing of this activity, mainly through *Riba* (interest)-based mechanisms as noted by some sources.[9]

Therefore, the interaction between Islam and finance took place within the context of the socio-economic conditions of the Arab communities at that time. Thorough investigations by Muslim scholars of the *Qur'anic* verses and the statements of the Prophet (PBUH)[10] in the transactions area, found that the approach taken by Islamic rules and regulations, to accommodate the prevailing financing regimes of that time and the regimes that might develop in the future, was 'progressive' rather than 'revolutionary'. Progressive in the sense of preserving the practices that do not contradict the general guidelines contained in the *Qur'anic* verses and the statements of the Prophet (PBUH) and the gradual removal of non-compliant practices. Thus, if a scholar is going to issue a *Fatwa* (a religious verdict) regarding a contemporary or unresolved issue in transactions, including financial ones, he is guided by the spirit of the axiom that states 'everything is allowed unless explicitly prohibited',[11] if these transactions have not been categorically regarded as illicit in the main sources of Islamic law"[12].

Throughout the history of Muslim societies in different parts of the world, people have been able to conduct their economic and financial dealings on the basis of this framework. As a result, their set-ups have influenced and have been influenced by the developments of other cultures and civilizations. But this interactive and progressive development did not result in a distinct discipline termed 'Islamic Finance' or even Economics. Rather, issues relating to these matters have been dealt with under different topics and headings, within the general textbooks of Islamic knowledge in particular *Fiqh* (Jurisprudence) and *Tafseer* (Exegesis).[13]

The rise of 'Islamic Finance' as a distinct discipline is recent in its origin. Most of the literature on this area traces the theoretical treatment back to the 1940s and 1950s. However, the call on the practical level may have been earlier than that. According to the sources we have been able to consult, the first call for the establishment of a financial institution on the basis of Islamic law can be traced back to the early part of the last century. In the late 1920s, Sheikh Ibrahim Abu Al-Yaqdhan, a North African reformist, called for the creation of a bank based on the rules of Islamic jurisprudence and managed with modern banking tools.[14] His call was swiftly smothered by the French authorities ruling North Africa at that time.[15]

It took until 1963 to see the realization of this dream, in Upper Egypt, with the Mit Ghamr Local Savings Bank in the Delta of the Nile. The originality of this experiment was to encourage savings behaviour among rural populations, designating those savings to local development while at the same time providing social services through the collection of *Zakat*, and providing the small savers with bank accounts without the stringent requirements of a minimum deposit amount. For political reasons the experiment was brought to end in 1967, but it allowed the crossing of a psychological barrier: the creation of a bank based on the rules of Islamic jurisprudence was seen to be plausible and desirable in enhancing financial inclusion of the financial systems of Muslim countries, and could be so again elsewhere. This then led to the creation of 'banks without interest' (or interest-free banks) that have become popular under the name 'Islamic bank' (*Bank Islami*). Others prefer the term 'finance house' (*Bayt Al-Tamwil*) or 'House of Islamic Money' (*Dar al-Maal Al-Islami*).

In spite of the huge developments and spread of Islamic Financial Institutions (IFIs) all over the globe during the past few decades, financial intermediation from an Islamic perspective remains problematic, as its true and distinct features from conventional practice remain the subject of heated debate among academicians, practitioners, *Fuqaha* (jurists), lawyers and financial regulators. The implications of the unsettled issue are apparent at the level of various conventional regulatory and supervisory bodies that have accommodated IFIs differently into their financial systems. In academia, the issue is far from over as the exact nature of 'the Islamic' financial intermediation is still being discussed and revisited from time to time.

In the prevalent debate, the term 'Islamic Finance' is often assimilated to one of the existing forms of the financial regimes; global or conventional finance, ethical, socially responsible and sustainable finance. These associations and assimilations have a great impact on the identity of Islamic finance and the educational programmes that are designed within this context. Hence there is a need to explore the relationship between IF and Islamic Economics, on the one hand, and IF and other forms of financial regimes on the other.[16]

Genesis of Islamic Economics education

Islamic Finance has entered the academic world through its parent Islamic Economics. The latter was introduced first as a course, before becoming a specialization and later a fully fledged programme was established at various departments, research centres, institutes or scientific Chairs.

The introduction of economics from an Islamic perspective in higher education institutions was relatively very early. The first course we are aware of was created in 1904 at Al Tha'alibiya high school in Algiers.[17] The course covered various economic topics such as production, distribution and consumption. With regard to financing, the course material seems to have advocated the use of participatory modes of financing over debt-based instruments. And in terms of consumption, it alerted consumers not to rely heavily on credit and to consume modestly according to one's real income rather than the 'potential' one created through credit and debt 'binge'.[18] Ironically, this call seems to have interacted with the analysis and diagnosis of the renowned French economist Paul Leroy-Beaulieu (1843–1916), who came to the conclusion that one of the prime causes of 'financial' crises is credit 'excessiveness'.[19] According to him, during the boom, economic agents behave on the expectations of the economic growth 'euphoria' that leads them to build their decisions on taking too much credit in the belief that the 'expected' revenues and capital gains are able to cover all future financial obligations that they have taken on interest-based credit.[20]

After the independence of Muslim countries, some faculties were opened hesitantly to this new discipline from the 1960s onwards. The Faculty of Commerce at Al-Azhar University in Cairo offered a course[21] in 1961.[22] Despite the inauguration of the first department entirely dedicated to Islamic Economics, at Umm Durman University in Sudan in 1965, the teaching of Islamic Economics was timid and very limited.[23] To overcome this slow process, the conference of Muslim scholars held in Cairo in September 1972 called for the introduction of Islamic Economics as a subject in the curriculum of the Bachelor degrees in Economics at the universities of the Muslim and Arab world. The organization of the First International Conference of Islamic Economics by King Abdulaziz University, from 21 to 26 April 1976, went further by calling for the teaching of Islamic law of financial contracts. Among the topics discussed in that conference were: banking without interest, and Islamic insurance. The recommendations of the conference emphasized the need 'of the governments of Muslim countries to support Islamic banking in practice', and 'to advance their theory [at the educational level] through the teaching of Islamic law of contracts and its fundamentals within faculties of economics, administration and business at the universities of Muslim and Arab countries'.[24] It is evident that the delegates of the conference did not mention, let alone discuss, the teaching of Islamic Economics within Western higher education.

In the introduction process of this 'discipline' the pioneers faced several difficulties in how to address economic issues from an Islamic perspective. On the methodological front, two main questions arose:

Is it better to create a 'new and distinct science'?
Is it preferable to introduce Islamic 'inputs' into conventional Economics courses?[25]

At the practical level, the second option seems to have prevailed in recent years, as evidenced by the mimicking of conventional products through the 'Islamic' financial engineering that has been endorsed by several *Shari'ah* advisory boards of IFIs.

This approach requires a serious and profound reflection on the relationship between substance and form on the one hand, and the conditions of the possibility of the emergence of Islamic Finance as a subject of knowledge on the other.

Impact of the crisis on finance education

The recent financial crisis that erupted in the US in 2008 has prompted a profound debate about the role of finance education curricula in the occurrence of such turbulence at a magnitude and scale that did not just affect the parties directly involved in the subprime 'scam' but brought the whole international financial and economic systems to a halt. In these circumstances, many aspects related to the financial system came under scrutiny. Higher education – responsible for the 'production' and training of the business 'elites' – has come under the critical spotlight. Business schools, finance departments, financial academics, even economists and the theory that they taught have not been spared either.[26]

From these reviews and examinations, 'ethics', 'values and 'responsibility' have been stressed as important elements that should be embedded in the finance and business curricula.[27] Thus ethical issues should be addressed at the forefront of university curricula in order that learners become aware of the impact of their financial decisions on the financial systems and economies.[28] The ethical dimension, in our view, should not be treated as an isolated subject; rather it should be integrated in an appropriate and lively manner throughout the programme.

In most institutions providing IF programmes, the debate on the impact of the crisis on the teaching of finance has not taken place yet. The flaws of the global economy – dominated by 'financialization' which led to a disconnection of the financial sector from the real world – highlighted some virtues of IF principles, particularly asset-backing, the prohibition of *Riba* (interest) and *Gharar* (*alea*). However, it should be noted that Islamic banks pose other risks to the financial system. These risks differ, in some respects, from those born by the practices of conventional banks, for example with regard to liquidity risk, operational risk and legal risks.[29] Furthermore, over the last few years, the 'Islamic financial innovation' has moved to complex legal arrangements. This complexity is likely, in the absence of a universal regulatory framework for accommodating Islamic instruments, to generate a systemic risk whose burden will be assumed by the whole society. This scenario may bring similar results to those which occurred in the conventional system during the deregulation era. In this perspective, IF appears to be providing an opportunity for conventional finance in addressing some of the crucial issues coming out of the crisis, but it has to draw lessons from the antagonism of conventional finance.

The dynamism of Islamic Finance education in the West

Since the beginning of the new millennium, IF education has experienced an unexpected surge in higher education. This trend builds on the liberalization of higher education initiated, internationally, by the General Agreement on Trade in Services (GATS) and, at the European level, by the Bologna process. The financial crisis has been particularly favourable to this tendency. According to Gérard Mestrallet, chairman of Paris Europlace, the organization in charge of promoting the French financial market, 'the global financial crisis calls into question the development models of conventional finance. This major upheaval gave Islamic finance momentum that it did not have a few months ago'.[30]

Islamic Finance in Western higher education is a phenomenon that is both complex and multifaceted. Despite its newness, teaching of the discipline has spread all over the globe, particularly in the Middle East, North Africa and Southeast Asia. Geographic proximity, linguistic affinity and historical ties seem to play major roles in this dynamism.

The study and the teaching of IF in the West could prove to be a useful tool for exchanging views, sharing experiences and knowledge transfer.[31] These two-way processes are presented in various aspects and are not limited to the Western hemisphere. For example, the creation of a Master's degree in Islamic Financial Management by a European school located in the Middle East forms a channel of dual benefit; on the one hand, the establishment has an access to European expertise in management and, on the other hand, it provides an opportunity for European business schools to learn from this experience in IF.[32]

The study and teaching of IF could lead, also, to a cognitive 'embeddedness' which considers IF as a component of global finance, an ethical alternative, or both, combining the ethics of Islam with the techniques of conventional finance. Islamic financial products could thus be treated, at the input, as conventional products indexed to interest and, at the output, as alternative financial products which take into consideration certain social, environmental, moral requirements of the consumers as does 'ethical' finance.

In this context, the evaluation of IF educational programmes is becoming a necessity from the point of view of their overall coherence and relevance vis-à-vis the mission assigned to them. The establishment of an evaluation system should generate reliable indicators, in terms of consistency, content and pedagogical quality so that education becomes a centre of excellence. If such a process is established, this may boost the emergence of IF as an entity 'distinct' from other forms of 'alternative' financing. This is a prerequisite for a fruitful interaction that leads to financial 'pluralism' and diversity bringing new possibilities and solutions to meet the financing needs of all economic agents regardless of their faith or ethnicity.

Without claiming to give a formal and homogeneous identity to the variety of IF examples in Western higher education institutions, this book sheds light on this phenomenon using the work of a group of academics who responded positively to the editorial team's request. Most of these authors play an active role in IF education in their respective institutions.

***

The book has been divided into three parts. Part I provides a detailed overview of IF education in the United Kingdom, France and Italy, its trends, developments and future outlook. At the same time, it provides an analysis of the top ten business schools that offer IF.

Part II, the central part of the book, provides a series of case studies from Western higher educational institutions in Europe and

Australia. It describes their particular experience with IF, including their educational taught programmes, career placements, research opportunities and activities in this sector. These institutions include Reading University, La Trobe University in Australia, Reims Management School, Newcastle University, Bangor University, the Markfield Institute of Higher Education (an affiliate of the Islamic Foundation), Strasbourg University, University of Leuven, and Liverpool Hope University.

Part III offers an insight into the research and other initiatives that have taken place in Western higher education institutions which include: the Islamic Finance Project of Harvard University, the Islamic Finance initiative at Sorbonne University, the Islamic Finance initiative at Westminster University, and the Saudi-Spanish Centre of Islamic Economics and Finance at IE Business School.

Notes

1. Warde, I. (2010) 'Islamic Finance and the Global Meltdown', Business Islamica, http://www.islamica-me.com/article.asp?cntnt=633
2. The conference was held from 19–21 December 2011 in Qatar, and it was organized jointly by the Faculty of Islamic Studies, an affiliate of Qatar Foundation, the International Association of Islamic Economics (IAIE – a UK-based organization), and the Islamic Research and Training Institute (IRTI – an affiliate of the Islamic Development Bank Group).
3. The 8th International Conference on Islamic Economics and Finance (2011) Communiqué. 21 December, Doha, Qatar.
4. The only book we are aware of is *Teaching of Islamic Economics & Finance at Islamic Schools in India*. The book has been published in Arabic, Urdu and English, by IFA Publications in India in 2010 and it was edited by Ausaf Ahmed. We thank our colleague Professor Abdul Azim Islahi of the Islamic Economics Institute for drawing our attention to this publication.
5. The dates may be earlier than that as, for instance, we found in France a thesis entitled 'L'usure en droit musulman et ses conséquences pratiques' (Usury in Islamic Law and its Practical Consequences) by Benali Fekar at the faculty of Law, Lyon University, 1908.
6. This may be the case of Durham University (UK) where Rodney Wilson – ex-professor and ex-director of the Durham Centre for Islamic Economics and Finance – played a vital role in maintaining this track.
7. Based on the information provided by the Ethos (Electronic Online Theses Service) of the British Library, http://ethos.bl.uk:8080/SearchResults.do, accessed on 10 May 2012.
8. 'Their covenants (covering) journeys by winter and summer', *Qur'an*: Surah 106, Verse 2.
9. Monzer Kahf and Tariqullah Khan (1409) 'Principles of Islamic Finance: A survey', *Islamic Research and Training Institute*, p. 4.
10. *Qur'an* and *Sunnah* are the two primary sources of Islamic Law (*Shari'ah*). There are other sources as well like *Qias* (analogy) and *Urf* (customs or traditions).

11. Matters discussed by jurists in *Shari'ah* are divided into two main categories: *Fiqh al-Ibadat* (Jurisprudence of Worship or rituals: e.g. issues of prayer (*Salat*)) and *Fiqh Al-Muamalat* (Jurisprudence of Transactions, e.g. financial dealings). Under the first category the general rule is guided by 'everything is prohibited unless explicitly allowed', while under the second the permissibility is the norm unless there is an explicit prohibition in a transaction or a deal.

12. This is based upon the famous axiom *Al-Asl fi Al-Ashi'a Al-Ibaha* (permissibility is the general guideline in deriving *Fatwas* (verdicts) relating to transaction matters). One has to be careful in the use and application of this axiom to avoid the two extremes of being either restrictive or permissive without referring to the authentic specific evidences in the *Qur'an* and the *Sunnah*.

13. Commentary books of the *Qur'an*, especially the books that deal with the verses of *Ahkam* (rules). Examples of *Akham* are permissibility of trade or sale and the prohibition of *Riba*. This rule has been derived from Verse 275 in *Surah* (Chapter) 2 of the *Qur'an*.

14. Abu Al-Yaqdhan (1928: 2).

15. The Sheikh was even interrogated because of this call. On the 3 May 1929, a French judge asked him: 'You wrote an article on the requirement for the nationals to form a local bank. You are trying to discriminate between locals and French citizens'. The sheikh replied: 'No! I have not tried to do that. I simply mentioned the need to create a local bank according to Islamic rules unlike modern banks [that operate on the basis of *Riba* (interest)]. We would be very happy, also, that young Muslims integrate foreign banks to learn modern techniques of management banking' (Nacer, 2006).

16. Nienhaus (2008).

17. Al-Médjaoui and Brihmat (1904).

18. Al-Médjaoui and Brihmat (1904: 57).

19. The author identified two main factors as 'causes of all causes' in the reoccurring of the financial crises. These were excessive speculation and excessive credits (Leroy-Beaulieu, 1913: part 3, p. 225).

20. Leroy-Beaulieu (1913). According to the translators, the book had been chosen by the then Education Minister of Egypt (1910–14), Ahmed Heshmat Pasha, to be translated into Arabic for teaching economics as a separate subject in Egyptian secondary schools. If that is the case, the book may have been the first Economics textbook of the twentieth century to be taught in the Arab world.

21. The course was first titled 'Economic Thought in Islam' before being changed in 1967 to 'Islamic Economics'.

22. Al Fangari (1994: 5–6).

23. El-Tayeb (2008: 11).

24. King Abdulaziz University (1976: 4).

25. We owe this observation to Dr Darwish Jastania, former director of the Islamic Economics Institute at the University of King Abdulaziz, who attended the conference. We thank him for that.

26. 'The Responsibilities of Management Intellectuals: A Survey', 'The Future of Finance and the Theory that Underpins It', 'Business Ethics education: Are Business schools Teaching to the AACSB Ethics education task Force Recommendations', and 'Freefall: Free Markets and the Sinking of the Global Economy'. These are just a few illustrative examples of articles, books and

headings in the spectrum of 'calls', 'pleas' and 'debates' that are coming out from the ashes of the recent financial turbulence. It is evident that the examination of the factors that led to this mess went beyond the markets' 'meltdown' to the 'core' and 'fundamental' foundations of financial and economic theories that might have given the rationale for such 'fallacies' and practices to prevail. Islamic Finance has also been called upon to review current trends in its practice; Liau Y-Sing and Frederik Richter quoted Richard Thomas, CEO of the London wholesale Islamic Bank (Gatehouse Bank) noting that 'Islamic finance may "return to roots"', *Reuters*, Monday, 15 February 2010. Willem Buiter, an ex-professor at the London School of Economics, for his part noted that 'A return to basics is likely now also in Islamic finance, which never strayed that far from its origins' (Buiter, 2009).

27. For instance Catholic colleges and universities in the USA have seen the crisis as a learning opportunity to 'teach their students the consequences of imprudent business decisions' and to 'draw the lessons on the issues of greed, selfishness and the need for sound moral judgment that offer great insight for young people at the start of their careers' (Casey, 2008).
28. Chesney (2010); Noyer (2009: 3).
29. Gérard Mastrallet, preface of Jouini and Pastré (2009).
30. Wilson (2007: 1).
31. Pierre Simon, President of Paris Chamber of Commerce and Industry: '*L'ESA doit rester un pôle d'excellence*' [The ESA should remain a centre of excellence], by Élodie Morel Lebbos, iloubnan.info.
32. Simon, Pierre (2009). "L'ESA doit rester un pôle d'excellence", entretien réalisé par Élodie Morel Lebbos, iloubnan.info, 23 février.

References

Abu Al-Yaqdhan, I. (1928) 'Hajat Al-Jazaïr Ila Masraf Ahli' [The need to create a bank for the natives in Algeria], *Wadi Mizab Journal*, 29 June.

Al Fangari, M. S. (1994) *Al-Wajiz fi Al-Iqticad Al-Islami* [An Introduction to Islamic Economics] (Cairo: Dar Al Shuruq).

Al-Médjaoui, A. and Brihmat, O. (1904) *Al-Mircad fi Masaïl Al-Iqticad* [Observations on the Economics Questions] (Algiers: Edition Orientale Pierre Fontana).

Buiter, W. (2009) 'Should you be able to sell what you do not own?' 16 March, blogs.ft.com/maverecon

Casey, E. (2008) 'Catholic colleges & universities: Financial crisis as a learning opportunity", *Catholic News Service*, 14 November, http://ncronline.org/node/2497

Chesney, M. (2010) 'Enseignement de la finance: la crise a-t-elle eu lieu?' *Le Temps*, 18 October.

El-Tayeb, E. (2008) *Al-Manahij wa Siyaghat Al-Nadhariya Al-Iqtisadiya Al-Kuliya* [Methodology and Formulation of Islamic Macro-economic Theory] (Khartoum: G-Town Publishing).

Jouini, E. and Pastré, O. (2009) *La finance islamique: Une solution à la crise?* (Paris: Paris Europlace & Economica), p. III.

King Abdulaziz University (1976) *General Recommendations of the First International Conference of Islamic Economics* (Jeddah: King Abdulaziz University).

Leroy-Beaulieu, P. (1913) *'Al-Mujaz Fi Ilm al-Iqtisad'* [Introduction to Economics], translated by H. Ibrahim and K. Mutran (Egypt: Al-Maarif Publishing).

Nacer, M. (2006) *Ibrahim Abu Al-Yaqdhan Jihad Al-Kalima* [Ibrahim Abu Al-Yaqdhan and the Struggle by the word] (Algiers: Alpha).

Nienhaus, V. (2008) 'Challenges and initiatives of human capital development through Islamic finance education at intermediate and undergraduate level, communication presented at the conference human capital development for Islamic financial industry: Challenges and initiatives', organized by the Islamic Research and Training Institute and the General Council of Islamic Banks and Financial Institutions, Jeddah, Hilton Hotel, 1 June.

Noyer, C. (2009) 'Global stability, the future of capital markets and Islamic finance in France', Speech at *The Euromoney Seminars, Islamic Paris Conference*, Paris, 29 September.

Simon, P. (2009). *'L'ESA doit rester un pôle d'excellence'* [The ESA should remain a centre of excellence], entretien réalisé par Élodie Morel Lebbos, iloubnan.info, 23 February.

Wilson, R. (2007) 'Islamic Finance in Europe', RSCAS PP 2007/2, Robert Schuman Centre for Advanced Studies.

Part I
Islamic Finance Higher Education: Cartography

2

Research in Islamic Economics and Finance: The State of the Art and an Agenda for Academic Cooperation

Olivia Orozco de la Torre

Introduction

During the last decade, news on Islamic Finance (IF) has been dominated by the expansion and growth of the industry and the creation of Islamic Banking (IB) institutions all around the globe. The industry has turned 50 years old in 2012, since the first experiments of financial institutions without interest appeared around 1963 (saving-investment banks in Mit Ghamr, Egypt; and some years earlier Tabung Haji, a saving-fund for pilgrims in Malaysia).[1] However, texts exposing the need to search for an alternative approach towards economic issues, based on the principles and values of Islam, emerged a bit earlier, around the 1950s, as part of what has been called the Islamic revival or resurgence.

However, modern Islamic Economics (IE) founded its grounds as a discipline around the 1970s. The First International Conference in Islamic Economics, organized in 1976 in Mecca, Saudi Arabia, by King Abdulaziz University, is considered the benchmark that symbolizes the starting point of IE as a modern paradigm or economic system. It is thus a relatively young model, although in almost half a century of history it has consolidated, generated different trends and schools, and keeps challenging its own premises and developments. Even if parallel, it is important to distinguish the process in which IE as a theoretical paradigm has developed from the expansion of the industry, as the implementation of the principles of IF, into practical cases. If the practice has been widely criticized for departing from its theory, certain gaps and pitfalls can be observed as well in the development of the discipline, which could respond or accompany those dynamics and outcomes in the more practical sphere.

17

In a context where the interest for exploring IF's meaning and implications is growing, consolidating and reorienting certain lines of research is essential to broaden up not only the horizons of IE and IF but also of social sciences in general. In this regard, a brief summary of the development of the discipline in these decades, accompanied by an analysis of the literature's current state, will help to identify some of the aspects that need to be tackled in order to develop a research agenda and possibilities for academic cooperation with European institutions of higher education.

This analysis, though, does not attempt to be a comprehensive evaluation and review of the literature, given the extensive work already done by different scholars in this regard, but simply offer a framework in which to place the current initiative and proposals in this book to enhance search and cooperation between academic institutions offering IE and IF programmes.[2]

Islamic Economics and Finance: Development of the discipline and state of the art

As mentioned, while first experiences of Islamic banks appeared in the 1960s, texts exploring theoretically the idea of what an Islamic approach to economics would be emerged some time earlier. The preliminaries of IE could be said to be a result of the confluence of two trends within Middle Eastern studies and research in the first half of the twentieth century: first, the literature dedicated to the revaluation of the Arab-Muslim heritage, the recovery of texts and works by thinkers and scholars of the past,[3] within and in response to Orientalism in the context of European colonialism; and second, the search for new paradigms and social models better fitted for the Islamic worldview within postcolonial literature.[4]

Works written between the 1930s and 1960s represent a bridge towards the creation of an IE vision or system, whose principles would be grounded in the 1970s.

In one of those earlier studies, 'Theory of Income Distribution under the Islamic Law, with Special Reference to the Function of Residual Income Recipients' (Georgetown University Thesis n. 1105, 1953) the author, Hesmat Ala'i, speaking already about 'Islamic economic[s]', highlights the inadequacy of current mainstream economics for dealing with complex phenomena, including the dynamics of the Islamic world.[5] Ala'i started his thesis with the *Muqaddimah* of Ibn Khaldun, in line with those other early texts exploring the economic ideas of medieval scholars, but went further in the economic analysis of Muslim values to speak about the Islamic perspective towards a whole set of economic aspects (consumption, income returns, management, credit, investments, social security, etc.), to finally reconsider the possibility of the 'Islamic economy' being integrated into the Western economic discipline or being made to conform into an interpretation of it.

Ala'i's thesis used what is probably one of the first modern collections of Islamic jurisprudence on financial issues made by a scholar, Nicolas Prodromou Aghnides, who was not a jurist himself and approached it as part of a 'theory' of finance: *Mohammaden Theories of Finance*.[6] Aghnides had made a review of Islamic jurisprudence dealing with exchanges, taxes and public finance, but emphasized the importance of analysing it with a 'historical perspective' in order to make its origins and practical implications understandable to the 'modern mind' (Aghnides, 1916: 5).

This historical approach would be dropped in a significant number of later works recovering the economic ideas of medieval Arab and Muslim scholars, or dealing with IE and banking later on; an aspect that has already been questioned from different forums and whose consequences and particular relevance will also be commented upon later.

Usually, the economic ideas of scholars in the past were, and still sometimes are, compared to contemporary concepts dominating the economic discipline and taken as alternatives to them, but without considering the different historical contexts they responded to. Moreover, the reinterpretations of older conceptions, both of medieval authors and of religious sources, were taken as the approach itself towards economics that Islam portrays and so appropriated as the pillars of what IE should be today, without mentioning how and by whom these reinterpretations were developed. This has made it sometimes difficult to discern which are the 'foundational axioms' (Asutay, 2007: 6) or conceptual foundations of IE; that is, the set of principles, values and objectives conforming the Islamic economic paradigm or system, as well as their hierarchy and order in the structure of that system.[7]

A methodical and theoretical construction of 'the' Islamic economic system, defining some of those main axioms or foundations, was undertaken from the 1950s to the 1970s by scholars whom Islahi qualified as the second generation of Islamic economists: 'pioneer Islamic economists' (Islahi, 2010: 166) or 'younger economists' (Siddiqi, 1981). It represents the transition towards IE as an economic system and model, the First International Conference on Islamic Economics in 1976 representing the benchmark or culmination of that period, and symbolizing such a transition towards the modern IE paradigm.[8]

Hence, the next generation, the third one according to Islahi's classification, is the one experiencing the expansion and recognition of IE as a new discipline (Islahi, 2010: 168). Their works and efforts entailed a complete process of reconstruction in which the simplest elements and determinants of the Islamic worldview (or worldviews) were identified to see their implications in economic aspects of life, in order to draw from there the set of principles (axioms), values and objectives of IE.[9] The values and principles embodied in the *Qu'ran* and the *Sunnah* were so revisited, and the economic implications of fundamental Islamic principles deduced and integrated into a coherent model of modern IE.

During the 1970s and 1980s, the implications of this new approach towards economics were so inferred into the different elements of the economic system, from consumer behaviour to investment criteria, banking and monetary policy, taxation, distribution of income, and development.

The mainstream group of texts and research proceeded by introducing the Islamic values and principles in the micro foundations of an economic system, in the individual preferences and utility functions, to then build up the different aggregated consumption, demand and investment curves. In this sense, the construction of the IE model was mainly based on the methods and structures of 'conventional economics', the Keynesian and neoclassical synthesis,[10] something criticized and even termed as those works made by 'Western-educated economists' (Akram Khan, 1989: 276).

The main argument against this mainstream approach was that those methodologies and tools were unable to grasp the 'comprehensive' nature of Islam (embedded in the *Tawhīd* principle or monotheism) and, so, Islamic agents' decisions and actions. In the 1990s, alternative approaches to the mainstream trend tried to propose new epistemological and methodological frameworks, more coherent and suitable to take hold of the 'holistic' nature of Islam, through the works of a heterogeneous group of authors, from Muhammad Akram Khan to Seyyed Vali Reza Nasr and Masudul Alam Choudhury. While Nasr called for a 'new Islamization of economics', arguing that the behaviour of the Muslim economic agent is not subject to moral 'constraints,' as some works of the literature stated, but to 'restraints', given that it is the individual who controls himself (Nasr, 1992: 17–18); Choudhury focused on the fact that individual preferences are 'embedded in social preferences' and ethics generated endogenously in the system; he worked so in the development of a Unitarian epistemological approach, called 'Islamic Political Economy', that would fit the holistic character of the Islamic worldview and interconnect economics with institutions, politics, society and science in a circular scheme of causal relations (Choudhury, 2000: 105, 116–18).

Other works try to face those epistemological and methodological challenges from the conceptual frameworks offered by the Philosophy of science or of Islamic science of Osman Bakar or S. Hossein Nasr. In this line, some authors had argued that Islamic individuals' choices and actions cannot be determined by maximizing criteria in 'mono-utility functions', that do not distinguish between needs and wants while reducing values to tastes. In this sense, neoclassical economics, being based still on the parameters of classical Newtonian physics, are dated by today's scientific standards, and so should experiment a transformation similar to the 'quantum' revolution that physics experienced during the first decades of the twentieth century with Einstein's Theory of Relativity (El-Ansary, 2006).

Current turning of the literature: From economics to finance

The distance between mainstream literature and those sections exploring new epistemological and methodological approaches has broadened up during the first decade of this new millennium, due to the increasing emphasis of the former on banking and finance (Muqorobin, 2008), at the expense of other areas and sectors of the economic system. Hence, if the 1950s uncovered the Islamic approach towards economic matters, the 1970s defined the elements and principles of an Islamic economy and the 1980s created modern IE, the 1990s and 2000s passed the baton over to IF.

The rapid expansion of the IF industry in this period has led to an increase as well in the sophistication and complexity of IB, in the scope of the services it offers and in the geographical areas and regulatory frameworks it operates. This has led necessarily to an intense development of the literature on financial issues, 'financial engineering' (capital markets, portfolio and risk management, capital requirements and profitability, regulations and standards, insurance, bonds and asset pricing, etc.). Of the current literature, 40 per cent is dedicated to banking and finance; theory and methodology still account for 20 per cent; while only a minor proportion deals with different areas of economic policy and macroeconomics (7% and 2% to fiscal and monetary policy, respectively), a mere 6 per cent deals with development, 3 per cent to economic history, 0.85 per cent to labour, and

0.5 per cent and 0.3 per cent to agriculture and industry, respectively (Muqorobin, 2008: 389).

Comparing training and education programmes nowadays with those from the earlier decades of the discipline, the contrast is self-evident, reflecting the mentioned shift from economics towards finance. As can be seen in other sections of this book, contemporary programmes are basically focused on IF to train the future executives of Islamic investment funds and financial institutions. An important part of the curricula verses on Islamic capital markets, *Sukūk*, derivatives, price assessments and risk-management. In contrast, an archetypal programme before would have focused on IE in general, studying IB and IF as part of the Islamic economic system, in addition to dealing with the whole set of policies and areas that conform to that system, from Islamic consumer, firm and investment behaviour, to market equilibrium, competition and market structures, distributive justice, taxes and public-sector and economic development in Islam (Iqbal, 1998: 15–16).

In a similar way, while the number of journals specialized on IE has been basically shrinking, with the exception of *Islamic Banker* and *New Horizon*, published since 1995 or the early 1990s, the rest of the magazines on IF today (8 of a total of 10) have been created in the last decade; the newest one, *Global Islamic Finance Magazine*, in 2009. The latest academic journals, the *Journal of Islamic Marketing* (JIMA) and the *Journal of Islamic Accounting and Business Research*, both founded in 2010, are also finance or business-related, as too is the *ISRA International Journal of Islamic Finance* and the *International Journal of Islamic and Middle Eastern Finance and Management*, created respectively in 2009 and 2008. From the dozen main academic journals on IE and IF launched in recent decades, nine at least are still being published but reflect as well the shifting interest from research to business-oriented matters.[11]

One of the facts that the development of IF over IE reflects as well is the gap between theory and practice in IF and, so, its departure from the original aims that were thought to be pursued – to offer an alternative model to capitalism, between capitalism and socialism, and to contribute to the development of Muslim countries (Asutay, 2010). Financial institutions, being closer to the values and views of the Muslim population, were expected to be able to bring into the banking system those sections of the population that were still out of conventional financial circuits in developing countries. Theoretically, this was thought to be an opportunity for enhancing processes of credit creation and, so, development. Especially, considering their community-oriented character, Islamic banks were thought to generate endogenous and local growth and reduce poverty in Muslim countries. However, Islamic financial institutions have been mainly focused in financing trade, big infrastructure and real estate projects, which, even if having an important impact on real economy, have not contributed to improving the situation and the development of rural and poor regions (Kuran, 2005). To recover the developmental aspects of IE and IF, numerous scholars, including some of those 'younger economists' who settled the grounds of IE in the 1970s and 1980s, propose prioritizing the principles, values and spirit of IE over the strict legal or *Shari'ah*-compliant criteria that govern nowadays the activity of Islamic financial institutions. In this line, going back to the comprehensive and primary principle of Islamic worldview, *Tawhīd*, they call for a revisiting of the concept of development in Islam in order to bridge the divide between the theory and practice of IF. Some of them do so from a political economy approach, based on functional and historically grounded Islamic institutions, such as *Zakāh*, *Hisbah*, *Waqf* and *Sadaqah* (Zaman and Asutay, 2009: 91–2). For a simplified scheme of the main trends and schools in the development of the Islamic Economic paradigm see Figure 2.1.

Main challenges and proposals for a research agenda

Some of the main critiques and successive debates about the state of the literature confirm the persistence of a series of unresolved issues. In particular, I would like to focus on four of them and make some qualifications and proposals in this regard:

1. Lack of an adequate methodology to the epistemological bases of the Islamic worldview. This deficiency has led, on the one hand, to the adoption of instruments and methods from neoclassical economics, which cannot be directly transferred to the Islamic economic paradigm (Choudhury, 1992: 104); and, on the other, to the supremacy of law over essence and principles.
2. Low implication and impact on development, both in terms of theoretical studies about the role of IF in development and the practice of IF institutions, not working with a developmental focus.
3. Concurrence of multiple structures and definitions of the IE model, which due to their conceptual nature (Akram Khan, 1989: 275), not being theoretical or grounded on empirical observation, do not offer a complete, coherent and ordered economic system.
4. Scarce historically grounded analysis of institutions and practices within Islam and in IF today, as well as of the ideas and texts by scholars writing in different historical and social contexts (Essid, 1995: 5).

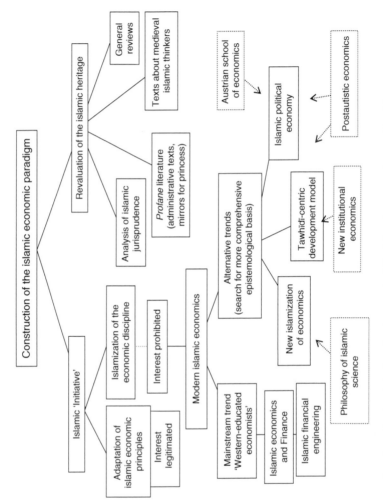

Figure 2.1 Phases, trends and schools in the development of the Islamic economic paradigm[12]

First of all, I would like to emphasize that some of the epistemological critiques and methodological problems exposed are not exclusive of the IE paradigm. The relation between ethics and economics or the role of values in economics (Siddiqi, 1981: 70) has produced a huge number of debates and dissertations in economic circles different to the Islamic ones (González, 1991). Besides, it is not only the choices and actions of Muslims which cannot be determined by maximizing criteria over 'mono-utility' functions. The anthropological reductions the neoclassical economic model entails have been questioned all around the globe. They not only model the behaviour of a maximizing and materialistic individual but that of a robot (Rubio de Urquía, 1991).

The 'Western' conceptions of economic theory, to which some Islamic economists refer (Zaman, 2008: 129), are not monolithic. Neoclassical economics is only the mainstream paradigm, but contested, in terms of methods, approach and objectives (the idea that science is 'value-free', the principle of maximization, of self-interest, the reduction of the human being to a simple machine that chooses between things, the monetization of all aspects of human life, etc.) from different and varied circles and traditions (Austrian school of economics, new institutionalism, postautistic economics, Christian economics, socially responsible and sustainable initiatives, ethical banking, etc.); trends and schools that in one way or another seem to share some elements, concerns and problems with IE and IF. Much could be learned and achieved if Islamic economists would explore and contact those other economic schools and trends that are trying to find new solutions for those epistemological and methodological challenges.

I would completely support, in this respect, Siddiqi's calls, in his paper about the obstacles to research, for bringing 'Muslim intellectuals out of their shell into the company of other intellectuals for exploring ways and means of delivering humanity from the unprecedented predicament it finds itself in' (Siddiqi, 2008: 10). With the aim of benefiting from the research traditions in the West, while allowing Western scholars to have a closer look at those ideas of IE, he adds that 'a strong center for research in Islamic economics located in the west' is needed (Siddiqi, 2008: 11). Maybe this is too ambitious, especially given the current economic crisis in Europe. My suggestion would be to make the existing IE and IF centres and programmes in Europe and North America work more closely with other departments (in those same universities or research networks) of economic theory, economic history and history of economic thought, in addition to other areas like philosophy, sociology and political sciences, in order to try to examine and tackle common topics, inquiries and debates.

In relation to the second point, about IF and development, Islamic financial institutions have been extensively criticized for departing from the risk-sharing principles inherent in its theory and for not investing in activities with a developmental impact – with the exception of some current initiatives in that direction, like Islamic microfinance (Obaidullah and Haji Abdul Latiff, 2008). Due to the low percentage of Profit and Loss Sharing (PLS) contracts in the portfolios of IF institutions, during the late 1990s there was certain debate and discussion about the agency problems and imperfect information constraints that these contracts faced. However, those debates seem to have vanished while the focus is now on studying the profitability and risk structures of different new derivatives and instruments, and there is little done about the real constraints that Islamic financial institutions confront. It has been justified that IB institutions had to compete with conventional banks, but few studies analyse the financial, regulatory and business contexts in which they had to develop their activity and which perhaps played a role in them focusing on mark-up contracts and commercial activities. With a few exceptions (Henry and Wilson, 2004), there have also been no studies that analyse the institutional and political economic contexts in which IF developed. Indeed, even the literature about the situation and reform of financial systems, in general, in Middle Eastern and North African countries (which could offer the context and background for those analyses) is scarce,. In sum, those different contexts and dimensions probably differ from the ideal framework of IE; a difference that may affect the operational capacities of IF institutions and whose dimensions and implications need to be examined in detail.

Linking this point and the last one, about the historical dimension, there is a need to understand and analyse contemporary economic realities in Islamic and Muslim countries, as well as in the past: how Muslims behave as consumers, producers, employers, traders and managers; as well as how Islamic and non-Islamic institutions operate in these countries (financial institutions but also institutions of charity and its impact on development, *Waqf, Zakāh* funds, inheritance, *Hajj*, etc., in line with those mentioned works by Zaman and Asutay, 2009); either thorough empirical studies (qualitative and quantitative) or historical works.

In relation to the last point, with few exceptions (Chachi, 2005: 15; Cizakca, 2011; Islahi, 2010) there is a significant lack and need of further studies on economic history and history of economic thought (analyses that, besides, would need to complement each other). For example, current claims in the literature about the need to go back to using the gold Islamic dinar (Mydin Meera and Moussa, 2004), cannot be approached without studying those past historical experiences with multi-metallic monetary systems in the Middle Ages and their implications for the stability of the monetary and financial system.

The historical vacuum becomes a particular acute problem given the lack of critical editions of the works by medieval scholars and philosophers, which in turn makes it difficult to compare and check interpretations or readings of their ideas (I am thinking of Ibn Rushd, in particular, but also of Ibn Taimiyyah, whose immense *Fatāwah* collections are hard to consult and compare, as well as al-Ghazali's works, among others).

As the importance of incorporating Islamic medieval scholars and institutions into the history of economic ideas in the Mediterranean has been widely claimed (the so-called big gap thesis; see Essid, 1987; Akalay, 1991), it is equally important to explore those *histoires croisées* (entangled histories) that show how scholars and monetary authorities in different parts of the Mediterranean dealt with and reacted to similar problems related to multi-metallic monetary systems (Orozco, 2008); as well as how they developed similar institutions, regulations and practices to deal with it – from the *commenda/Mudārabah* mercantile contracts (Grice-Hutchinson, 1978; Udovitch, 1962), to the *almotacén/Al-muhtasib* and the institutions in charge of the regulation of the markets (Glick, 1971; Chalmeta, 1973), or of hosting travellers and merchants, taxing trade and housing economic transactions (Constable, 2003).

Aslam Haneef adds in his comments to Siddiqi's paper about 'Obstacles to Research in Islamic Economics', that Islamic and Western history of civilizations should be taught together. Indeed, that exercise might lead to reconsideration of the reasons for maintaining that mirage of speaking about two and not one single civilization, grounded in common values, principles and institutions (of Judeo-Muslim-Christian origin).

The same then as now: as the economic crisis showed, economic discipline has to deal with similar problems of resource allocation, speculation, greed and management all around the globe. Economists of different countries and backgrounds are trying to face those same problems. I would like to ask those designing the curricula and research agenda of IE centres to take this into account, go deeper in the study of the economic discipline and economic thought in its different trends, now and in history.

Notes

1. It seems that another previous attempt was made in the late 50s to create an Islamic bank in a rural area of Pakistan. See Traute (1983) and Wilson (1983) as quoted by Chachi in: Abdelkader Chachi, "Origin and Development of Commercial and Islamic Banking Operations," *Journal of King Abdulaziz University: Islamic Economics* 18, No. 2 (2005): 3–25, p. 15.

2. Some extended critique evaluations of the Islamic economics paradigm may be found in M. A. Choudhury's *The Islamic Worldview*, Akram Khan's *Islamic Economic: The State of Art*, S. V. R. Nasr's *Islamization of Knowledge: A Critical overview* and M. U. Chapra's *What is Islamic Econonomics?*. Literature reviews and appraisals of the state of art in the literature are also numerous and generate continuous debate. See the conference papers of *7th International Conference on Islamic Economics and Finance* (1–3 April 2008), and other roundtables and discussion, like the ones organized by the Islamic Research and Training Institute and the Arab Planning Institute, including works in this respect by Akram Khan, M. N. Siddiqi, Abdul Azim Islahi, Kamal Tawfiq Hattab and Khaled A. Hussein, among others.

3. According to Islahi, one of the first works in this respect was an article, written by Salih in 1933, that discussed the economic ideas of Medieval Muslim scholars ('Arab Economic Thought in the Fifteenth Century'). Abdul Azim Islahi, "Thirty Years on History of Islamic Economic Thought: Assessment and Future Directions," in *The 7th International Conference in Islamic Economics: Thirty Years of Research in Islamic Economics. Solutions & Applications of Contemporary Economic Issues, 1–3 April 2008*, 2008 (pp. 347–70), p. 347.

4. For Essid it is result of two trends, the "reawakening of the Arab world" and the emergence of the "Islamic initiative". Yassine Essid, (1995), *A Critique of the Origins of the Islamic Economic Thought*, E. J. Brill, New York, (pp. 4–5). Asutay sees the modern variant of Islamic economics owning its development in 1970s to the identity politics. Mehmet Asutay (2007), "A Political Economy Approach to Islamic Economics: Systemic Understanding for an Alternative Economic System," *Kyoto Bulletin of Islamic Area Studies* 1, N° 2, (pp. 3–18), p. 3.

5. Other earlier works, like Hameedullah's (1936) and Qureshi's (1946), among others, are commented in Mohammad Nejatullah Siddiqi (2006), "Islamic Banking and Finance in Theory and Practice: A survey of state of the art," *Islamic Economic Studies*, Vol. 13, No. 2, p. 2.

6. Ala'i does not date it but includes it in a text of Columbia University by Seligman, "Studies in History, Economics & Public Law", edited by Edwin Robert Anderson supposedly in the thirties. Hesmat Ala'i, *Theory of Income Distribution under the Islamic Law, with special reference to the function of Residual Income Recipients*, Georgetown University Thesis (n. 1105), 1953, p. 46. It is probably part of Aghnides' thesis: Nicolas P. Aghnides (1916), *Mohammedan Theories of Finance*, New York: Columbia University. Available online at: http://archive.org/stream/mohammedantheor01aghngoog (05/05/12).

7. For example, in a comprehensive attempt to bring together and synthesize those essential elements, Asutay includes eight axioms (Taw îd, Al-'adl wa`l-ihsan, Ikhtiyar, Fard, Rubūbiyyah, Tazkiyah, Khilâfah, Maqasid al-Sharî'ah) while in a later work by Azid Islamic economics is defined by six basic assumptions (Taw îd, Rubūbiyyah, Guidance, Khilâfah, Tazkiyah, and Spiritual Accountability) plus eight groups of goals and objectives. Both authors, however, quote some common leading Islamic economists (Ahmad, Chapra and Naqvi). See previously cited Mehmet Asutay (2007) and Toseef Azid (2010) "Anthology of Islamic Economics: Review of Some Basic Issues," *Review of Islamic Economics* 13, 2, 165–94.

8. The previous generation has been considered that of the "founders or pioneer scholars" writing from the 1920s to the 1950s. Abdul Azim Islahi (2010), "Four Generations of Islamic Economists," *JKAU: Islamic Economics*, 23, 1, pp. 163–9 (p. 166). That generation is the one that started in fact writing on the economic approach or 'economic teachings' of Islam, while criticizing Western contemporary theory and policy. It was developed mainly by religious scholars, *'ulama*, in addition to "the lefties and Muslim social thinkers and reformers;" Muhammad Akram Khan (1983), *Islamic Economics: Annotated Sources in English and Urdu*, Leicester, England: the Islamic Foundation, p. 7, quoted in Esposito & Voll (2001, pp. 47–8).
9. Linking with the mentioned confusion about which are those elements and axioms, Nasr will argue that the problems encountered by Islamic economists in building up the Islamic economic system are due to the lack of "an internally consistent worldview at hand." S. V. R. Nasr (1992), *Islamization of Knowledge: A Critical overview*, International Institute of Islamic Thought, Islamabad, p. 4.
10. Fahim Khan even structures his book following the different parts of a neoclassical economics manual, with a theory of Consumer Behavior, a function of Macro Consumption and of Investment Demand "in an Islamic framework". M. Fahim Khan (1995), *Essays in Islamic Economics*, The Islamic Foundation, Leicester.
11. Among others, the *IIUM Journal of Economics and Management* seems to have not published new volumes since 2010.
12. This charter attempts to be only a mere scheme to orientate in some of the main trends and development within the development of the Islamic economic paradigm. It does not try to offer a systematic and comprehensive picture.

References

Abdul Mannan, M. (1984) *The Making of Islamic Economic Society: Islamic Dimensions in Economic Analysis* (Jeddah: International Center for Research in Islamic Economics).

Ahmad, K. (ed.) (1980) *Studies in Islamic Economics* (Leicester: The Islamic Foundation, Leicester).

Ala'I, H. (1953) *Theory of Income Distribution under the Islamic Law, with Special Reference to the Function of Residual Income Recipients*, Georgetown University Thesis (n. 1105).

Aghnides Nicolas, P. (1916) *Mohammedan Theories of Finance*, New York: Columbia University. Available online at: http://archive.org/stream/mohammedantheor01aghngoog (05/05/12).

Akalay, O. (1991) *Le grand vide de Joseph Schumpeter: brève histoire de la pensée économique en Islam* (Casablanca: Wallada).

Akram Khan, M. (1989) 'Islamic Economic: The State of Art', *Toward Islamization of Disciplines: Proceedings and Selected Papers of the Third International Conference of Islamization of Knowledge* (Kuala Lumpur, 24–31 July 1984) (Virginia: International Institute of Islamic Thought), pp. 273–92.

Asutay, M. (2007) 'A political economy approach to Islamic economics: Systemic understanding for an alternative economic system,' *Kyoto Bulletin of Islamic Area Studies*, 1, 2, pp. 3–18.

—— (2010) 'Considering the dichotomy between the ideals and realities of Islamic finance', *New Horizon* (published by IIBI, London), 174, 32.

Azid, T. (2010) 'Anthology of Islamic economics: Review of some basic issues', *Review of Islamic Economics*, 13, 2, pp. 165–94.

Cizakca, M. (2011) 'The Islamic Gold Dinār – myths and reality', *ISRA International Journal of Islamic Finance*, 3, 1, pp. 49–63.

Chachi, A. (2005) 'Origin and development of commercial and Islamic banking operations', *Journal of King Abdulaziz University: Islamic Economics*, 18, 2, pp. 3–25.

Chalmeta, P. (1973) *El 'Señor Del Zoco' En España: Edades Media Y Moderna: Contribución Al Estudio De La Historia Del Mercado* (Madrid: Instituto Hispano-Árabe de Cultura).

Chapra, M. U. (1985) *Towards a Just Monetary System. A Discussion on Money, Banking and Monetary Policy in the Light of Islamic Teachings* (Leicester: The Islamic Foundation).

—— (1996) *What is Islamic Econonomics?* (Jeddah: Islamic Research and Training Institute, Islamic Development Bank).

Choudhury, M. A. (1992) *The Principles of Islamic Political Economy: A Methodological Enquiry* (New York: St. Martin's Press).

—— (2000) *The Islamic Worldview* (London: Kegan Paul International).

Constable, O. R. (2003) *Housing the Stranger in the Mediterranean World: Lodging, Trade, and Travel in Late Antiquity and the Middle Ages* (Cambridge: Cambridge University Press).

El-Ansary, W. (2006) 'The quantum enigma and Islamic sciences of nature: Implications for Islamic economic theory', *The 6th International Conference of Islamic Economics and* Finance, 21–4 November 2005, pp. 143–75.

Esposito, J. L. and Voll, J. O. (2001) *Makers of Contemporary Islam* (New York: Oxford University Press).

Essid, Y. (1987) 'Islamic economic thought', in S. Todd Lowry (ed.) *Pre-Classical Economic Thought: From the Greeks to the Scottish Enlightenment* (Boston: Kluwer-Nijhoff Publishers), pp. 77–102.

—— (1995) *A Critique of the Origins of the Islamic Economic Thought* (New York: E. J. Brill).

Fahim Khan, M. (1995) *Essays in Islamic Economics* (Leicester: The Islamic Foundation).

Glick, Thomas F. (1971) "Muhtasib and Mustasaf: A Case Study of Institutional Diffusion", *Viator*, 2, pp. 59–81.

González, M. J. (1991) 'Lo ético en la Historia del pensamiento económico', *ICE*, no. 691, March, (pp. 17–30).

Grice-Hutchinson, M. (1978) *Early Economic Thought in Spain 1177–1740* (London: George Allen & Unwin).

Henry, C. M. and Wilson, R. (eds) (2004) *The Politics of Islamic Finance* (Edinburgh: Edinburgh University Press).

Islahi, A. A. (2008) 'Thirty years of research in the history of Islamic economic thought: Assessment and future directions', in *Thirty Years of Research in Islamic Economics: Solutions & Applications of Contemporary Economic Issues*, The 7th International Conference in Islamic Economics – Conference papers, IDB-IRTI-KAU-IAIE-IERC.

—— (2010) 'Four generations of Islamic economists', *JKAU: Islamic Economics*, 23, 1, pp. 163–9.

Iqbal, M. (1998) 'Teaching programs in Islamic economics: A comparative study', in M. Oreibi (ed.) *Contribution of Islamic Thought to Modern Economics: Proceedings of the Economic Seminar held Jointly by al Azhar University and the International Institute of Islamic Thought (Cairo, 1988/1409)*, Second edition, The International Institute of Islamic Thought, pp. 8–53.

Kuran, T. (2005) *Islam and Mammon: The Economic Predicaments of Islamism* (Princeton: Princeton University Press).

Muqorobin, M. (2008) 'Journey of Islamic economics in the modern world,' in *Thirty Years of Research in Islamic Economics: Solutions & Applications of Contemporary Economic Issues*, The 7th International Conference in Islamic Economics – Conference papers, IDB-IRTI-KAU-IAIE-IERC, pp. 385–404.

Mydin Meera, A. K. and Larbani, M. (2004) 'The Gold Dinar: The Next Component in Islamic Economics, Banking and Finance,' *Review of Islamic Economics*, 8, 1, pp. 5–34.

Nasr, S. V. R. (1992) *Islamization of Knowledge: A Critical Overview* (Islamabad: International Institute of Islamic Thought).

Obaidullah, M. and Abdul Latiff, H. S. (2008) *Islamic Finance for Micro and Medium Enterprises*, IRTI-IDB & Centre for Islamic Banking, Finance and Management – University Brunei Darussalam.

Orozco, O. (2008) *Monetary Thought in Islamic and Christian Scholars (13th and 16th century): A Comparative Perspective on Debasement and the Rise of the Quantity Theory of Money*, Ph.D. thesis (Florence: European University Institute).

Rubio de Urquía, R. (1991) 'Ética y procesos de asignación de recursos', *ICE*, no. 691, March, (pp. 7–16).

Siddiqi, M. N. (1981) *Muslim Economic Thinking: A Survey of Contemporary Literature* (Leicester: The Islamic Foundation).

—— (2006) 'Islamic banking and finance in theory and practice: A survey of state of the art', *Islamic Economic Studies*, 13, 2, pp. 1–48.

—— (2008) 'Obstacles of research in Islamic economics,' in *Thirty Years of Research in Islamic Economics: Solutions & Applications of Contemporary Economic Issues*. The 7th International Conference in Islamic Economics – Conference papers, IDB-IRTI-KAU-IAIE-IERC.

Udovitch, A. L. (1962) 'At the origins of the Western Commenda: Islam, Israel, Byzantium', *Speculum*, 37, 2, pp. 198–207.

Zaman, A. (2008) "Experiences of IIIE: 1983–2007" in *Thirty Years of Research in Islamic Economics: Solutions & Applications of Contemporary Economic Issues*, The 7th International Conference in Islamic Economics – Conference papers, IDB-IRTI-KAU-IAIE-IERC, (pp. 123–34).

Zaman, N. and Mehmet, A. (2009) "Divergence between Aspirations and Realities of Islamic Economics: A Political Economy Approach to Bridging the Divide", *IIUM Journal of Economics and Management* 17, 1, pp. 73–96.

3
Islamic Finance Higher Education at a Glance: A Global Picture

Ahmed Belouafi and Abderrazak Belabes

Introduction

Before looking at the Islamic Finance education programmes (IFEPs) at various higher education institutions in the West, it is important to present a global picture of the development and current state of the IFE phenomenon. The major aim is to gather as much accurate information as possible to provide a well-documented track of its features and trends. It should be noted that the term 'Islamic Finance higher education', in this chapter, refers to an educational programme leading to a specialized degree in IF.

Sample database

The database for this chapter is part of a research programme of the Institute of Islamic Economics about IFE around the world. It covers programmes offered in Arabic, English and French. The sample for the present study consists of 129 programmes and the range of covered degrees, in the three languages, is as spelled out in Table 3.1.

The emergence of Islamic Finance higher education programmes

Since the beginning of the millennium, several IFEPs emerged in different parts of the World. Table 3.2 provides an account of the early developments in this regard:

It is clear from the previous table that the number of IFEPs has been relatively limited and some of them have disappeared altogether, as is the case at Loughborough University, and some of them have continued on an interrupted basis. However, the year 2006 saw a significant landmark

Table 3.1 Classification of surveyed degrees in IF awarded in English, French and Arabic worlds

English world		French world		Arabic world	
Utilized abbreviations	**Degree titles**	**Utilized abbreviations**	**Degrees titles**	**Utilized abbreviations**	**Degrees titles**
	Certificate		Certificate		
	Diploma		Diploma		Diploma
	Higher Diploma	DU	University Degree		Higher Diploma
BSc	Bachelor in Science				Bachelor in Science
	Postgraduate Diploma				
MSc	Master of Science			BSc	
MA	Master of Art			MSc	Master
MBA	Master of Business Administration			MBA	
EMBA	Executive Master of Business Administration			Ph.D.	Doctorate
LLM	Master of Law				
Ph.D.	Doctorate of Philosophy				

Source: Authors' classification.

Table 3.2   Institutions that have been involved in establishing IFEPs since the year 2000

Institution name	Country	Year of establishment of IFEP	Note
Loughborough University	UK	2000	Ceased in 2005
Durham University	UK	2000	Ceased in 2003. The initiatives have been on and off till 2012 where new degrees have been launched
Yarmouk University	Jordan	2002	
International Institute of Islamic Finance	Pakistan	2003	
Arab Academy for Banking and Financial Sciences	Jordan	2003	
Sudan Academy for Finance and Banking Sciences	Sudan	2003	
Emirates Institute for Banking and Financial Studies	United Arab Emirates	2003	

Source: Authors.

with the establishment of a unique institution fully dedicated to IFEPs; the International Centre for Education in Islamic Finance (INCEIF) that was inaugurated by Bank Negara (the Central Bank of Malaysia) in 2005 and started its operations effectively from the year 2006.

Another turning point in the spread of IFEPs has been the international financial crisis. According to the information we have, the crisis seems to have boosted the supply of IFEPs. This may be due to the attention that has been given to the industry because of the extraordinary growth rates that it has achieved during the turbulent years of the crisis, and to the crucial importance of taking seriously into consideration the question of 'values' and 'ethics' to instil 'moderation' into the behaviour and organization of the financial system and its players. This epistemological, moral and ethical questioning is meaningful only if it goes along with a reflection on the teaching of finance and business which should focus on social responsibility of business and policymakers (Chesney and Dembinski, 2011: 66). Within this dynamic context, the teaching of IF seems to have changed noticeably as shown in Figure 3.1.[1]

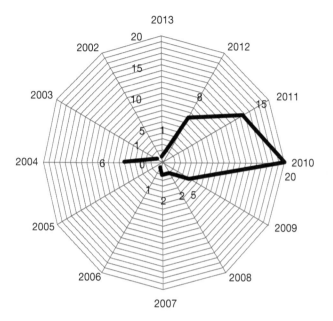

Figure 3.1 The number of IFEPs introduced per year in the world from 2002 through 2013
Socurce: Authors.

This evolution of IFEPs in the aftermath of the crisis is even more apparent in the Western world as shown in Figure 3.2, particularly in the United Kingdom, which saw the opening of fully fledged Islamic banks from 2004, and in the active role taken by the French authorities in promoting Paris as a hub for IF since 2008.

Distribution of IFEPs by continents

Figures 3.3 and 3.4 display the distribution of IFEPs across four continents. Asia comes first with 79 (61%), followed by Europe with 36 (28%), Africa with 13 (10%) and finally Oceania with 1. The American continent does not host any programmes yet. The cartography shows that IFEPs in the Western world occur mainly in Europe. But this does not mean that the USA does not offer courses or research programmes in IF in their territory or abroad. For example, the Fletcher School of Tufts University offers a course entitled 'Islamic Banking and Finance' which provides a comprehensive introduction to Islamic Banking (IB) and IF. Moreover, the Harvard Law School at Harvard University

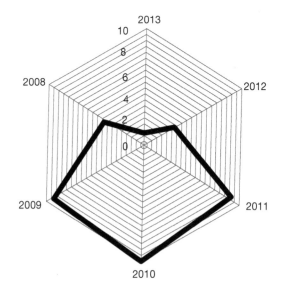

Figure 3.2   The number of IFEPs introduced per year in the Western world from 2002 through 2013
Socurce: Authors.

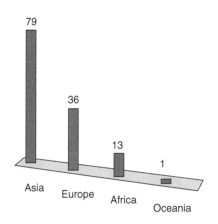

Figure 3.3   Distribution of IFEPs by continents (value)

developed an Islamic Finance Project.[2] Moreover, the American University of Leadership offers in Morocco, as part of its MBA, a specialization stream in IF. The International Institute of Islamic Thought, established in the United States in 1981, introduced a degree in IE

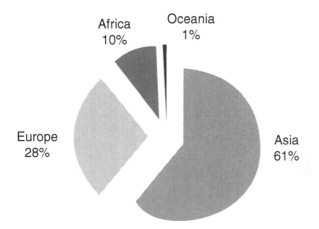

Figure 3.4   Distribution of IFEPs by continents (%)

and IF in France for two consecutive academic years (2009–10 and 2010–11).

At first glance, the leading position of Asia may be explained by the number of Muslim inhabitants in this area, but this explanation loses its relevance for Africa. Thus, the presence of Muslims does not appear to be a determinant factor in explaining the diffusion of IFEPs in Asia. Other factors seem to play an important role as the political and economic will of the actors and communication strategy promoting IF. Based on this argument, the case of Malaysia can be singled out from the proactive role its government and society are playing in promoting the country as an international hub for IF.[3] At the European level, the cases of the UK and France are the most revealing ones. In 2006 the UK chancellor of the exchequer, Gordon Brown planned to make *'Britain the gateway to Islamic finance and trade'*. For her part, Christine Lagarde, France's minister of economy, declared on 2 February 2008 that 'We will adapt our legal system so that the stability and the innovation of our financial centre can be beneficial for Islamic finance by welcoming its activities to Paris as has been the case in London and other financial centres' (Jouini et Pastré, 2008: 111). Moreover, she told the French Senate in September 2010: 'London has not the upper-hand monopoly of Islamic finance. By taking appropriate tax injunctions, in that way I think I have fulfilled my roadmap that Paris could become a hub for Islamic finance' (Marini, 2010: 293).

Distribution of IFEPs by economic blocs

In terms of economic blocs (Figures 3.5 and 3.6), the European Union leads with 36 programmes (44%), followed by ASEAN with 28 (35%), GCC with 17 (21%) and BRICS with 2 (2%). Thus, Europe again occupies a prominent place.

Moreover, the previous results reveal a paradox: while the Gulf countries are undeniable leaders in many segments of the IF products market, their competitive position in IFEPs is lagging vis-à-vis EU and ASEAN. Despite this delay, the Gulf, especially Bahrain, has a competitive advantage in terms of the position that this region has. For instance, to fill in the gap of its deficit in properly qualified human resources in IF, Senegal sent to Bahrain, in December 2010, a group of 12 executives from six institutional entities, to undergo an accelerated education as future trainers in IF (Fall, 2011). This initiative has been

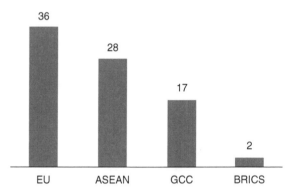

Figure 3.5   Distribution of IFEPs by economic blocs (value)

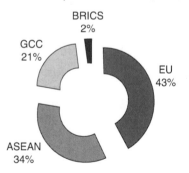

Figure 3.6   Distribution of IFEPs by economic blocs (%)

carried out despite the language difference between the two countries.[4] The traditional 'prestige' of French higher education institutions has been put aside in this situation.

Distribution of IFEPs by countries

Figure 3.7 gives an idea of the supply of IFEPs by countries. Britain leads with 27 programmes (21%) followed by: Malaysia with 22 (17%); United Arab Emirates with 11 (9%); Pakistan with 10 (8%); Jordan with 8 (6%); Bahrain with 6 (5%); France, Indonesia and Nigeria with 4 (3%); Sudan, Kuwait, Qatar, Brunei and Syria with 3 (2%); India and Algeria with 2; and a set of 12 countries with a single programme.

This picture shows that IF higher education is no longer confined to Arabs or Muslims, but has transformed into an interest for other areas outside these traditional locations. In addition, these programmes seem to attract students of different nationalities and backgrounds. For example, the launch of Strasbourg Management School's 'university degree' (*diplôme universitaire*) attracted a diversity of students from Belgium,

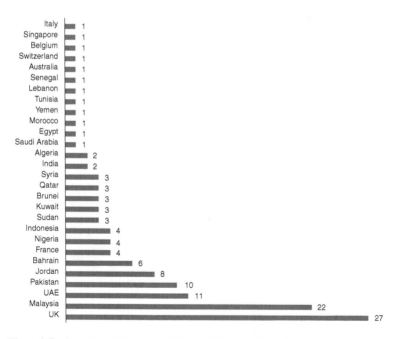

Figure 3.7   Attractiveness of IFEPs by countries (number of programmes)

Luxembourg, Germany and Switzerland besides the French (Gadric, 2009). For its part, La Trobe University in Melbourne, Australia, attracts students from Vietnam, Hong Kong, the United States, Pakistan, India and Saudi Arabia in addition to Australians (Grooch, 2010). The case studies covered in this book may shed more light on the attractiveness of the programmes with reference to learners' origins and backgrounds.

Distribution of IFEPs by the medium of instruction

Concerning the IFEPs' distribution by the medium of instruction (Figure 3.8); English leads with 97 programmes (75%), followed by Arabic with 25 (20%), and French with 6 (5%). This result is not surprising given that English is the language of the international business community. But this does not imply that native English speakers have the advantage in the workforce market. On the contrary, in this dynamic and globalized world, language proficiency has become an additional asset. Consequently, the major IF institutions may prefer to hire staff who speak at least two languages as compared to those limited to English only. Some French and Arab business schools attempt to take advantage in this respect by providing IFEPs entirely in English like ESA Beirut, Reims Management School, Effat University Jeddah, TAG-Org[5] Amman or HBMeU[6] Dubai. In the Western world, the position of the English language is even more evident with 91 per cent, while the share of the French language increased to 9 per cent, and as it is anticipated the Arabic language is not present (Figure 3.9). In order to shed more light on this feature, it is important to look into the distribution of these two respective languages by countries.

Figure 3.10 gives an idea of the distribution of IFEPs taught in English by country; the UK leads with 27 programmes (30%), followed by

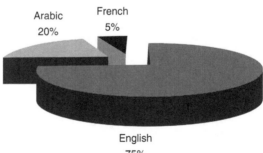

Figure 3.8   Distribution of IFEPs by language in the world (%)

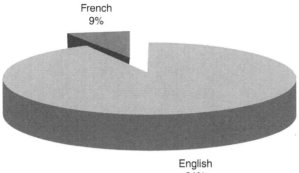

Figure 3.9   Distribution of IFEPs by language in the West (%)

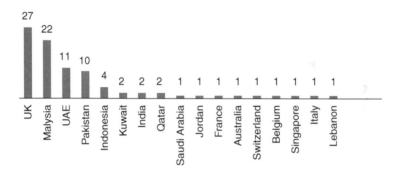

Figure 3.10   Distribution of IFEPs among English-speaking countries

Malaysia with 22 (25%), and United Arab Emirates with 11 (12%). The contribution of non-Western countries appears significant with a percentage share of 64 per cent. Interestingly, the presence of France and Saudi Arabia should be noted. France – which traditionally has been known for its 'resistance' to English – created a certificate in Islamic banking and finance delivered entirely in English. Saudi Arabia, generally regarded as 'conservative', opened an Executive Master degree in Islamic Financial Management in English at Effat University, a leading private non-profit institution of higher education for women, operating under the umbrella of King Faisal's Charitable Foundation.[7]

Figure 3.11 shows the distribution of the IFEPs in French speaking countries. The percentage share of 42.85 per cent of non-western countries appears to be significant as well.

Figure 3.11   Distribution of IFEPs among French-speaking countries

Distribution of IFEPs by level of study

In terms of educational level (Figures 3.12 and 3.13), master degrees lead with 70 programmes (54%) followed by diplomas with 17 programmes (13%), bachelors with 12 programmes (12%), certificate, postgraduate diploma and Ph.D. with 7 programmes (5%), advanced diploma, high diploma and university degree with 2 programmes (2%). Two observations can be made findings:

- The first; most of these programmes are confined to a master degree.
- The second; is the fact that executive degrees seem to take over academic programmes.

Regarding the type of degree (Figures 3.14 and 3.15), the title Master leads with 26 programmes (39%), followed by the MBA with 15 (23%), MSc with 14 programmes (21%), MA with 4 (6%), Executive Master with 3 (5%), LLM with 2 (3%), MPhil and EMBA with 1 (1.5%). The title Master includes MSc, MA, and Executive Master. But we preferred to present it as such to give an idea of the subtleties of the comparison. Among those degrees which are called Master's, nine are academic and 17 executive. This confirms the previous analysis and shows an increase in IF executive programmes to meet industry demand for properly qualified personnel.

Distribution of IFEPs by type of instruction

Concerning the type of instruction (Figure 3.16), the c-learning (i.e. conventional learning) leads with 116 programmes (90%) followed by the e-learning with 13 (10%). The teaching of IF by e-learning allows students to form themselves outside of any temporal or geographical

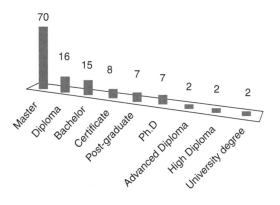

Figure 3.12 Distribution of IFEPs by level of study (number)

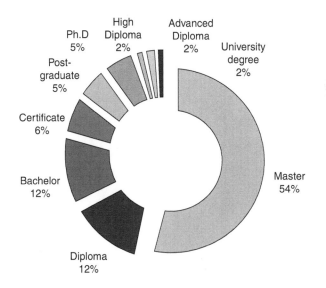

Figure 3.13 Distribution of IFEPs by level of study (%)

constraints; to be able to start a programme at any time and teaching at their own pace according to their availability and constraints. In the Western world (Figure 3.17), the share of e-learning has increased to 25 per cent. In this part of the world, the e-learning infrastructure seems to be more developed.

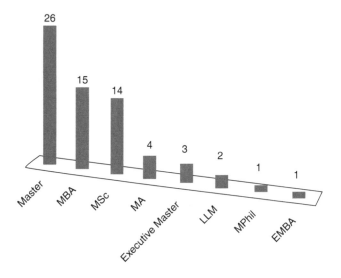

Figure 3.14   Distribution of IFEP by titles of Master's degrees (number)

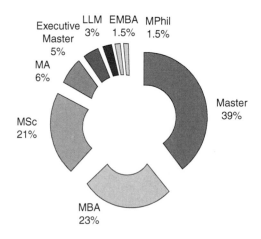

Figure 3.15   Distribution of IFP by titles of Master's degrees (%)

Conclusion

Based upon the previous analysis, the following observations can be made:

- Historically, the emergence of IFEPs took place in the United Kingdom in the early twenty-first century. In this field, the Western

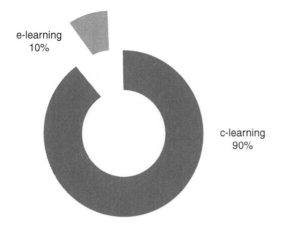

Figure 3.16   Distribution of IFEPs by the mode of education in the world (%)

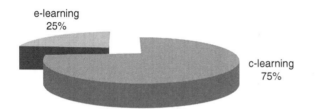

Figure 3.17   Distribution of IFEPs by the mode of education in the West (%)

world is mainly represented by Europe. The distribution by countries shows that the United Kingdom occupies a leading position, closely followed by Malaysia.

- Regarding the medium of instruction of the delivery of IFEPs in the world, English leads with 75 per cent, followed by Arabic with 20 per cent and French with 5 per cent. In the Western world, the position of English is reinforced with 91 per cent and also the French with 9 per cent.
- The distribution by educational level shows the dominance of Executive Master degrees to meet industry demand for human capital development.

Notes

This chapter draws from some developments of a previous paper presented at the seminar 'Reforms in Islamic Higher Education in Meeting Contemporary

Challenges', organized by Graduate School of Education and Human Development, Nagoya University and Japan Society for the Promotion of Science, 30–1 July 2011.

1. Due to the lack of dates information for all programmes, it should be noted that the information displayed in the previous chart is based on 67 programmes only.
2. In fact this project has been running for quite a long period. It was founded in 1995 by the Harvard University Center for Middle Eastern Studies (CMES), and in late 2003, the IFP became a part of the Islamic Legal Studies Program (ILSP) at Harvard Law School (ifp.law.harvard.edu/login/about).
3. The initiatives taken in this regard are numerous. The amendments to the Banking Act in 1983 and the establishment of the International Islamic University Malaysia (IIUM) in the early 1980s are very old ones. In recent years the establishment of INCEIF, IFSB, ISRA and others clearly demonstrate the role played by Malaysia. In education there has been official talk about the accreditation of IFEPs since 2011.
4. The Senegalese élite generally uses French as the language of work.
5. Talal Abu-Ghazaleh Organization.
6. HBMeU: Hamdan Bin Mohammed e-University.
7. In 1419 H (corresponding to 1999 G), it started offering its academic programmes under the name of Effat College and n the 3rd of Safar 1430 H (corresponding to 30 January, 2009 G), Effat College acquired University Status as a private institution of higher education for women (source: effatuniversity.edu.sa).

References

Chesney, M. and Dembinski, P. (2011) 'La finance doit être au service du bien commun', L'Hebdo, Interview réalisé par Geneviève Brunet, 9 novembre, pp. 64–6.

Fall, K. N. (2011) 'Finance islamique au Sénégal: combler d'abord le déficit en ressources humaines', http://www.e-financeislamique.com/actualites/actualites-scientifiques/125-finance-islamique-au-senegal-combler-dabord-le-deficit-en-ressources-humaines.html

Gadric, A. (2009) 'Paris-IX versé dans la finance islamique', Libération, 18 août.

Gooch, L. (2010) 'Asia-Pacific Universities Adding Islamic Finance Courses', The New York, September 26.

Jouini, E. and Pastré, O. (2008) Enjeux et les opportunités du développement de la finance islamique sur la place de Paris, Paris: Paris Europlace.

Marini, P. (2010) Rapport fait au nom de la commission des finances (1) sur le projet de loi, adopté par l'Assemblée nationale, de régulation bancaire et financière, Paris: Sénat, 14 septembre, http://www.senat.fr/rap/l09-703-1/l09-703-11.pdf

4
Islamic Finance Higher Education in a Complex World

Ahmed Belouafi, Abderrazak Belabes and Mohamed Daoudi

Introduction

Over the past few years, Islamic Finance (IF) higher education has attracted worldwide attention. This chapter proposes to study the geo-educational dynamics of the development of this newly emerging discipline. In this geo-educational rivalry, some interesting facts are coming out. For instance, in terms of the number of programmes provided by higher education institutions, Britain is outpacing the mother countries of IF such as Saudi Arabia and Bahrain. Malaysia, on the other hand, is striving to consolidate its position to become an educational hub for IF. What does this dynamism tell us about the current and future cartography of IF education? Which countries and/or regions are going to take a lead? What sort of realities might develop at universities, departments and other higher educational institutions? Finally what sort of implications will these developments have for the flows of IF discipline?

The context of Islamic Finance education development

The liberalization of trade in goods made since 1948, led under the GATT in 1994 to the signing of a new agreement called the 'General Agreement on Trade in Services' (GATS) and the creation in 1995 of the World Trade Organization (WTO). With the establishment of the GATS, the process of trade liberalization has extended to include what have been generally regarded as 'public services'. Education is a typical example of such services. Despite its classification in this category, the fact that the vast majority of countries are still reluctant to open the doors freely to education and other 'service commodities'[1] and 'the resentment of the academia community to the "commodification" of higher education or the subordination of the values of higher education to commercial interests alone' (Bashir, 2007: 8), the last decade or so has witnessed a tremendous growth in international trade in education services, especially at the tertiary level (Sauvé, 2002: 4).[2] Interestingly, the forms of studying abroad are changing. The largest segment is still 'student mobility', however other forms such as 'service mobility' through satellite campuses and/or partnerships between local and overseas institutions are gaining momentum.

> In the UK, the second biggest destination for overseas students after the US, for example there are now 340,000 students taking UK university courses in their home countries, either through partnerships between UK and local universities or else through UK universities setting up branch campuses, such as Nottingham in Ningbo in China. More than 160 branch campuses have been opened in more than 50 countries – mostly by US universities.
>
> Coughlan (2011)

Despite the fact that IF as an emerging phenomenon that came into being over the past few decades or so, it has picked up dramatically, at the international platform, since the mid-1990s. The growth of its assets maintained a double-digit pace on the international financial scene. Thus, it is anticipated that the development and transformation of aspects relating to IF, including education, are not going to be spared the effects of these interactive and very dynamic developments that are taking place internationally.

Sample of the study

Our working sample consists of 123 IF programmes; degrees bearing an IF spearhead title, which cover five continents and are distributed over 26 countries. This database was created as part of an ongoing research programme of the Islamic Economics Institute (IEI) at the University of King Abdulaziz, dedicated to IF higher education. The sample has expanded since our last survey (Belouafi and Belabes, 2011). All findings and analysis that follow are based on this database.

Geo-education of Islamic Finance

The geo-education explores the relationship between power and space; a virtual space in the sense that its borders are constantly changing in a dynamic and evolving manner. The object of the geo-education is the international educational flow and interaction of its actors reported by their ability to influence, persuade and/or attract. The interest of the

Table 4.1 Combinational analysis of IF education

Cases	A	C	Corresponding countries
Scenario 1	0	0	Rest of the world
Scenario 2	0	1	USA, Netherlands, Canada
Scenario 3	1	0	Pakistan, Jordan, Bahrain, Indonesia, Kuwait, Syria, Sudan, Brunei, Qatar, Algeria, India, Saudi Arabia, Yemen, Egypt, Tunisia, Morocco, Senegal, Italy, Switzerland, Belgium, Australia
Scenario 4	1	1	UK, Malaysia, UAE, France

geo-educational approach (GEA) is to distinguish between territorial attractiveness (A) and external competitiveness (C) with their respective weightings α and β.

$$GEA = \{\alpha C, \beta A\}$$

In the combinational analysis, the interaction between these two variables produced four possible scenarios (Table 4.1); 0 denoting the absence of the variable, and 1 denoting to its existence.

Table 4.1 shows that the vast majority of the countries which have some activities in IF education fall into Scenario 3, and this category is dominated by Muslim and Arab countries relying mainly on their territorial attractiveness. On the other hand, advanced countries that are coming late to the race are relying upon their external competitiveness. Will the prestigious image and well-established infrastructure of these educational institutions work in their favour? The dynamism and the fierce competition between these institutions to consolidate their ranking positions in the 'job market' and 'cutting-edge research' might give a positive affirmation to this scenario.[3] However, the realities on the ground – in terms of 'ease' and 'quick' employability of the graduates from these programmes – might not support that. We think that 'clear-cut' conclusions in this regard are difficult to arrive at given the very recent inauguration of these programmes. The turning point has been 2009, according to Belabes and Belouafi (2011).

Educational attractiveness

In this study, the educational attractiveness of a country is defined as its ability to attract higher education courses in IF to its territory. In this competition, each country tries to become the hub of education on a regional or perhaps international level. Figure 4.1 shows a world map of the educational attractiveness in IF at the continental level. Asia comes

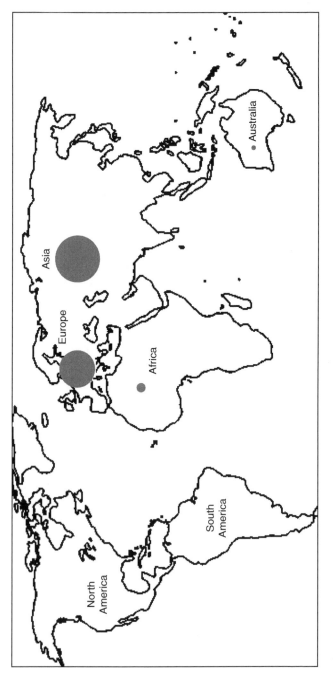

Figure 4.1 Educational attractiveness in IF by continents

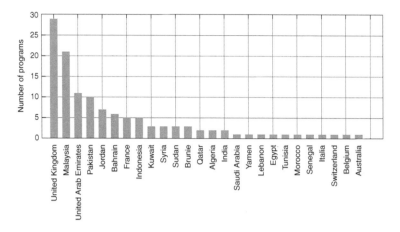

Figure 4.2 Educational attractiveness in IF by country

in first position, followed by Europe, Africa and Australia respectively. The American continent does not host an IF programme yet in its higher education system.

The distribution by country (Figure 4.2) shows Britain in a leading position with 28 programmes, closely followed by Malaysia with 21, and the UAE with 11.

Educational competitiveness

The educational competitiveness of a country is defined in this case by its ability to gain educational space outside its geographical borders. Figure 4.3 shows a world map of educational competitiveness in IF. Unlike in Figure 4.1, the American continent appears in this scenario. Thus, the two dimensions – attractiveness and competitiveness – are complementary and one cannot substitute for the other.

The details of this mapping (Figure 4.4) show some conventional couplings between the United States and Morocco, France and Saudi Arabia, Malaysia and France. These combinations can be explained (Table 4.2) by adapting the language of instruction to that of the welcoming country's élite (Scenarios 1 and 2) or to that of the country of origin (Scenario 3). Thus, the teaching of IF by a US institution in Morocco is done in French, by a French-speaking (i.e. the country delivering the programme) institution in Saudi Arabia in English, by a Malaysian institution in France in English. In the geo-educational

52

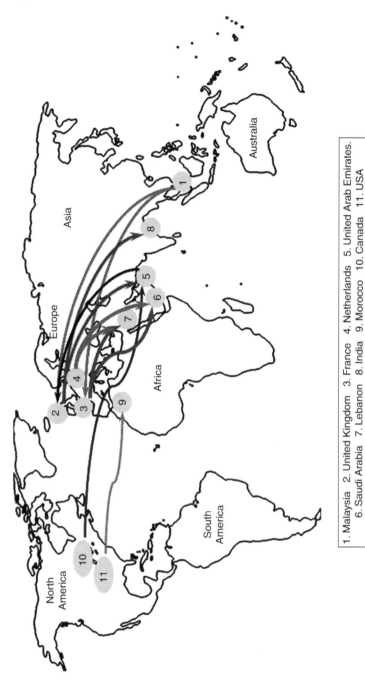

Figure 4.3   Educational competitiveness in IF

1. Malaysia 2. United Kingdom 3. France 4. Netherlands 5. United Arab Emirates.
6. Saudi Arabia 7. Lebanon 8. India 9. Morocco 10. Canada 11. USA

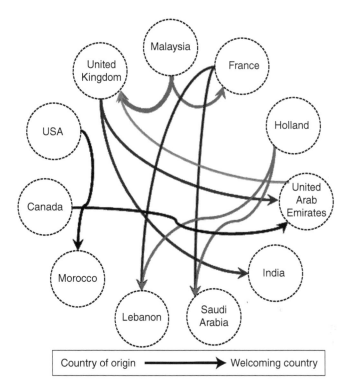

Figure 4.4 Dynamics of educational competitiveness by country

Table 4.2 Medium of instruction of IF in non-conventional situations

Case	Welcoming country	Country of origin	Medium of instruction
1	USA	Morocco	French
2	France	Saudi Arabia	English
3	Malaysia	France	English

rivalry, the language of the country of origin seems relegated to the background in favour to the conquest of an educational space.

Islamic Finance education: The 'soft power' tools of standardization and accreditation

Some researchers have noticed a close relationship between IF education and the central banks of Malaysia and Lebanon via the International

Centre for Education in Islamic Finance (INCEIF) and Ecole Supérieure des Affaires (ESA) of Beirut respectively (Chaar and Ourset, 2008). INCEIF was established in December 2005 by the Central Bank of Malaysia. ESA of Beirut has been managed since its inception, in April 1996, by the Chamber of Commerce and Industry of Paris, the French Ministry of Foreign Affairs and the Central Bank of Lebanon. The entry of the Central Banks of Bahrain and Singapore came to accentuate this trend. The Central Bank of Bahrain (CBB) has, for instance, launched on 13 July 2011 a special fund (the Waqf Fund) to finance research, education and training in IF; and is also active in working with industry and other stakeholders to develop industry standards and the standardization of market practices in IF industry.

On the other hand, the International Islamic Law and Finance Centre was established in Singapore following a collaborative initiative between Singapore Management University's School of Law and Lee Kong Chian School of Business, which works closely with government bodies, particularly the Monetary Authority of Singapore (Singapore's financial regulator) and the Ministries of Finance and Law.

In general, central banks adopt disparate postures that oscillate between proactive, neutral and oppositional. Proactive postures harness the energy of the actors, both internal and external, and set up an anticipation process and strategic integration. The objective, in this case, is to spread the standards, not through enforcement but rather through persuasion. The 'battle' of standards is not limited to the compliance or arbitration of Islamic law; rather, it extends to the development of international referential academic standards. In this regard, the accreditation[4] and quality will become, in the near future, indispensable tools in the geo-education of IF. Recognition of qualifications will depend not only on factors relating to the form and substance, but also on the quality of the curriculum and the institution which offers them, certified by the accreditation body.

Interestingly, a Malaysian project is been developed in this direction via the Association for Islamic Finance Advancement, as evidenced by the following remark of the prime minister of Malaysia, Mohd Najib Abdul Razak, on 19 April 2011:

> It [the Economic Transformation Program (ETP)] will also establish the Association for Islamic Finance Advancement (AIFA), which will accredit programs and advance and promote Islamic Finance education globally. With a GNI impact of RM1.2 billion by 2020, it will see the creation of about 4,300 related jobs.
>
> Abdul Razak (2011)

As noticed by some observers,[5] behind the 'surface' facet of the initiative to boost human capital development and to ensure the quality of the graduates of Islamic Finance education programmes there is the Malaysian ambition to establish Kuala Lumpur as an educational hub for IF. In this regard it is reported that last year Malaysia attracted 2,000 local and international students to its various Islamic Banking and IF courses. And the country is aiming to target 55,000 locals and 28,000 international students by the year 2020.[6]

Conclusion

In a globalized world where competing powers seek new fields of operation; the geo-educational approach provides an additional reading grid of international relations. It sheds light on the redrawing of the educational map. Behind the announcement effects of a particular country aiming to become the educational hub in IF, there are hidden power rivalries that do not appear on the surface. Among the issues of this rivalry that may appear at this stage are the standards – jurisprudential, prudential, rating, and accounting and auditing – that relate to IF industry. Arbitration appears to be gaining momentum. All such developments will have far-reaching consequences for the development of the IF discipline and its curricula at higher learning institutions, especially if they gain recognition from an international standards-setter like the Bank for International Settlements (BIS), and the backing of an international institution like the International Monetary Fund (IMF), and, perhaps regional backing from, for example, the Islamic Development Bank (IsDB). Such realities are possible if we take into consideration the close links between these organizations and the IFSB (the Kuala Lumpur-based standards setter for IF industry).

Notes

This chapter is based on a paper that was presented at the 4th World Conference on Education Sciences (WCES, 2012), Barcelona, 2–5 February 2012.

1. According to the data available at the WTO web page, only five WTO members – Australia, Japan, New Zealand, Switzerland and the USA – have to date tabled negotiating proposals on education services under the GATTS. These members are out of the 21 members who have included commitment to higher education and 44 members who have made commitments to education in general: www.wto.org (accessed 10 April 2012), Sauvé (2002: 19); Knight (2002: 10).
2. For instance, the number of international students around the world rose by more than 75% between 2000 and 2009 (Coughlan, 2011).

3. This scenario might also be supported by the current changing forms such as 'service' or 'camps' mobility instead of students mobility as part of the international trade in education noted earlier.
4. Some academics have regarded the accreditation route as 'highly political and ... fundamentally about a shift of power' (Harvey, 2004: 5).
5. Such as *Islamic Finance News* (IFN Reports 1 June 2011), the *Islamic Globe* (27 April 2011) and *Finance News* (9 May 2011).
6. The *Islamic Finance Globe*, 2011, "Malaysia Seeks to be a Global Educational Hub".

References

Abdul Razak, M. N. (2011). 5th Progress Update of the Economic Transformation Programme (ETP), 19 April, *Office of the Prime Minister of Malaysia*, http://www.pmo.gov.my

Bashir, S. (2007). 'Trends in international trade in higher education: Implications and options for developing countries', *Education Working Paper Series Number 6*, March, World Bank.

Belouafi, A. and Belabes, A. (2011). 'Islamic finance programs at higher education institutions: Overview and prospects'. Paper presented at the *International Seminar on Reforms of Islamic Higher Education in Meeting Contemporary Challenges*, Graduate School of Education and Human Development, Nagoya University and Japan Society for the Promotion of Science (JSPS), 30–1 July.

Chaar, A. M. and Ourset, R. (2008). 'Formation et conceptualisation de la finance', Jean-Paul Laramée, *La finance islamique à la française: un moteur pour l'économie, une alternative éthique* (Paris: Secure Finance), pp. 273–90.

Coughlan, S. (2011). 'Record numbers of international students', *BBC News Education*, 10 March.

Harvey, L. (2004). "The power of accreditation: Views of academics", in *Accreditation Models in Higher Education*, Di Nauta, P., Omar, P. L., Schade, A., and Scheele, J. P. (ed.) *European Network for Quality Assurance in Higher Education* (Helsinki: ENQA Workshop Reports), pp. 5–19.

Knight, J. (2002). 'Trade in higher education services: The implications of GATS', the *Observatory on Bordless Higher Education*, Report, International Strategic Information Service, London.

Sauvé, P. (2002). 'Trade, education and the GATS: What's in, what's out, what's all the fuss about?' Paper prepared for the OECD/US Forum on Trade in Educational Services, 23–4 May 2002, Washington, DC.

The Islamic Finance Globe (2011). 'Malaysia seeks to be a global educational hub', 27 April.

5
Islamic Finance Education in the UK: Opportunities and Challenges

Abul Hassan

Introduction

Islamic Finance (IF) is among the fastest growing components of global finance. Its growth is estimated to have reached $1.3 trillion in 2011, 150 per cent up over the previous five years (UKIFS, 2012). The market potential of the Islamic Banking (IB) and IF sector has attracted the UK in a big way (Dar and Presley, 1999). The interest has found expression not only in the field of business but education as well. The UK banks, stock markets, accounting standards and rating agencies are keen to enter into the IF field. There is a notable convergence of IF to mainstream positions of both business and academics. It seems that Western countries in general and the UK in particular are much interested in such convergence (Dar and Presley, 1999). All over the world, universities are eager to initiate or expand programmes for teaching and research in IF at the higher level. Almost a dozen UK universities have started courses and postgraduate qualifications in IF. In fact, Islamic investment has become one of the fastest-growing sectors of the global banking industry, expanding by 15–20 per cent a year (NBR Analysis, 2008). However, the programmes for education in IF were hurriedly drawn up to meet the expanding demand (Hasan, 1998). The haste resulted in unsuitable curricula frames, and the design of courses and lack of competent teachers in some cases compromises the quality of instruction. Therefore, theory and practice exhibited a little divergence. The purpose of this presentation is to give an overview of IF as an academic programme in UK universities/higher education institutions and of the challenges it is facing.

Islamic Banking and Finance in the UK at a glance

In the UK, interest in IF reflects the government's commitment to promoting Britain as an IF centre. It has been providing IF services for the past three decades, but it is only in recent years that this service has begun to receive greater acclaim. As an IF service provider, the UK is the leading Western country, largely based on five fully *Shari'ah*-compliant banks and HSBC Amanah (UKIFS, 2012).

An important feature of the development of London as the hub of IF markets and Great Britain as the key Western centre for IF has been the supportive government policies intended to broaden the market for Islamic products (Karbhari, Naser and Shahin, 2004). The outcome is reflected in the establishment of various aspects of IF: 22 banks including five fully *Shari'ah*-compliant ones; 37 Sukuk issues raising $20bn listed on the London Stock Exchange; around 25 law firms supplying services in IF (UKIFS, 2012).

In 2008, the UK Treasury published a paper setting out the government's aim for London to be 'Europe's gateway to international Islamic finance'. This acknowledged that the industry was still young and therefore not yet experiencing skills shortages, but predicted that it soon would be. It stated: 'The pool of potential applicants in the UK will have to keep up with the rapid growth of the market'.[1]

Furthermore, the development of IF has enjoyed cross-party support over the past decade. There has been a key policy objective of the UK government: to ensure that nobody in the UK is denied access to competitively priced financial products on account of their faith.

Islamic Banking and Finance education: A bonus for UK universities

'"There is an extent to which, to a westerner, Islamic Finance products look very similar to ethical finance products," says Stefan Szymanski, professor of economics at Cass. "There is a demand for morally upright investment vehicles and Islamic finance is the Islamic version of that."'[2] Therefore, expanding IF needs increasing manpower. Education, research and training assume importance. The sort of knowledge and skills the market seeks largely determine the form and level of instruction for various academic disciplines. Education has to follow the market (Hasan, 2008). The UK already leads Europe in the number of IF courses; for example, diploma, certificate, leading to entry to postgraduate level at several universities (IF Newsletter, 2003). These new courses are not just seen as something for

Muslims only. They are for anyone interested in a fast-developing industry that in the UK has been quite busy in the past few years accommodating forms of investment in finance that are *Shari'ah*-compliant.

The IB and IF service industry has experienced profound growth in the past few decades. This growth is expected to accelerate further the global expansion in demand for *Shari'ah*-compliant financial products and services (Karbhari, Naser and Shahin, 2004). To sustain and support the future growth of the industry, human intellectual capital plays a pivotal role in driving the performance and market competitiveness of the industry. In fact it will be the defining actor. The fast pace of innovation in global financial services in general and in the IF services sector in particular will require new expertise and skills. Therefore, there will be an increase in demand for adequately qualified professionals. In this environment, the creation of a substantial pool of talent and expertise is thus indispensable for the future growth of IF. Strengthening research and development capabilities is also important for enhancing the capacity for innovation to meet the diverse requirements of the rapidly changing global economy.

The introduction of IB and IF courses in British universities thus arises from the recognition of this sector and from the need to produce human capital to advance the industry to greater heights. This will ensure an adequate supply of capable, trained staff with knowledge and understanding of the industry, and that can only strengthen the industry itself (IF Newsletter, 2000).

Islamic economics as an academic discipline

In order to promote the discipline of Islamic Economics (IE), banking and finance in British academia, the Islamic Foundation, UK, first successfully negotiated and finally succeeded in October 1995 in introducing the teaching of IE and IF as one of the MSc modules at the University of Loughborough, UK (Rahman, 2004). It later started a fully fledged MSc IB and IF course as well as a Ph.D. programme in 1996, the first of their kind in the Western world. The Islamic Foundation not only sponsored the salary of the research fellow appointed at Loughborough University, but also gave a grant to enrich the library with the necessary books and materials (IF Newsletter, 2003).

Universities offering courses on Islamic Finance

The demand for IF courses is increasing every year in universities in the UK that offer this course. Universities in the UK have not only responded enthusiastically but are also taking the lead in positioning Britain as a leading centre of learning in IF.

Islamic finance at the postgraduate level

A bold step in the promotion of IE as an academic discipline was the establishment of the Markfield Institute of Higher Education (MIHE) in 2000, an academic project of the Islamic Foundation, UK. The degrees of MIHE were initially validated by Portsmouth University, and later by Loughborough University (IF Newsletter, 2003). The purpose of this project was to contribute towards the global development of human capital that was required to support future growth and development, particularly in the area of the global IB and IF industry. This gave the Islamic Foundation stature and recognition as an International learning centre, and its students now come from more than 29 different countries in Europe, Asia, America and Africa. Later, the purpose-built complex of MIHE was formally inaugurated by His Royal Highness the Prince of Wales, in 2003 (IF Newsletter, 2003).

MIHE now offers a wide range of courses. It provides an opportunity for students to pursue postgraduate certificates and diplomas, MA, MPhil and Ph.D. courses in Islamic Banking, Finance and Management. Also, MIHE has been recognized as an excellent institution for producing high-calibre young graduates, professionals and researchers for the benefit of the IB and IF industry. MIHE's decade of experience in IF will also provide a training environment including internships for developing IF professionals.

Besides MIHE, some other universities in the UK like Aston University, Bangor University, City University, Durham University, Newcastle University, University of Glamorgan, University of Reading and University of Salford are offering Masters and Ph.D.s in the area of IF and related subjects.

Islamic finance course by CIMA

The Chartered Institute of Management Accountants (CIMA) has developed an advanced diploma course in IF and a diploma course in IF with a prestigious advisory group of *Shari'ah* experts.[3] This is a fairly comprehensive course and takes two to six months of distance learning to complete. The course is geared towards mature students who have a strong background in finance. This certificate course assists employers in the UK and other major financial centres throughout the world in equipping their employees to develop financial products and management accounting from an Islamic perspective.

The challenges

In this section, we will look at the curricula, reading materials and quality of students and instruction in the field of IB and IF. With a few general observations, we will discuss some of the challenges that post-graduate instruction and research at British universities face in these areas.

Curricula

A curriculum is a set of educational experiences organized more or less deliberately (Barnett and Coate, 2005). Curricula are central to the student experience, and therefore, curriculum development is a key activity in higher education institutions. However, there is no particular approach in curricula development that focuses mostly on methodological issues in IE. It fully relies on negative filters. Thus, we see a scattering of criticism by mainstream economists who claim that IE and IF should not be treated as disciplines. This unclear approach promotes divergence and confrontation too. In this aspect, we see a 'step by step approach' (Kayed, 2008). The scholars in the areas of IB and IF have increasingly taken this route. This approach works on the principle that what cannot be shown in violation of the ethics of IB and IF and at the same time process would fulfil the UK standard norms of curricula so that business graduates in IF should not face any problem in the job market. That is why MA/MSc programmes in IF at British universities are a mix of mainstream and IB and IF subjects.

IF education at the graduate level is not currently in a very satisfactory state. This is partly reflected in the increasing departure of financing expedients from the major goals of IF and IB to achieve welfare objectivity. Economic problems of a society in general and humankind in particular are essentially similar everywhere, however their treatment differs according to the perception, norms and priority of various social systems (Hasan, 2008). The validation of mixed banking opened the doors for convergence with the mainstream presumably to the disadvantage of IF in the long run, and in education too. Some other points may be mentioned here. First, the unidirectional convergence of IF with the mainstream in practice is directing its educational approach and structure as well. It has some immediate advantages but has also the potential to promote divisive and deviant tendencies in the area of IF. Secondly, there is much diversity in the academic programmes and course structures in the area of IF within British universities. Some degree of standardization with flexibility margins is desirable and feasible as well. The crux of the matter is how to design the overall course structure in such a way that it maintains students' competitiveness in the job market.

The position of the Ph.D. programme in the areas of IF, IB and accounting in British universities is somehow better in terms of research contributions. But IE is losing students to other alternatives, and most students prefer to pursue their Ph.D. in the areas of IB and IF (Kayed, 2008). Since the total number of students seeking Doctoral degrees is increasing every year (e.g. in Durham), their admission should be restricted to selected institutions where faculty and facilities could be strengthened to promote excellence. This would also allow pooling of teachers coupled with stricter screening of students. Furthermore, creation of research environments, foundational infrastructures based on a positive filtering approach, sharing of knowledge and experience, cooperative teaching and ample funding may help build the critical mass to speed up research and build skills in the area of education.

Reading materials

The pace of IB and IF has been fast as a popular discipline, and the subject is now being taught at Master's level in more than 18 universities in UK with IF being a recognized area for accepting students in their Ph.D. programmes. The department/business schools facilities seem to expand at a faster rate than the availability of suitable and adequate reading materials for the students studying the subject at various levels.

However, there is an acute shortage of textbooks for the courses provided by British universities. Currently, for IF courses, the students are asked to refer to articles, monographs and books which do not meet the requirements in terms of analytical depth or coverage for graduate-level students. The Islamic Foundation, UK, the Islamic Research and Training Institute (Islamic Development Bank Jeddah) and the Islamic Economics Research Institute of King Abdulaziz University have all done laudable work in publishing useful reading material, but for a variety of reasons do not sometimes serve the purpose. The materials assembled in the books was not originally meant to serve the students, being largely collections – compiled or translated – of authors' writings or contributions to conferences or journals. Many of these materials need immediate revision, improvement and updating. Some of the materials used at the university level are not entirely free of errors in formulation and faulty equations or diagrams. Without ignoring these materials, there is a need for purposefully written and published books. It may be mentioned that this observation is not meant to detract in any way from the value of numerous learned contributions in the fields of IB and IF made by individual scholars and institutions. There is no doubt, however, that they seldom cover more than the fringe requirements of an academic programme.

Quality of students and instructions

There has been a continuous increase in the number of students who follow programmes offering Masters/Ph.D. degrees or diplomas in IF. The quality of students seeking Masters and Ph.D. degrees in IF is no different from that in other courses at business schools/departments of Economics and Finance at British universities. Most of the students are pursuing IF programmes to advance their careers. It is naïve to proceed on the assumption that they have any prior background needed for the subject; even a knowledge of the basics in banking and finance, especially an aptitude for quantitative applications, is conspicuous by its very absence (Hasan, 2008). In the case of language, the vehicle of ideas is often found to be broken despite the requirement that students should have an International English Language Testing System (IELTS) score of 6.5. To teach and guide in these circumstances is indeed a nightmare.

In the matter of instruction, the tutors too occasionally do not have appropriate and adequate knowledge of what they teach. Most British universities ask their existing tutors/lecturers to cover the IB and IF-related modules, about which they do not have sufficient knowledge. Therefore there is a need to recruit the right quality of academics to teach in these areas.

In summary, we can say that with the expansion of the IF service industry worldwide every year, there will no doubt be growing demand for postgraduate specialization in IF. By developing a need-based curriculum in the area of IB and IF, British universities can meet the challenges of a global requirement for graduates. On the other hand, those students who complete such study will have an advantage in finding positions within the quickly expanding IF sector. But in the bigger picture, IF education can help to ensure an adequate supply of capable, trained staff with knowledge and understanding of the industry, and that can only strengthen the industry itself.

Conclusion

The market potential of IF has attracted the UK in a big way. The interest has found expression not only in the field of business but also in education. New books and journals on IF are mushrooming. Seminars and conferences on Islamic economics now mostly focus on financial and monetary issues. However, in the future, success of IF will depend on the coordinated and concerted collaborative efforts of all stakeholders, namely the IF practitioners, educators and researchers. In this regard, all parties should make relentless efforts to continuously promote the development of IF into a field which is dynamic, responsive and sustainable. So long as the increasingly competitive environment raises the pressures to produce immediate results, no doubt there will be investment in human capital. Otherwise universities/higher educational institutions themselves may even face the challenge of finding qualified lecturers to teach the courses as well as to pursue research programmes. Moreover, there is a need to measure how many billions of pounds/dollars IF already handles every year and a need to understand how the IF institutions escaped the worst effect of the credit crunch. In any case, if its growth continues over the coming years, no doubt IF will become a universal part of every university's curriculum.

Notes

1. See http://www.hm-treasury.gov.uk/d/consult_sukuk101208.pdf
2. Harriet Swain (28 July 2009), 'Islamic finance courses give universities a bonus', http://www.guardian.co.uk/education/2009/jul/28/business-schools-islamic-finance
3. See http://www.cimaglobal.com/Study-with-us/Islamic-finance-qualifications/

References

Barnett, R. and Coate, K. (2005) *Engaging the Curriculum in Higher Education* (Berkshire: OUP).

Banker, The (2008) *Special Supplement: Top 500 Islamic Financial Institutions*, November, www.thebanker.com.

Dar, H. A. and Presley, J. R. (1999) 'Islamic Finance: A Western Perspective', *International Journal of Islamic Financial Services*, 1, 1, pp. 9–20.

Hasan, Z. (1998) 'Islamization of knowledge in economics: Issues and agenda', *IIUM Journal of Economics and Management* (Special issue), 6, 1, pp. 1–40.

——— (2008) 'Islamic Finace Education at Graduate Level: Current Position and Challange', MPRA paper No. 8712, University Library of Munich, Germany. Available at: http://mpra.ub.uni-muenchen.de18712/

IF Newsletter (2000) 'Markfield Institute launched', *The Islamic Foundation (IF) Newsletter*, No. 18, pp. 1–2.

——— (2003) 'Prince visits foundation', *The Islamic Foundation (IF) Newsletter*, No. 21, pp. 1–3.

Karbhari, Y., Naser, K. and Shahin, Z. (2004) 'Problems and challenges facing Islamic banking system in the West: The case of the UK', *Thunderbird International Business Review*, 46, 5, pp. 521–43.

Kayed, R. N. (2008) *Appraisal of the Status on Research on Labour Economics in the Islamic Framework*, a paper presented at the 7th International Conference held on 1–3 April 2008 in Jeddah.

NBR Analysis (2008) 'Islamic Finance: Global trends and challenges', *National Bureau of Asian Research*, 18, 4, p. 3.

Rahman, S. (2004) 'Founded on ideals: The Islamic foundation', *EMEL*, No. 8 (November–December), pp. 24–5.

UKIFS (2012) 'Financial Market Series: Islamic Finance', The CityUK Report, Date of access 2 April 2012.

6
Islamic Finance Education in France: An Unexpected Surge

Abderrazak Belabes and Ahmed Belouafi

Introduction

Since the year 2008, Islamic Finance (IF) has attracted wide attention in France. The French government has become proactive in its initiatives to promote Paris as a potential hub for IF. The media and academic communities, on their part, have joined the race by looking at and exploring the opportunities that this emerging phenomenon may bring to the national economy in particular, and members of society in general. For instance, in a recent article the famous French magazine *Le Point*, the equivalent of *Time* and *Newsweek* magazines, noted that IF is: 'On the rise, and seems to be immune to the crisis, as is the case with educational programmes'.[1] However, the creation of an Islamic Finance education programme (IFEP) in France has been on the table since the year 2006. The crisis, in this respect, has been an accelerating and not a triggering factor as the number of activities relating to IF has increased on French soil since its eruption in 2008.

Despite this dynamism and interest, Islamic Finance Education (IFE) seems to have received little attention from researchers and other members of the academic community. As a result, the number of academics involved, in one way or the other, with aspects of IFE remains limited.[2]

As in most countries, IFE has emerged in France as a research topic and then as a module in an established conventional academic programme, and finally it has become a subject of national and international research projects and programmes. One of the remarkable breakthroughs in this development has been the establishment of the Chair of Ethics and Financial Norms, a project jointly created by the University Paris 1 Pantheon – Sorbonne and King Abdulaziz University through its Islamic Economics Institute (IEI) affiliate. According to Pierre-Charles

Pradier, chair coordinator, in order for themes 'to put Islamic finance at the service of human development', research must be developed in this field.[3] Some other chairs might appear in the near future at other establishments such as the Universities of Strasbourg and Paris Dauphine.

The year 2011 saw the introduction of IF as an elective course in the world's top 10 Master's in finance. French business schools have taken the lead in this process.[4]

It should be noted that, at present, employment opportunities in the educational supply of IFE programmes appear to be very limited in mainland France. As there is only one institution offering Islamic financial products in France (the Chaabi Bank, a subsidiary of the Banque Populaire of Morocco, which has 17 branches in France), most IF employment opportunities seem to lie outside education in both French and foreign banks. The major French banks, such as Société Générale, BNP Paribas or Crédit Agricole Corporate and Investment Bank, have all created offshoots in the Gulf region and in London dedicated to IF products specializing in corporate and investment operations.

In the absence of sufficient and detailed data, the present chapter attempts to provide a general overview about the development of IFE in France, while the contributions in the next parts will shed more light on the experiments of some higher institutions in this area.

The role of the French National Research Agency

From the information we have been able to consult, it seems that France has been able to single itself out by announcing in June 2008 its support of a programme entitled 'Islamic Banking and Finance' by government rather than a private institution; that is the National Research Agency (ANR). In order to understand the rationale of this support, it is worth describing briefly the role carried out by the agency in promoting research in mainland France.

The ANR is a national funding agency that was established in 2005. Initially it was established as a public interest group, and in 2006 gained the status of a public establishment of an administrative character.[5] The agency's main objective is to support research projects proposed by the scientific communities at various higher education institutions. To secure funding, the proposal has to be evaluated and then approved by the agency according to normal procedures such as peer-review that govern this sort of programme.

Within this context, the agency has granted financing to a research programme entitled 'Islamic Banking and Finance', under the theme 'human and social science',[6] for a period of four years (2009–12). The ANR is the only European public research agency we are aware of that supports a programme dedicated to IF. The programme is coordinated by the Institute of Finance of Strasbourg (a partnership of research laboratories CDE – that is, Center for Corporate Law – and LARGE – that is, Research Department of Management and Economics). This programme has enabled Strasbourg University to launch a university degree in IF at its Management School. The project has also enabled the University to organize other activities such as workshops, conferences, the creation of postdoctorates in Islamic finance, and to launch *Les Cahiers de la finance islamique*, the first French academic 'journal' exclusively devoted to IF.

The projects selected by the ANR are funded for a period of three to four years. The ending of this funding should drive those who are in charge of running the IF programme to seek partnerships with institutions that could support them, including funding for Ph.D. students, symposia and publications. Currently, Southeast Asia and the Gulf Cooperation Council region might be potential backers of this kind.

Institutions offering educational programmes in Islamic finance

In terms of French educational supply in IF, it is necessary to distinguish between courses that are taught in the French territory and those given by French institutions abroad.

IFEPs provided to date earn their attendees a certificate, diploma, or a university degree which is, in France, a certification created and empowered by a university, unlike the Master's which is a national degree. The university degree was awarded a specific educational status, designed to meet needs not covered by national degrees. The access mode, the period of study, and the methods of evaluation differ depending on the purposes of the educational programme.

As noted earlier, the data reveals that all IFEPs have been created after the financial crisis (Figure 6.1), but interest in them began well before that.

Until recently, there were five IFEPs in France (Table 6.1), provided by four French institutions and a private US institute called the International Institute of Islamic Thought (IIIT). After the closure of the IIIT's division in France, the supply decreased to four educational programmes. A Master of Science, planned since 2009,[7] may be launched in the near future at the University of Strasbourg.[8]

The French educational supply in IF abroad is provided by the Ecole Supérieure des Affaires in Beirut (Table 6.2), associated pole of

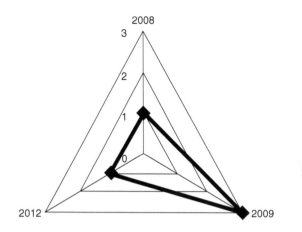

Figure 6.1   Temporal dynamics of IFEP creation in France

Table 6.1   IFEPs in France

Launch date	Institution	Name
25 November 2008	French Institute for Islamic Studies and Sciences (IFESI)	Islamic Finance Degree
21 January 2009	Strasbourg Management School	University Degree in Islamic Finance
18 November 2009	University Paris-Dauphine	University Degree 'Principles & Practices of Islamic Finance'
23 November 2009	International Institute of Islamic Thought	Islamic Economics & Finance Degree
January 2012	Reims Management School	Certificate 'Islamic Banking and Finance'

Table 6.2   French IFEPs provided abroad

Launch date	Institution	Name
31 October 2006	Ecole Supérieure des Affaires and the Chartered Institute for Securities & Investment (London)	The Islamic Finance Qualification (IFQ)
9 October 2008	Ecole Supérieure des Affaires provided in partnership with the Rotterdam School of Management	Executive Master in Islamic Financial Management

ESCP-EAP European School of Management, managed by the Chamber of Commerce and Industry of Paris in partnership with the French Ministry of Foreign Affairs, via the French Embassy in Beirut, and the Central Bank of Lebanon.

The French Institute for Islamic Studies and Sciences

The French Institute for Islamic Studies and Sciences (IFESI) is a private higher educational institution specializing in Islamic studies and Arabic language. It started its operations in 2001 in the Val de Marne, and has progressively developed to settle at Boissy-Saint-Léger in southeast Paris.

On 13 May 2006, the ADIMM[9] hosted, in the IFESI, a conference on the theme of 'Overview and critique of Islamic finances today'. The meeting ended with the presentation of a specific case of real-estate financing, showing not only the need for IF but especially laying out the prospects of what will be possible in France in the near future.[10] Following this conference, many students and professionals have expressed the wish to have a career in IF. Overwhelmed with this enthusiasm, those in charge at the IFESI have launched an initiative to examine the feasibility of establishing an IFEP in France.

It took several months for the project to mature and take its anticipated shape in a context where the government was not yet open to IF. The organization of the first French forum on IF, on 6 December 2007, opened a new era as shown by a statement in the programme's brochure:

> Whereas President Sarkozy asserted on 12 June 2007 his will to 'reinforce the attractiveness of the Paris market place' and 'turn it as soon as possible into the competitiveness pole of the financial technologies-innovation industry, it is essential – and urgent – for French institutions, companies and financial houses to understand the competitive challenges and opportunities for development offered by the *Shari'ah*-compliant financial industry.[11]

In September 2008, the IFESI announced the creation of the Department of Islamic Finance, through which it intended to propose thematic seminars and a degree in Islamic finance (launched on 25 November of the same year). This was the first educational programme of its kind to be created on the French mainland.

Due to its area of concentration, the Institute designates a significant portion of the programme to law and jurisprudence through which it seeks to highlight the Islamic dimension of finance. The educational programme consists of three major themes: Islamic law of economy and finance, IF and conventional finance (CF), practical aspects (banking products and services, insurance, bonds, etc.).

In terms of communication, the Institute emphasizes its leading role in creating the first educational programme in the field of IF in France, and the important part reserved for the Islamic law of contracts. Will this strategy be sufficient for the appearance of new entrants who have the human, technical and financial means to be major players in this domain? Only time will tell! With limited resources it is possible to do great things, provided strategic positioning is achieved in line with developments.

Strasbourg Management School

The Strasbourg Management School is the Business school of the University of Strasbourg, the largest university in France since January 2009. The University came into being as a result of a merger between three universities; March Bloch, Louis Pasteur and Robert Schuman.

The School's mission is to train managers to be able to adapt themselves to the management and economic challenges of globalization. The three core values of school are sustainability, ethics and diversity in order to train future managers to exercise of their social, societal and environmental responsibility. We can understand why the school established, on 21 January 2009, the first university degree in IF in France. This decision, which seemed risky in the French context, was facilitated largely by the concordat (an element of local Alsace and Moselle law in which region religion has had a special status since 1801)[12] and the financial support of the ANR.

The idea of the University's degree was born following the organization of an international conference on 'Islamic Banking and Finance' at Robert Schumann University on 11 January 2008.[13] As noted by Michel Storck, professor of Law at the University, 'In January, we organized a symposium on this theme, where the professionals have expressed their difficulty in recruiting specialists. Hence, the idea of the educational programme introduced for the next school year'.[14] In a report dated April 2008, the French evaluation agency for research and higher education noted the interdisciplinary intention of the Centre for Corporate Law, headed by Michel Storck, to extend its field of investigation: in particular with the mixed research unit 'Society law and religion' on Islamic finance.[15]

According to Michel Kalika, the ex-director of the Strasbourg Management School, the creation of a university degree in IF has been motivated by three reasons:

- Islamic finance is an important topical subject for the financial sector as a whole (banking and insurance). We believe that our School of Management should not miss out on this opportunity.

- The program may open the door for a reflection on our teaching methods at the School to take into consideration the relationship between management and our culture. It is interesting in a management school to understand that the tools depend on cultural context. Moreover, because of its location, Strasbourg is a multicultural city and in the history of Alsace, the religion fact has a special place.
- The university has a large research group in the field of finance.[16]

A distinguishing feature of the university degree in IF is that the distribution of modules does not follow the traditional classification 'conventional/Islamic'. Rather, the programme of 270 hours, which includes theoretical teaching, practical applications supplemented by simulative stock market classroom, is divided into eight modules: Islamic economics, Islamic banking and finance law, Islamic banks, Islamic financial markets, regulation of Islamic financial institutions, governance and management, additional materials, simulative stock market classroom. The brochure of the programme does not provide information on the educational team, and so on.

In terms of communication strategy, the school has positioned itself as a pioneer in offering the first university degree in IF in France. This strategy has been paying off. When we asked some Parisian students why they had enrolled on the programme when similar establishments existed back home, their response was that this was the first university of its kind in France and for them possessed symbolic value.

After four years, the results appear to be positive. 'Over a hundred people, from professional backgrounds and different countries, were trained in Strasbourg, and we have already received more than thirty applications for next year', said Sâmi Hazoug,[17] the new coordinator of the programme. The initial project of the University of Strasbourg was and still is ambitious and progressive:

- Opening a university degree in IF for professionals.
- Opening a continuous education for students.
- Launching an online educational programme which enhances the 'internationalization' of the university through the introduction of an IF degree.[18]

University Paris Dauphine

Under the Master 222 Asset Management, Paris Dauphine University organized, in May 2007, a conference on 'Islamic finance and *Shari'ah*-compliant funds'. The creation of the university degree in

IF at the Strasbourg Management School has led the University Paris Dauphine, especially renowned for the high quality of its finance educational programme, to create a university degree in Principles and Practices of Islamic Finance. The complex of the capital or the sin of pride seems to have played a significant role in this matter. As noted by Ilyès Jouini (2009), the initiator of the programme: 'The University of Strasbourg in France was a pioneer in launching a year ago a university degree in Islamic Finance. As for the Dauphine University, I proposed, in April 2009, to create a specialized educational programme in this area. Everything went smooth with the proposal, but in June we obtained all things we have requested from the administration'.

The stated objective of this programme is to train experts in IF and enable them to master the concepts, methods and techniques related to this theme. The course is based on three teaching schedules:

- Seminars organized in five major modules: Fundamental Finance; International Environment; Conceptual Approaches; Banking, Insurance and Markets for IF; Islamic Techniques of Finance.
- Conferences and discussion (Module 6) to which are invited French and foreign personalities.
- Development of a dissertation (Module 7) supervised by a member of the teaching staff in terms of its design, achievement and dissemination.

As such, the educational programme is meant to be in continuity with the teaching tradition followed by the university in the field of economics and finance. But the profile of students is not limited to these two specialties; 'some have a master in finance, others in law, and others are professionals in banking, finance and insurance', said Kaouther Jouaber, the individual responsible for the degree.[19] On average, two-thirds of the intake are professionals and one-third are students.

In terms of communication strategy, it is not a surprise that the University Paris Dauphine highlights its international reputation in the field of finance. As noted by Ilyès Jouini,[20] 'students must first master the basics of conventional finance, to which we add the essentials, legal and technical, of Islamic finance'. That is why the university degree in IF was inaugurated at the Palais Brongniart, the former location of the Paris stock exchange and mythical seat of French finance.

International Institute of Islamic Thought

The International Institute of Islamic Thought (IIIT) was established in the United States in 1981 to revitalize and reform Islamic thought and its methodology. The IIIT France's branch started its operations in the year 2000 at Saint-Ouen, in Paris, to make a scientific contribution in the 'Francophone' world on Islam and Muslim societies today. On 23 November 2009 the Institute launched a degree in Islamic Economics and Finance (DEFI). The stated objective was to 'address the theoretical and practical aspects of Islamic economics and finance in relation to current thinking on the development of Islamic finance in Europe and worldwide'. For contributing to major debates that have been taking place across Europe on the development of an alternative economic ethics, the Institute created, in 2009, a scientific research group dedicated to Islamic Economics (IE) and IF at the European (GREFIE or Groupe de Recherche Economie et Finance Islamique en Europe [Research Group for Islamic Economics and Finance in Europe]) (GREFIE) level. The website of the Institute does not communicate accurate information about the programme or the teaching staff. However, we managed to get a copy of the DEFI's programme 2009–10[21] and 2010–11.[22] It should be noted that the content of the second programme was updated in the light of the rapid evolution of the IF industry. It includes 12 modules distributed as follows:

- Five modules in the first semester: Global Objectives of the *Shari'ah*; General Principles of Islamic Law; History of Islamic Economic Thought; Theory of IF; Philanthropic Dimensions of Islam.
- Seven modules in the second semester: Governance Regulation and Standardization in IF; Organization and Functioning of an Islamic Bank; Organization and Operation of a Structure of Islamic Insurance; Risk Management in IF; Market Instruments in IF; Socially Responsible and Ethical Finance: Practical experiences; IF from a Geo-Economic Perspective.

For reasons that remain unknown, the IIIT Paris closed its operations in 2011. The suspension of the DEFI, after two years of service (2009/2010 and 2010/2011) is therefore not related to the failure of the educational programme itself. Hence, the disappointment of former students who had close ties with the various activities of the IF programme.

In terms of communication strategy, the initiator of the educational programme seems to emphasize the need to connect IF to its mother matrix, political economy from an Islamic perspective.[23]

Reims Management School

The Reims Management School has introduced IF into its existing programmes through a specialized course entitled 'Islamic Banking and Finance'. The course is taught in English to students enrolled in Master I or II, who are called to choose from 100 courses to build their careers. The objective is to enable acquisition of knowledge about the principles and rules governing the functioning of Islamic banking and insurance.[24] Some students are of German, British or Chinese origin; 'We were expecting between 35 and 40 to be enrolled, but we received 90 applications. We accepted only 50', said Ghassen Bouslama, the coordinator of the course.[25]

This unexpected influx led to thinking about the possibilities of creating an educational programme. But it appears that the task was not easy, perhaps for fear of taking risks, or lack of a sufficient teaching framework or visibility on the future of IF in France. Given these uncertainties, Reims Management School has finally opted to create a certificate in 'Islamic Banking and Finance' in partnership with the International Centre for Education in Islamic Finance (INCEIF) – a way to meet demand without saturating the market with a new Master's.

The stated goal of this certificate is 'to meet the growing interest in the Islamic financial industry by offering professionals and students the opportunity to study the functioning of Islamic banking and capital markets'.

The courses in this certificate are consistent with Part 1 of the Chartered Islamic Finance Professional (CIFP) programme given by the INCEIF. This explains why the four modules of Reims Management School's certificate are entirely taught in English and include only IF courses: *Shari'ah* Rules in Financial Transactions; Islamic Economics; Deposit and Financing Operations of Islamic Banks; and the Islamic Capital Market.

In terms of communication strategy, Reims Management School is positioned as a pioneer in France, offering the first certificate in IF by playing on the notoriety of the INCEIF.

Ecole Supérieure des Affaires

The Ecole Supérieure des Affaires (Business High School) (ESA), which is a French business school located in Beirut, currently offers two educational programmes: The Islamic Finance Qualification (IFQ) and The Executive Master's in Islamic Financial Management (XIFM).

The IFQ, launched on 31 October 2006, is a joint initiative between ESA and the Chartered Institute for Securities and Investment (London) to develop a 'world-class' qualification in IF. Despite its success, the IFQ requires regular updating to take into account, on the one hand, the qualitative and quantitative development of IF around the world and, on the other hand, the specificities of each country.

The XIFM programme is delivered at the ESA in conjunction with the Rotterdam School of Management (RSM), Erasmus University. Its mission is 'to equip managers of Islamic and conventional financial institutions with the needed financial management techniques, in order to enhance the competiveness of their firms in today's highly competitive financial markets'.[26] The curriculum consists of two main parts: IF courses (seven) and CF courses (nine) delivered over 16 months period with two months for the professional thesis. According to Pierre Simon (2009), president of the Chamber of Commerce and Industry of Paris, 'the transfer of competence between ESA and France may take place in both directions: the competence of ESA in Islamic finance, for example, greatly interests our Western business schools, which are just beginning to become familiar with this aspect of global finance'.

In October 2009, the XIFM was inaugurated at the Effat University, a leading private non-profit institution of higher education for women in Saudi Arabia, operating under the umbrella of King Faisal's Charitable Foundation. It remains to this day the first higher educational programme in IF created in Saudi Arabia.

In terms of communication strategy, ESA highlights the fact that XIFM is the first university programme that applies the techniques of financial management in IF, and considers the relationship between IF and CF in terms of synergy. In this regard, IF would benefit from the technical capacities of CF, and CF would draw ethical aspirations from IF.

In terms of competitive strategy, for Abdel-Maoula Chaar, the initiator of the programme, 'the 'Islamic' label and the more or less sophisticated capacities of IF engineering are no longer enough for them to count among the great players. Certainly, the technical ability remains a key skill, but no longer constitutes a competitive advantage. In fact, as in conventional finance, competitive advantage most probably lies in the managerial talent of the makers: in their ability to assess situations, to manage risk, to adopt the relevant decisions and organize their business in order to make it as efficient as possible'.[27] This strategy is based on the new competitiveness banking approach that gives an overriding role to the organization and management over the cost and efficiency factors.[28] Jaap Spronk, professor of finance and academic dean of MBA programmes at the RSM confirms this by saying:

> The XIFM is an offspring of the Master in Financial Management programme which is wholly owned and supported by RSM. The field of Islamic finance has indeed reached a turning point. Its recent strong development alters the nature of its competitive advantages, which means that the management of Islamic banks and financial

services must move from technical and operational to strategic financial management.[29]

Conclusion

Until recently, nobody could have imagined that IF can be taught in French higher education institutions. The emergence of these educational programmes is motivated by three main factors: the willingness of political authorities to host IF the interest of the French financial actors in this new form of finance; and a lack of specialists in the field internationally. IF is, therefore, presented as a new opportunity that complements CF. Even if the introduction of Islamic financial products in France still falls far behind expectations, the job opportunities abroad remain important since French degrees have a 'good reputation'.

Currently, the most common formula is that of creating an educational programme entirely dedicated to IF. Other formulas may emerge in the future through an IF specialization in, for example, curricula of law or banking, risk management, and even in Islamic studies.

For most IF programmes, the field of interest of the initiator affects to a large extent the identity of these initiatives. For instance, Strasbourg Management School's degree has a legal orientation, while that of the University Paris Dauphine is more financial, and that of ESA more management-oriented.

The available data on the educational supply in Islamic finance in France are not detailed enough and do not therefore allow for reliable comparisons of, for example: the composition of teaching staff and their diversification (share of academic and professional teachers); stability in staffing; risk of redundancy owing to rival programmes; the influence of the specialization of each tutor; the language of teaching for each module; internationalization; employability of learners; and finally the link to research.

Notes

1. Lefebvre (2012: 138).
2. Belabes (2009, 2010) and Leclerc-Olive (2011a, 2011b).
3. Lefebvre (2012: 140).
4. See Chapter 8, 'Islamic Finance Education at Top 10 Business Schools'.
5. Decree No. 2006-963 of 1 August 2006 on the organization and functioning of the National Research Agency, JORF No. 178 of 3 August 2006, p. 11567, text no. 18.
6. ANR, *Programme Blanc* (2009–12), 267/2008, p. 22.
7. Haquani (2009).
8. Jacques (2011) and Hazoug (2012).

9. AIDIMM (Association d'Innovation pour le Développement Economique et Immobilier): Association for Innovation in Economic Development and Real Estate created in Paris in 2005 with the primary objective of facilitating the general public's access to real estate in accordance with Islamic ethics.
10. Bamba (2006).
11. Arab-French Chamber of Commerce and Secure Finance (2007). The French finance industry and the Paris money market in the era of Islamic Finance: Issues and Perspectives for Companies and Financial Institutions Operating in France, The first international forum on Islamic Finance to be held in France, Paris, 6 December, p. 3.
12. The University of Strasbourg has a faculty of Catholic theology and a faculty of Protestant theology, and the University Paul Verlaine of Metz has a Theology department. These are the only French public universities where theology is taught.
13. http://sdre.misha.fr/IMG/pdf/prog_11janvier2008.pdf.
14. Dufrêne (2008).
15. AERES (2008: 5).
16. Corcos (2008).
17. Hazoug (2012).
18. Corcos (2008).
19. Lefebvre (2012: 140).
20. Jouini (2009).
21. We thank our colleague Professor Mohammed Boudjellal, the initiator of the Islamic Economics and Finance Degree, for providing us with the 2009–10 programme. He is a professor in the Faculty of Economics at the University of M'sila and also visiting professor in the University Degree of Islamic Finance at the Strasbourg Management School.
22. We thank our colleague Faouzi Houha, coordinator of the DEFI for 2010–11, for providing us with the programme. He is currently studying at Laurentian University in Greater Sudbury, Ontario, after a short stay in France.
23. Professor Mohammed Boudjellal, contacted by e-mail, has approved this conclusion on the communication strategy after reading it. We would like to extend warm thanks to him for responding positively to our request.
24. Gaudenz (2009).
25. Haquani (2009).
26. ESA 'Executive Masters in Islamic Financial Management', http://www.esa.edu.lb/fr/Xifm, accessed on 18 September 2012.
27. Chaar (2008).
28. Lamarque (2005).
29. RSM (2009).

References

AERES (2008) *Rapport du comité d'experts sur l'unité de recherche: Centre du droit de l'entreprise, EA 3397 de l'université de Strasbourg 3* (Paris: AERES), www.aeres-evaluation.fr/content/download/.../AER_STBG3_004.pdf

ANR (2008) *Programme Blanc*, Paris: ANR, http://www.agence-nationale-recher-che.fr/fileadmin/user_upload/documents/aap/2008/selection/Blanc-2008-V2.pdf, p. 22.

Bamba, A. (2006) 'La finance islamique bientôt en France', *Saphirnews.com*, 24 mai, http://www.saphirnews.com/La-finance-islamique-bientot-en-France_a3317.html

Belabes, A. (2009) 'The Islamic finance degree of the Strasbourg Business School: A field investigation', *Wednesday Seminar 2008–2009* (Jeddah: The Scientific Publishing Center, King Abdulaziz University), pp. 273–92.

—— (2010) 'Research and education on Islamic finance in France: From niche to mainstream', presented at the *International Conference on Research and Training in Islamic Economics and Finance*, the International Institute of Islamic Thought in cooperation with IRTI & CIBAFI, Paris, 18 March.

Corcos, A. (2008) 'Un nouveau diplôme universitaire en finance islamique à l'Ecole de management de Strasbourg', propos recueillis par, *Focus*, 16 juillet.

Chaar, A-M. (2008) 'Former les dirigeants de la banque islamique de demain', *L'Orient du jour*, 23 janvier, repris dans RIBH, le Journal de la finance islamique, http://ribh.wordpress.com/2008/01/23/former-les-dirigeants-de-la-banque-islamique-de-demain/

Dufrêne, C. (2008) 'L'émergence des formations en finance islamique', *L'Argus de l'Assurance*, 31 octobre.

Gaudenz, C. (2009) 'Reims Management School lance un cours en finance islamique', *La Tribune.fr*, 20 avril.

ESA (2012) Executive Master in Islamic Financial Management, http://www.esa.edu. lb/sites/default/files/ESA%20xifm%20RV%20%20Low%20Res%20Final.pdf

Haquani, S. (2009) 'La France rattrape son retard dans la formation charia', *AGEFI Hebdo*, 11 juin.

Hazoug, S. (2012) 'Formation continu en finance islamique: bilan positif pour le DU de l'EM Strasbourg', entretien accordé à *Ribh le Journal de la finance islamique*, 9 avril, http://ribh.wordpress.com/2012/04/09/formation-continue-en-finance-islamique-bilan-positif-pour-le-du-de-lem-strasbourg/

Jacques, A. (2011) 'Le religieux sur les bancs de la fac', *Le Point.fr*, 16 juin.

Jouini, I. (2009) 'Face à la crise, la finance islamique permet d'ajouter une corde à son arc', propos recueillis par Caroline Boudet, *Les Echos*, 17 novembre.

Lamarque, E. (2005) *Management de la banque: Risques, Relation Client, Organisation* (Paris: Pearson Education).

Leclerc-Olive, M. (2011a) 'La crise financière a-t-elle quelque chose à dire aux sciences sociales? De l'expertise à l'espace public'. Propositions pour une enquête partagée, Institut catholique de Paris, *Cahiers de Recherche de la Chaire Ethique et Finance,* n° 2011/1.

—— (2011b) 'Mathématiques financières, éthique et centralités', in M. Leclerc-Olive, G. Scarfò Ghellab and A-C. Wagner (eds) *Les mondes universitaires face au marché. Circulation des savoirs et pratiques des acteurs* (Paris: Editions Karthala), pp. 365–80.

Lefebvre, C. (2012) 'Apprentis banquiers halal', *Le Point*, 10 mai, pp. 138–40.

RSM (2009) Unique Master Programme in Islamic Finance, *Rotterdam School of Management, Erasmus University*, 10 July, http://www.rsm.nl/about-rsm/news/detail/1732-unique-master-programme-in-islamic-finance/

Simon, P. (2009) 'président de la Chambre de commerce et d'industrie de Paris: "L'ESA doit rester un pôle d'excellence"', entretien avec Élodie Morel Lebbos, iloubnan.info, 23 février.

7
Islamic Finance Education in Italy: Current Trends

Valentino Cattelan

As is well known, during the last decade the Islamic financial (IF) market has constantly grown at the remarkable rate of 10–15 per cent per year. At present, with assets estimated at over $1.6 trillion worldwide, it represents an appealing investment area investment for Western economic operators.

Considering the emergence of this transnational market, many European countries, like the United Kingdom, Luxembourg and France, have already promoted forms of integration of IF in their national jurisdictions, following a strategy of diversification and attraction of capital from the Gulf, Middle East and South Asia. Accordingly, academic programmes have been established in these countries in order to meet a demand for education necessary for a proper development of the market.

With specific regard to Italy, on the contrary, both structural factors (such as the limited internationalization of the national financial system, as well as the lack of a large Muslim population) and the persistence of traditional immigration policies (scarcely open to cultural pluralism) have determined a certain delay in the elaboration of proper initiatives for the implementation of the sector. In fact, unlike the United Kingdom (where the academic system has multiplied the educational projects on Islamic finance 'following' the demand of the market[1]) and France (whose government has played a direct role in supporting *Shari'ah*-compliant investments through specific tax instructions, following the contribution of the *Rapport Jouini et Pastré*[2]), Italy continues to remain a permanent borderline actor both in the integration of the IF market and in offering comprehensive educational programmes.

Given these preliminary remarks, this chapter aims at providing a brief (while comprehensive) outline of the Italian experience in IF higher education, showing how, despite a persistent interest on the matter (Section 1), the national academic system still provides only a few dedicated initiatives (Section 2), while more coherent programmes (at the level of Master's degree or Ph.D.) are at a preliminary stage or only partially referable to the scientific field of Islamic Economics (IE) and IF (Section 3). The chapter will conclude with final considerations (Section 4) on the current and prospective trends of Islamic Finance Education (IFE) in Italy, both in relation to the level of internationalization and competitiveness of the Italian academic system and with special reference to the ongoing political evolution of the Mediterranean.

Islamic Finance, Italian institutional actors and academia: Evidence of a permanent interest

Without any doubt, several initiatives in the last 20 years have shown Italian institutional and academic actors' persistent interest in IF. In particular, institutional and economic operators to a certain extent forestalled academia in seeing the potential of the field.

Looking at the former actors, in fact, the first workshop on the matter was promoted as early as 1994 by Banca di Roma (today part of the group Unicredit), that organized a conference on Islamic Banking (IB) open to investors and academics. In 1997, a pioneering project for the urban regeneration of Palermo's city centre in Sicily was supported by the municipality: the project, named Genoardo (from the Arabic *jannat al-ard*, 'paradise on earth', recalling the name of the central park of Palermo during the Arab domination) was intended to favour the meeting of local and the Muslim cultures and the social integration of Arab immigrants. The project, inspired by the attempt to rebuild the 'unity' of the Mediterranean through the application of IF (specifically, by structuring the operation via *Ijara* contracts) was characterized by the participation of lawyers, bankers, architects and social operators, but remained unfortunately at a stage of preliminary definition. Later on, in 2002, it was the turn of the national network of banking institutes, Associazione Bancaria Italiana (ABI)[3] to promote a conference on the opportunities related to IB, in cooperation with the Islamic Research and Training Institute (Islamic Development Bank) and Camera di Commercio Italo-Araba (Italian-Arab Commerce Chamber) (the proceedings are collected in Aliboni, 2003). Five years later, in 2007, ABI also signed a memorandum of understanding with the Union of Arab Banks (UAB), which was perceived by many commentators not only as a means to a permanent dialogue and cooperation between the two associations, but as a renewed step forward towards the integration of

IF in Italy: notwithstanding, the memorandum did not lead to relevant developments on the matter. Last but certainly not least, in 2009 Banca d'Italia (the Italian central bank) organized a seminar dedicated to IF, followed by the release of a related research paper on supervision and stability issues (Gomel, 2010). In his opening speech to the seminar, the former governor of Banca d'Italia, Mario Draghi, underlined that:

> The growth of Islamic finance in recent years is one of the aspects of the increased role being played in the global financial system by a number of emerging economies. This is of course a welcome development ... [but] as the recent crisis has taught us, growing complexity calls for enhanced international cooperation by policymakers and regulators.[4]

Despite this consciousness, the seminar by Banca d'Italia did not lead to any comprehensive study or action in favour of a coherent integration of IF into the national financial system.

As far as Italian academia is concerned, pioneering investigations on IE and IF could already be found in the 1980s, under the field of Islamic Studies (the 'discovery' of the subject in Italy was made by Scarcia Amoretti, 1986 and 1988),[5] while the first study of the topic of IB by an Italian legal scholar is dated ten years later (Piccinelli, 1996). More recently, specific seminars on IF have been promoted by a variety of academic institutions, with a related increase in the number of publications on the topic, adopting legal (Gimigliano and Rotondo, 2006), economic (Vadalà, 2004; Giustiniani, 2006; Borracchini, 2007; Hamaui and Mauri, 2009; Porzio, 2009; Dell'Atti and Miglietta, 2009), sociological (Atzori, 2010) interdisciplinary (Khan and Porzio, 2010) and educational (Cattelan, 2011) approaches.

At any rate, these texts are mainly intended for professionals and researchers, and are not addressed to students either at an undergraduate or postgraduate level. In other terms, although they certainly contribute to the analysis of the peculiarities of IF and its current evolution as part of the international financial system, their fundamental limit, from an educational perspective, is the barrier of access for young people, since they are not intended as textbooks or course texts: as a consequence, IF maintains in Italy the 'aura' of a 'closed realm', reserved for a small network of specialists.

Regrettably, the present academic offering of educational programmes on IF in Italy confirms this impression. In fact, the opportunities for undergraduate and graduate students to have access to the study of the subject are still quite limited both in number and duration, implying the objective difficulty of providing them with a comprehensive outline of IF principles and mechanisms, apart from an introductory discourse on the fundamental issues related to this complex emerging discipline.

State of Islamic finance educational programmes in Italy

Next to an increase in academic publications, as shown in the previous section, Italian higher education centres have recently promoted specialized courses on IF. As just remarked, these courses are still very limited in number and duration.[6]

In this section, two initiatives already ongoing will be briefly described: the course on Marketing and Islamic Finance, organized by the Società Italiana per l'Organizzazione Internazionale (SIOI), and the teaching module Integrating Islamic Finance in the EU Market, launched by the University of Rome Tor Vergata in relation to a grant by the European Commission (Lifelong Learning Programme – Jean Monnet Action). As will be remarked later, it is relevant to note that both these initiatives cannot properly be said to represent a 'direct' expression of Italian academia, but, more precisely, an 'indirect' educational investment in IF by public entities institutionally orientated to an international dimension, which by definition overcome local instances. Further considerations of this point will be included in the chapter's Conclusions.

Corso di alta formazione in marketing e finanza islamica

The Corso di alta formazione in marketing e finanza islamica (advanced course in marketing and Islamic finance) is an initiative by SIOI,[7] launched in 2010 and this year (2012) in its third edition.

The course (taught in Italian) comprises ten weekly meetings, from April to July, and has the fundamental objective to provide a specialized expertise on the mechanisms regulating commercial traffics in a prospective interaction between Western and Islamic markets in the light of increasing internationalization. Accordingly, it is addressed to executives with an interest on the process of market globalization, as well as to diplomats, economic, financial and legal advisors and postgraduate students orientated to a diplomatic or international career. The course's contents cover aspects of Islamic culture, marketing, IE and IF, cross-cultural negotiation, with meeting-events and workshops aimed at linking the theory and practice of intercultural commerce.

The stress on the internationalization of the markets through an intercultural approach certainly represents the major feature of the course: from this perspective, it confirms the attention always given by SIOI to international affairs, from the year of its foundation in 1944, with the institutional aim of supporting the role of the Italian state in the international community, as well as that of Italian operators as globalizing actors.

The European module integrating Islamic Finance in the EU market

The Education, Audiovisual and Culture Executive Agency (EACEA) is the entity responsible for the management of European Union funds addressed to programmes in the educational, culture and audiovisual fields[8].

Among the programmes and actions managed by the EACEA, the Lifelong Learning Programme (LLP) supports learning opportunities such as the Comenius, Erasmus, Leonardo da Vinci, Grundtvig and Jean Monnet programmes, which are well known to scholars and students involved in European integration studies. Within the Jean Monnet programme, a European module[9] has been granted, after due application for cofinancing, to the University of Rome Tor Vergata on the topic of Integrating Islamic Finance in the EU Market, for the period September 2010–August 2013.

With regard to its educational contents and objectives, the module underlines how, in the current globalization of financial markets, the recent emergence of IF in Europe enjoys the peculiarity of raising further concerns for the promotion of adequate social, intercultural, inter-religious and migratory policies in the EU; it also raises new issues for a better integration of religious minorities in Europe, as well as for the tenability of the application of religious laws within a secular polity. Considering all this, the module aims at promoting a deeper understanding of the phenomenon, thanks to a comparative approach to law and economics. On the one side, it explores the rationales of conventional finance (CF) and IF and their divergences in risk management; on the other side, it analyses the development of IF products and services and its impact in the European Union both as an instrument of social and economic integration of Muslim minorities, and as a factor of financial integration of the EU member states with the regions of the Middle East and North Africa (MENA) and the Gulf.

The module is addressed to practitioners and financial advisors, as well as to students of international economics and finance, aiming at specializing in IE and IF pluralism. As a consequence, the module comprises a variety of integrated activities, embracing the largest spectrum of audience. In particular, besides the publication of an edited volume on IF in Europe (Cattelan, forthcoming), these activities can be summarized as follows.

Postgraduate course on Islamic Finance

The module comprises, first of all, a total of 12 teaching hours to postgraduate students, which have been inserted within the University of Rome Tor Vergata's Master's in Development Economics and International Cooperation (MESCI), for further details of which see Section 3).

This introductory course to IF has been conceived according to an approach willing to highlight the impact of current globalization on the financial market: consequently, challenging the universality of conventional capitalism, the course interprets IF as part of a plural financial system, where different conceptions of economic justice(s) can coexist and influence each other.

Accordingly, within a framework of property rights pluralism, IF is presented as the outcome of a theory of justice (*'adl*) where a specific *Qur'anic* paradigm brings about the conceptualization of the 'right' (*haqq*) as the result of the divine 'decree' (*hukm*). Islamic property rights are summarized around three fundamental rationales: the centrality of the object in the transaction as something 'tangible' (*haqiqi*) to be traded; the fundamental need for equilibrium in the exchange (prohibitions of *riba, gharar* and *maysir*); asset-backed risk and investment risk-sharing as logical manifestations of the principle of profit-loss sharing.

After the depiction of these rationales in relation to the contract (*'aqd*) as a means for maintaining the justice given by God, the course focuses on the current practice of IF as a growing transnational market. In particular, it analyses:

- the contractual instruments employed by IF institutions (sale-based transactions: *murabaha, ijara, salam, istisna'*; partnership transactions: *mudaraba* and *musharaka*);
- The products and services provided by Islamic banks, as well as the emerging market of Islamic insurance (*takaful*), Islamic securities (*sukuk*) and the issues related to the admissibility of Islamic derivatives.

Interpreting IF as a viable means for fostering local development, the course also discusses the potentialities of Islamic micro-finance and project financing, with a final focus on IF's growth in specific geographical areas, namely Southeast Asia, MENA and Europe, according to a case-study approach.

Rome Islamic Finance Summer School

The European module also comprises a summer school, which takes place in July.

The first edition (30 June–1 July 2011) was dedicated to the topic 'Islamic Finance in Europe: Tools for the development of a plural financial system', with more than 30 participants and around 15 lecturers and discussants involved. The fundamental aim of the initiative was to provide attendees with proper tools to understand the present evolution of IF in relation to the EU market, from an economic and legal standpoint, according to a multidisciplinary approach. Within this framework, IF was inserted within the broader context of contemporary globalization, highlighting: the process of hybridization of economic and legal structures, as a result of the meeting between foreign cultures and the West; the attempt to meet the needs of a changing world, where developed and developing economics face new challenges. In this way, the summer school was intended to interpret IF in the light of an emergent plural financial system on a global stage, where new ethical demands affect the request for innovative economic development.

Maintaining this perspective, but with a stronger concentration upon the emergence of a plural financial system at a global level, the second edition of the summer school (4–6 July 2012) was dedicated to 'Islamic Finance and Pluralism. Managing diversity as an opportunity for growth', with a major focus on the effect of globalization on the international financial market, and in particular the potential impact of the Arab springs on IF and commercial relations in the Mediterranean. Accordingly, the summer school explored the current evolution of IF as an emergent transnational market, providing attendants with fundamental means for dealing with globalization through alternative tools for portfolio diversification and risk management, as well as for the promotion of socially responsible investments and sustainable growth.[10] The three days comprised lectures, workshops and round tables on the following thematic areas: economic development, pluralism and Islam; IF on a global stage, from theory to practice; IF, Europe and the Arab spring impact on the MENA region.

The teaching of Islamic Finance at Master's degree level in Italy

As previously noted, the existing educational projects in IF available in the Italian academic system seem more influenced by the external international evolution of the market than an internal will to embrace the subject. This perception is confirmed by the fact that no Italian academic institutions at the moment offer a comprehensive programme of education in IF at the level of Master's degree or Ph.D. programmes.[11]

At any rate, two academic institutions have recently inserted IF in their Master's degree curricula: the University of Rome Tor Vergata and the University Luiss Guido Carli.

Master's in Development Economics and International Cooperation – University of Rome Tor Vergata

MESCI is a one-year international postgraduate programme (taught in English), characterized by an in-depth application of an interdisciplinary methodology to development issues.[12]

Its educational programme – targeted at students and professionals looking for a career in international organization, private companies and non-governmental bodies working in the field of development policies – comprises modules of economic quantitative and qualitative methods, courses on development economics, international development assistance, as well as sustainable development.

Within the section of development economics, an introductory course on Islamic Finance has been inserted as a compulsory component since 2011. The contents and objectives of the course – cofinanced by the EACEA and part of the module Integrating Islamic Finance in the EU Market – have already been described in Section 2.

Master's in Economia e Istituzioni nei Paesi Islamici – School of Government, University Luiss Guido Carli

This Master's degree on the Economy and Institutions of Muslim Countries (taught in Italian) represents a point of innovation in the educational offer by the School of Government of the University Luiss Guido Carli,[13] and will have its first edition in the academic year 2012/2013.

Aimed at providing advanced tools and methods to interpret new political, economic and financial challenges related to the Muslim world, with an eye specifically on the Mediterranean, the Master's includes in its curriculum not only a module on Islamic law, but also a specific course on finance and Islamic banks.

The course, inserted in a Master's degree related to the area of global governance, clearly shows a growing awareness of the likely evolution of the international financial system, and in particular of the Mediterranean area, towards a paradigm of financial pluralism in which IF will play an increasing role also as a factor of intercultural dialogue. In other words, in a context of deeper social and economic integration between Europe and the Mediterranean area, IF is seen as a remarkable tool able to contribute to an appropriate management of the challenges of globalization.

Conclusions: Assessing the competitiveness of the Italian economic and educational system with regard to Islamic finance

This chapter has shown how the existence of educational experiences of IF in Italian academic institutions remains quite limited.

In particular, while education on the matter is already provided by an institution devoted to international affairs (Corso in marketing e finanza islamica – SIOI), the only specific course on IF existing today at a Master's degree level (within MESCI, University of Rome Tor Vergata) appears to be the result of a fortunate match between the host institution's attempt to internationalize its educational offer and the European Union's interest, through the EACEA, in exploring a matter of clear appeal for the future of the Euro-Mediterranean area. This interest is certainly shown also by the School of Government – University Luiss Guido Carli, which has inserted a module on IF in the curriculum of a Master's degree dedicated to students willing to specialize in the economy and institutions of Muslim countries.

How should one interpret this permanent lack of comprehensive educational projects (Master's degree or Ph.D. programmes) specifically devoted to IF in Italy?

Looking at economic and demographic factors, it must first be considered that the Italian financial system has never experienced a level of internationalization comparable to that in other European countries (such as the UK or France); at the same time, the limited size of the national Muslim population (around 2%, while it reaches the 8–9% in France) may give another interpretative clue for the scant 'appeal' to Italian universities of a field like IF, which may be (wrongly) perceived as targeted at Muslim students.

Apart from these variables, it is probably the absence of a governmental commitment by the Italian state towards the integration of IF within the national financial system which has done most to prevent (or, at least, not to promote) the launch of advanced educational projects in this subject. Clearly, this limit constitutes an obstacle to the Italian economic system's effective capability in competing from an educational perspective at a European level (with IF being present in the curricula of other European countries).

In the light of an even faster integration of economic and financial phenomena being an inescapable effect of globalization, Italian academia's educational delay will certainly represent a further burden for the growth of the national economy, especially given the growing migratory flows in the Mediterranean, as well as the likely impact of the Arab springs in the future evolution of commercial relations in the MENA and Gulf regions. The increasing mobility of young people in the Mediterranean, combined with the request for financial instruments (able to satisfy cultural peculiarities of migrant customers but also the possible request for *Shari'ah*-compliant assets by small and medium-sized companies in MENA), will in future constitute a variable which must be considered for the competitiveness of European countries as they seek a new area of economic development in the Mediterranean.

To sum up, missing the educational opportunity of IF is not only downgrading Italy to being a 'host country' of an expertise forged elsewhere, but will represent in the medium to long term a factor of exclusion from proactive activity in the economic as well as intercultural dialogue of the Mediterranean.

Notes

This chapter is dedicated to Professor Emeritus Biancamaria Scarcia Amoretti, for her exceptional contribution to the study of Islam.

1. The long-established presence of specialized courses on IF in UK academic curricula is well known. In particular, the IF programme at the University of Durham (www.dur.ac.uk) comprises a summer school, an MA, an MSc as well as a Ph.D. programme in Islamic Finance, Banking, Management and Economics. Besides Durham, courses on Islamic Law and Islamic Finance are taught at the School of Oriental and African Studies (SOAS) at the University of London (www.soas.ac.uk); an MSc programme is also available at the Aston Business School of Birmingham (www.aston.ac.uk).
2. After the creation of the Union for the Mediterranean in July 2008, aimed at relaunching the Barcelona Process, the political commitment of the French government towards the promotion of IF was officially signalled by Christine Lagarde, who declared in the same year the government's objective to make France more competitive also through its support of the IF market. Contemporarily, the agency Paris Europlace (www.paris-europlace. net) published in 2008 the *Rapport Jouini et Pastré* (after the names of the two authors), released with the express aim to fostering France's ability to attract capital from the Middle East through IF. Accordingly, looking at educational programmes, from 2009 a *Diplôme universitaire en finance islamique* has been introduced at the Ecole de Management of the University of Strasbourg (www.em-strasbourg.eu); other educational projects have also been launched

at the University of Lille, Montpellier, Sorbonne and Paris-Dauphine, with an increasing number of conferences, workshops and seminars specifically dedicated to the topic.

3. The Italian Banking Association (ABI) gathers all the major actors of the Italian banking and financial system, representing and promoting their interests both at a national and international level (www.abi.it).

4. The full speech by Mario Draghi and all the documents related to the event can be found on the website of Banca d'Italia (www.bancaditalia.it).

5. While Italian translations of primary works by Chapra and Ismail date back respectively to 1979 and 1980.

6. It must be noted, at any rate, that already in 2008 an attempt to launch IF education in Italy was made by the University of Rome La Sapienza through the announcement of a Master's in Mediterranean and Arab Finance and Banking (MMAFB). Organized with the cooperation of Istituto di Studi Economici e Finanziari per lo Sviluppo del Mediterraneo (ISME), ABI, Union of Arab Banks (UAB) and Intesa Sanpaolo (one of the top banking groups in Italy), MMAFB intended to train new professionals with a combined knowledge of IF and CF, to serve merchant and corporate banking for the Mediterranean and Middle East markets. This ambitious educational plan (which can be considered as the first example of an IF Master's degree project in Italy) was active for only two years; unfortunately no data are available on the success of the initiative with regard to the number of attendees.

7. The SIOI is an international non-profit organization that has been operating since 1944, subject to the Ministry of Foreign Affairs's supervision. SIOI's institutional aims are diplomatic and international training, gathering research and information on topics in international organization, international relations, international cooperation and international protection of human rights (www.sioi.org).

8. For any information on the Agency, please refer to http://eacea.ec.europa. eu/index_en.php

9. For a detailed explanation of the didactic and administrative features of a 'European module', please refer to the EACEA website, as specified in the previous note.

10. The specific contents of the summer school can be found at www.islamicfinance.it

11. It must be said, at any rate, that unofficially some projects of Master's degrees in IF, of which I have had direct vision, have circulated among a tight circle of academics and professionals. However, this preliminary stage has not evolved into the factual launch of any Master's programme. On this subject, a certain reluctance to invest in educational projects in IF is perceivable: this reluctance is usually justified by decisionmakers within university governance with reference to the presence of equivalent programmes in neighbouring European countries (even if the educational market for IF is very far from being saturated), as well as by an assumed lack of a national educational demand for the topic. As a consequence, Italian students are currently obliged to move to the UK or France to acquire specific competences in IF. The Conclusions of this chapter will

try to advance an interpretation of this short-sighted approach, and to highlight how it clearly signals a loss of competitiveness for the Italian national system.

12. MESCI is an initiative of the Centre for Economic and International Studies (CEIS), Faculty of Economics, University of Rome Tor Vergata. For any further information, please refer to http://www.ceistorvergata.it/master/mesci

13. All the activities of the School of Government can be found at http://sog.luiss.it

References

Aliboni, R. (ed.) (2003) *Banca e finanza islamica: autonomia e cooperazione* (Roma: Camera di Commercio Italo-Araba).

Atzori, D. (2010) *Fede e mercato: verso una via islamica al capitalismo?* Collana dalla Fondazione ENI Enrico Mattei (Bologna: Il Mulino).

Borracchini, N. (2007) *Banche e immigrati: credito, rimesse e finanza islamica* (Pisa: Pacini).

Cattelan, V. (2011) 'Educare alla finanza islamica in Italia, per essere competitivi in Europa', in E. M. Napolitano and L. Visconti (eds) *WelcomeBank – Migranti and Marketing Bancario* (Milano: EGEA), pp. 159–63.

—— (ed.) (2013) *Islamic Finance in Europe: Towards a Plural Financial System*, Studies in Islamic Finance, Accounting and Governance (Cheltenham; Southampton, MA: Edward Elgar Publishing).

Chapra, M. U. (1979) *Obiettivi dell'ordine economico islamico*, translated by P. Visani (Carmagnola: Arktos).

Dell'Atti, A. and Miglietta, F. (eds) (2009) *Fondi sovrani arabi e finanza islamica* (Milano: EGEA).

Gimigliano, G. and Rotondo, G. (eds) (2006) *La banca islamica e la disciplina bancaria europea. Atti del Convegno Internazionale di Studi, Napoli, 8–9 aprile 2005* (Milano: Giuffrè).

Giustiniani, E. (2006) *Elementi di finanza islamica* (Torino: Rist).

Gomel, G. (ed.) (2010) *Finanza islamica e sistemi finanziari convenzionali. Tendenze di mercato, profili di supervisione e implicazioni per le attività di banca centrale*, Questioni di Economia e Finanza, Occasional Paper no. 73 (Roma: Banca d'Italia).

Hamaui, R. and Mauri, M. (2009) *Economia e finanza islamica* (Bologna: Il Mulino).

Ismail, I. M. (1980) *L'Islam e le teorie economiche odierne*, translated by P. Visani (Carmagnola: Arktos).

Jouini, E. and Pastré, O. (2008) *Rapport Jouini et Pastré. Enjeux et opportunités du développment de la finance islamique pour la Place de Paris. Dix propositions pour collecter 100 miliards d'euros* (Paris: Paris Europlace).

Khan, M. F. and Porzio, M. (eds) (2010) *Islamic Banking and Finance in the European Union: A Challenge*, Studies in Islamic Finance, Accounting and Governance (Cheltenham; Southampton, MA: Edward Elgar Publishing).

Piccinelli, G. M. (1996) *Banche islamiche in contesto non islamico: materiali e strumenti giuridici* (Roma: I. P. O).

Porzio, C. (ed.) (2009) *Banca e finanza islamica. Contratti, peculiarità gestionali, prospettive di crescita in Italia*, CAREFIN, Centre for Applied Research in Finance (Roma: Bancaria).

Scarcia Amoretti, B. (1986) 'Il concetto di libertà nei testi di economia islamica: alcune osservazioni', in *Alifba*, no. 6/7, pp. 47–54 (Palermo: Centro Culturale Al-Farabi).

—— (1988) *Profilo dell'economia islamica* (Palermo: Centro Culturale Al-Farabi).

Vadalà, E. (2004) *Capire l'economia islamica* (Patti: Yorick).

8
Islamic Finance Education at the Top Ten Business Schools

Ahmed Belouafi, Abderrazak Belabes and Cristina Trullols

Introduction

Despite the 'reservations' and the 'critiques' that surround their application, classification, ranking and accreditation of business and finance higher, education programmes and institutions are becoming more and more of a pushing factor for 'quality assurance' and 'assessing' tools that business schools and finance departments cannot ignore. Since the year 1988, which saw the production of the first rankings of US business schools, by *Business Week* magazine, the ranking 'heap' has seen significant developments through the involvement of other 'media outlets' and the widespread attention given to these rankings (Devinney, Dowling and Perm-Ajchariyawong, 2008: 195). The annual work carried out by the *Financial Times* (FT) has been one of the prominent rankings in this field.

According to the FT ranking of 2011, the Top Ten Business Schools in finance comprise the following institutions: HEC Paris, IE Business School, ESSEC Business School, Saïd Business School, Warwick Business School, Grenoble Graduate School of Business, ESCP Europe, Imperial College Business School, Skema, EM Lyon Business School. Six of these institutions are French, four British and one Spanish.[1]

Contrary to expectations, the analysis of these business schools' programmes reveals that half of them offer a module specific to Islamic Finance (IF). The teaching of IF has become a competitive advantage for the best Master's in finance programmes in the world.

If one refers to the classification criteria of the Master's, namely research opportunities, diversity and internationalization, IF is involved in almost all of these criteria. According to Geneviève Causse-Broquet, emeritus professor at ESCP Europe:

> Islamic Finance is one of the asset classes that grew the fastest in the world, before the financial crisis in August 2007, and continues to grow. Born in the 1970s, IF has developed in the oil countries. If it is still highly concentrated in the Persian Gulf and Southeast Asia, it recently exported to the United States and Europe due to the excess liquidity from the Gulf countries due to the strong increase in oil prices.[2]

A brief statement regarding the modules presented in IE Business School's Master's in Finance supports this position:

> Islamic finance is becoming an increasingly important field of investment as Gulf investors have become pivotal actors in the world's capital markets. Islamic law (*Shari'ah*) only permits very specific products. Therefore a deep understanding of the mechanism used to issue *Shari'ah* compliant products will be a big asset for any future financier.[3]

IE's Master's in Finance courses changed from having all core courses to having 80 elective courses, one of these being IF. This is a full-time programme designed for recent graduates with an outstanding academic record who wish to pursue a career as a certified financial analyst in the financial industry. The programme was awarded second place worldwide in the *Financial Times* Master's in finance ranking for 2011. In addition, the *Financial Times* awarded IE´s MBA programme with a third-place European ranking in Europe and an eighth-place worldwide ranking.

Table 8.1 shows a contagion phenomena in the education field where each institution aspires to be the first to offer a course in IF. This reflects the leading position of French business schools in the conquest of educational space in IF.

If almost all available modules have an elective status, in ESSEC business school, the students of the Advanced Master's in Financial Techniques have a core course of 12 hours in IF. The rationale behind this development, as stated by one of the programme initiators, is to expand the students' horizons and minds as future fund managers and traders. 'It's a great way to show that we can integrate some ethics in finance. Whether you are in Islamic, Catholic, ethical and solidarity finance, the approach is the same', said Cedomir Nestorovic, ESSEC's professor of Management.[4] Moreover, in October 2012, IE Business School's Professor Ignacio de la Torre, academic director for the Finance

Table 8.1 Top Ten business schools offering Islamic Finance courses

Ranking	Institution	Name	Character
1	HEC Paris	Islamic Finance	Elective
2	IE Business School	Islamic Finance	Elective
3	ESSEC Business School	Islamic Finance	Core
6	Grenoble Graduate School of Business	Islamic Finance	Elective
9	Skema	Islamic Finance	Elective

Master's programme, will introduce a first degree in Finance of 'which Islamic finance will be a core component'.[5]

This educational strategic decision is motivated by the fact that the future leaders of finance must master the fundamentals and standards of this new, alternative form. It also aims to broaden the market opportunities in areas of finance before the rise of unemployment in Europe. Top Ten business schools seek to develop managers with expertise not only in the field of conventional finance (CF) but also in that of IF.

Reasons behind the Islamic Finance programmes

The interest of the Top Ten institutions in IF may not be motivated by business considerations only. IF offers new perspectives for research in Financial Economics. In this regard, some business schools have established research programmes or research centres dedicated to IF.

The IE Business School has established the Saudi-Spanish Centre for Islamic Economics and Finance in collaboration with the Institute of Islamic Economics of the King Abdulaziz University based in Jeddah, a big city for business in Saudi Arabia.

Following an international conference on 'Beyond the Crisis: Islamic Finance in the new financial order', held on 16–17 June 2010, the two institutions have published a book entitled *Islamic Economics and Finance: A European Perspective.*[6]

A second conference – 'Islamic Finance in the 21st Century', held on 1 December 2011 – served as a platform to discuss the main challenges facing education in the field of IF and has led to the current book: *Islamic Finance in Western Higher Education: Developments and Prospects.*

Ironically, while the Top Ten business schools use the teaching of IF as a competitive advantage in the global context of the liberalization of higher education, most business schools in the Muslim and Arab world stick to the ideological stand in this perspective. The integration of IF into the curriculum is seen as a nuisance factor in the image of the institution and its attractiveness.

Conclusion

The value of the Top Ten business schools for IF will not be limited to the supply of an elective and core course. The mapping of IF education in the world shows that other scenarios are possible: the creation of an IF stream within a conventional curriculum or the simple creation of a pure degree in IF are examples of such possibilities.

The institutions that currently offer educational programmes in IF should consider this challenge from the Top Ten business schools, through the continuous improvement and innovation of curricula content to better meet market needs and developments of skills in the world of finance. With this improvement, the leading business schools will show to others the image of their own future.

Notes

1. *Financial Times*, Masters in Finance Pre-experience 2011.
2. ESCP Europe (2012).
3. IE Business School, Master in Advanced Finance – Course Description: 6.
4. Quoted by Lefebvre (2012: 138).
5. Quoted by Parker (2011).
6. Langton, Trullols and Turkistani (2011).

References

Devinney, T., Dowling, G. R. and Perm-Ajchariyawong, N. (2008) 'The Financial Times business schools ranking: What quality is this signal of quality?' *European Management Review*, 5, 4, pp. 195–208.

ESCP Europe (2012) 'Programmes impact: Finance islamique, http://www. escpeurope.eu

Financial Times, Masters in Finance Pre-experience 2011, http://rankings.ft.com/ businessschoolrankings/masters-in-finance-pre-experience-2011.

IE Business School, Master in Advanced Finance – Course Description, http:// www.ie.edu/business/programas/MASTERS%20IN%20FINANCE/GMIF/ Overview/course.pdf

Langton, J., Trullols, C. and Turkistani, A. (2011) *Islamic Economics and Finance: A European Perspective* (London: Macmillan).

Lefebvre, C. (2012) 'Apprentis banquiers halal', *Le Point*, 10 mai, pp. 138–40.

Parker, M. (2011) 'Madrid aims to become education hub of Europe', *Arab News*, 12 December.

Part II
Islamic Finance Higher Education in the West: Cases and Experiments

9
Islamic Finance at Henley Business School, Reading University

Simon Archer

Introduction

This chapter is concerned with experience in teaching and research in Islamic Finance (IF) over 15 years in two UK universities at which the writer has worked. In the International Capital Markets Association (ICMA) Centre at Henley Business School (part of the University of Reading), there is a taught MSc in Investment Banking and Islamic Finance and a Ph.D. programme which admitted its first students this year. There is also a programme of executive education. In the School of Management at the University of Surrey, there was a less formal Ph.D. programme in IF which ceased when I left in 2003; the research topics are mentioned briefly further.

Academic work in IF in the UK faces challenges resulting from the fact that the subject area is a new area of practice and hence of research and teaching. This chapter draws attention to these challenges and describes how they have been addressed in the two universities mentioned previously.

Modern IF is a very recent development, and started to become prominent only in the 1990s. This has obvious implications for teaching and research in the field. Specifically, for a European university to offer taught courses in IF, it has to overcome two difficulties. The first is finding teaching staff with an adequate knowledge of the field. The second is the paucity of suitable textbooks and research literature. These two difficulties reinforce each other. The lack of really good textbooks – such as exist for conventional finance (CF), where a number of excellent texts, mostly American, exist – means that it is hard for a lecturer who has no higher degree in IF to perform competently as a teacher in the subject.

The amount of research literature is growing, which is beneficial for both taught postgraduate and Ph.D. programmes. With regard to the latter, however, the difficulty in finding lecturers with an adequate knowledge of the subject is reflected in a similar difficulty in finding suitable Ph.D. supervisors. Moreover, the existing research literature is far from rich in terms of theoretical development. This is a handicap for Ph.D. students in developing their research design.

Experience in education and training (executive education): University of Reading

Taught degree programmes

University of Surrey

During the period 1995–8, consideration was given to introducing a taught Master's degree in IF here. This was to be a part-time, block-release programme involving a partner institution in a GCC country. Teaching was to be carried out by staff of this institution together with myself and a specialist in IF who was a visiting professor and Ph.D. cosupervisor at the University. In the end, the project was not brought to fruition, owing to various problems of which perhaps the crucial one was that, at that time, the University of Surrey had no Master's degrees in CF which could have provided suitable modules to be included in the proposed degree programme. In addition, there was a lack of firm commitment from the partner institution.

University of Reading

In 2008, the University of Reading introduced a Master of Science (MSc) in Investment Banking and Islamic Finance (MScIBIF), in collaboration with the International Centre for Education in Islamic Finance (INCEIF), an university-level institution in Kuala Lumpur, Malaysia offering both degree and professional programmes. The degree is offered through the ICMA Centre, which is a specialised school of Finance ('the business school for financial markets') established some 20 years ago with the support of the ICMA.

Thanks to the collaboration with INCEIF and to the employment as visiting professors of academics experienced in IF, the Centre has been able to develop its MScIBIF as part of a portfolio of MSc degree programmes in Finance. This portfolio includes MSc programmes in:

International Securities, Investment and Banking
Investment Management

Financial Risk Management
Financial Research
Capital Markets Regulation and Compliance
Corporate Finance
Financial Engineering
International Shipping and Finance
International Business and Finance
Real Estate Finance

The current structure of the MScIBIF degree is as follows:

Autumn Term
Securities, Futures and Options
Fixed Income and Equity Investments
Financial Analysis
Financial Markets
Introductory Quantitative Methods
Spring Term
Corporate Finance
The Principles of Islamic Finance and the Nominate Contracts (ten credits)
Design, Implementation and Risk Aspects of Islamic Financial Products and Services (20 credits)
Islamic Financial Institutions and Markets (ten credits)
Plus one of:
    Essentials of Financial Engineering
    Financial Regulation and Regulatory Policy
    International Securities Markets
    Managing Securities Operations
    Topics in the History of Finance
Summer Term (at INCEIF)
Any three, totalling 30 credits, from:
    Islamic Capital Markets
    Islamic Economics
    Wealth Planning and Management
    Research Project.

Thus, out of a total requirement of 180 credits for the degree, courses in Islamic Finance contributing 40 credits are taught at Reading during the Spring Term (January–March), 30 credits by two members of Reading staff (visiting professors who have a substantial record of research and publications in the field), and 10 credits by a member of INCEIF staff who visits Reading. Courses in IF contributing a further 30 credits are taken during the Summer Term at INCEIF in Kuala Lumpur. Hence, 70 out of 180 credits, or more than one-third, are provided by IF courses. Students may also stay on in Kuala Lumpur to complete INCEIF's professional qualification of Chartered Islamic Finance Professional.

The arrangements just described indicate how the University of Reading has addressed the problem of finding teaching staff with an adequate knowledge of IF, namely the use of senior visiting faculty and an agreement with another university-level institution that specializes in IF.

While the majority of students are from Middle Eastern countries, to these should be added students from Kenya, Nigeria, the UK and Continental Europe.

The requirement to spend the Summer Term in Kuala Lumpur, together with the additional costs associated with this, was found to be viewed less favourably by some potential applicants. Hence, it is proposed that as from the 2012–13 academic year, another version of the MScIBIF will be introduced allowing students to take all 180 credits in Reading. The 30 credits obtained in Kuala Lumpur will be replaced by 30 additional credits taken in Reading in the Spring Term in the form of a dissertation and/or taught courses.

Ph.D. programme

The Ph.D. programme at the ICMA Centre is intended for students who have achieved distinction level in a relevant Master's programme – a relatively demanding requirement. It is a full-time, three-year programme incorporating a first year in which students take courses in research methods, and may take certain MSc courses that are relevant to their research topic. Most of the Ph.D. students are employed as teaching assistants, as in German universities. The situation as regards IF is discussed further under the 'Research' subheading further.

Executive education

The ICMA Centre developed a programme of executive education in the fundamentals of IF in conjunction with the Institut de Formation Bancaire de Luxembourg. The programme is designed for young professionals in Finance and Commercial Law and consists of a set of two-day modules comprising the following:

Foundation Modules
Islamic Finance: Introduction

Risk Management in Islamic Finance
Islamic Insurance (*takaful*)
Islamic Securitization (*sukuk*)
Advanced Modules
Asset Management in Islamic Finance
Corporate Governance in Islamic Finance
Islamic Project Finance

Each module is assessed by means of a multiple-choice question paper. A candidate who passes the four foundation modules is awarded a Foundation Certificate in Islamic Finance. On passing the three advanced modules, a holder of the Foundation Certificate receives an Islamic Finance Diploma.

Experience in research

Research by members of academic staff

Members of academic staff who teach IF have ongoing research activities in the field and have published their work in peer-reviewed journals and edited volumes. A number of such publications are listed in the Appendix later. Much of this work has been concerned with various challenges facing IF institutions, and in particular prudential concerns such as the regulation, supervision and corporate governance of Islamic banks and insurance (*takaful*) undertakings. Work carried out as consultants for the Islamic Financial Services Board has provided an additional dimension to this research. Another theme is the study of *fiqh al mua-malat* (Islamic commercial jurisprudence), which provides the juristic underpinning of Islamic finance. It is essentially a body of contract law, but as a juristic underpinning for a complex and fast developing practice of Islamic Banking and insurance it raises a number of important research issues.

Doctoral research supervised by members of academic staff

University of Surrey

Prior to taking up my present post at the University of Reading, I was professor of Financial Management at the University of Surrey, Guildford. In this capacity, in 1995 I started a Ph.D. programme in IF. This I did at the instigation, and with the indispensable participation, of Dr Rifaat Ahmed Abdel Karim, at that time secretary-general of the Accounting and Auditing Organization for Islamic Financial Institutions (AAOIFI), who was appointed visiting professor at the University. I considered Professor Karim's active participation as a Ph.D. cosupervisor to be indispensable, as my own grasp of IF at that time was insufficient for supervision of Ph.D. research in this field.

Professor Karim and I cosupervised six Doctoral research projects, on the following topics which were related to the financial reporting of, and corporate governance in, IF institutions:

The 'True and Fair view' – An Islamic perspective
Risk in Islamic Banks
The Implementation of AAOIFI's Financial Reporting Standards in Sudanese Islamic Banks
The Effect of AAOIFI's Financial Reporting Standards on Disclosures in the Annual Reports of Islamic Banks
Corporate Governance of Islamic Banks in the GCC Countries
A Model for the Valuation of Islamic Banks.

All of the previous projects except the fifth involved a substantial amount of primary data collection. All but the last two required data collection via questionnaires and interviews (an onerous process), while the fourth project demanded the codification by hand of large amounts of secondary data (published annual reports).

One challenge in such research is the development of an adequate theoretical motivation. For the projects listed before, this was based mainly on the literature on transparency, corporate governance and market discipline.

Of the five Doctoral students, two were young academics on scholarships from their universities (in Bahrain and Malaysia, respectively), who were able to study full time, while two were senior managers in public sector institutions (central bank and ministry of finance) who studied part time, and one was a manager in a central bank who started on a full-time basis and transferred to a part-time basis.

Part-time Doctoral study is very demanding on the student, and may be equally demanding on the supervisor. On the other hand, admitting only full-time Ph.D. students has the effect of excluding candidates whose practical knowledge of IF may enable them to develop insights, and in some cases to obtain access to research sites, which would not be available to students whose background is purely academic. My personal experience leads me to suggest that it is preferable to insist on periods of full-time study of, say, six months at the beginning of the

Doctoral studies and at least three months at the end, the former in order to complete the literature review and research design (and to take courses in research methods and other relevant subjects) and the latter to complete writing-up.

The ICMA Centre, University of Reading

As mentioned before, the ICMA Centre currently admits only full-time Ph.D. students, and this, together with the demanding admissions criteria, has limited the number of Ph.D. students in IF. There have been numerous applications which have not been accepted.

There are currently two Ph.D. students in IF, both fully externally funded, that is not employed as teaching assistants, and both in the first year of Doctoral studies. One has been working as a lecturer in a college of Business Studies in Kuwait, and the other is a central banker in Saudi Arabia. Their chosen topics are:

Corporate Governance of Islamic Financial Institutions
National Risk Management Programme for Managing Sovereign Assets, with Particular Reference to Saudi Arabia.

As the second topic only partially concerns IF, as well as having a macro-economic dimension, we have a cosupervisor in the Department of Economics whose research covers this area.

Conclusions

Universities in Europe have much to offer in terms of Ph.D. studies for candidates from countries in which IF is practised. They may also benefit from developing their research in this rapidly developing and challenging area of finance. However, in order to provide appropriate supervision for such Doctoral students, universities need to have academic staff with an adequate theoretical and empirical knowledge of the field and of the particular challenges it presents to the researcher. There is no dearth of applicants for Doctoral studies in IF, but many do not meet stringent admissions criteria and hence would require closer than average supervision. Anecdotal evidence together with my own experience as an external examiner suggests that these requirements, and especially the need for adequately qualified supervisors, are not always met.

Appendix

Research publications in Islamic Finance

John Board is dean of the Henley Business School and professor of Finance, University of Reading. Simon Archer, Rifaat Ahmed Abdel Karim and Volker Nienhaus are visiting professors at the ICMA Centre, Henley Business School, University of Reading.

John Board

Chapter in book

'Development of Islamic capital markets', in Islamic Financial Services Board (2011) *Strategies for the Development of Islamic Capital Markets: Infrastructures and Legal Aspects of Islamic Asset Securitisation* (Kuala Lumpur: Islamic Financial Services Board).

Simon Archer

Chapter in book

'Capital requirements, counter-cyclicality and Islamic finance', in Islamic Financial Services Board (2010) *The Changing Landscape of Islamic Finance* (Kuala Lumpur: Islamic Financial Services Board).

Simon Archer and Rifaat A. A. Karim

Papers in refereed journals

'Agency theory, corporate governance and the accounting regulation of Islamic banks', *Research in Accounting Regulation*, special international issue, Autumn 1997.

'Financial contracting, governance structures and the accounting regulation of Islamic banks: An analysis in terms of agency theory and transaction cost economics', *Journal of Management and Governance*, Autumn 1998 (with T. Al-Deehani).

'On capital structure, risk sharing and capital adequacy in Islamic banks', *The International Journal of Theoretical & Applied Finance*, December 2005.

'Corporate governance, market discipline and regulation of Islamic banks', *The Company Lawyer* 27, 5, May 2006.

'Risks in Islamic banks: Evidence from empirical research', *Journal of Banking Regulation*, 10, 2, 2009 (with N. M. Ariffin).

'Supervisory, regulatory and capital adequacy implications of profit sharing investment accounts in Islamic finance', *Journal of Islamic Accounting and Business Research*, 1, 2, 2010 (with V. Sundararajan).

'Profit-sharing investment accounts in Islamic banks: Regulatory problems and possible solutions', *Journal of Banking Regulation*, 10, 4, 2010.

Chapters in books

Islamic Finance: The Regulatory Challenge (2007) (Singapore: John Wiley (Asia) Pte Ltd).

'Supervision of Islamic banks and Basel II: The regulatory challenge'.

'Measuring risk for capital adequacy: The issue of profit sharing investment accounts'.

'Specific corporate governance issues in Islamic banks'.

'Concluding remarks: The challenges to financial sector regulators and supervisors, to the Islamic financial services industry sector and to governments and legislative authorities'.

Simon Archer, Rifaat Ahmed Abdel Karim and Volker Nienhaus

Chapters in books

Takaful Islamic Insurance: Concepts and Regulatory Issues (2009) (Singapore: John Wiley (Asia) Pte Ltd).

'Conceptual, legal and institutional issues confronting *Takaful*'.

'Corporate governance and stakeholder rights in Islamic insurance'.

'Concluding remarks: The structure of *Takaful* undertakings and resultant unresolved issues'.

Volker Nienhaus

Chapter in book

'Islamic finance and financial crisis: Implications for Islamic banking', in Islamic Financial Services Board (2010) *The Changing Landscape of Islamic Finance* (Kuala Lumpur: Islamic Financial Services Board).

10
Islamic Finance Education at La Trobe University

Ishaq Bhatti

Introduction

Australia is the fourth largest investment fund holder in the world. With its large investment base and its geopolitical position near some of the world's largest Islamic countries, Australia is well placed to take part in the rapidly emerging area of Islamic Finance (IF). To be seen as a leader in IF, Australia will need to develop a finance workforce with expertise in conventional finance (CF), IF and *Shari'ah*-based regulatory complexities. There are a limited number of educational institutions providing this mix of training to cater for the needs of the global IF industry. Only those that can tap into advanced computing technologies will be able to build bridges between multidisciplinary areas and to structure courses that will meet the needs of an ever expanding and complex financial management industry including the IF industry.

According to Kearney, the finance industry will require more than 30,000 IF experts[1] in the Gulf in the next decade if the growth rate in IF continues at its current rate. At the moment, the expected growth rate in IF is approximately 15 per cent annually,[2] resulting in a rapidly growing need for highly qualified IF experts who can work in the industry with innovative products to earn a living for the investors and themselves. Currently, IF is around 2 per cent of the total CF, implying that the volume of transactions, investment, liquidity and accounts activities in the IF industry is still lower compared to CF. However, its future growth prospects are promising if it can successfully offer financial alternatives to international corporations, individual investors, firms and banks in the context of sophisticated products which can accommodate the needs of the expanding Muslim population looking for halal financial services.

The main objective of this chapter is to demonstrate how to create the human capital needed in the IF industry in the Western world where Muslims are in the minority. This chapter proposes the structure of an IF curriculum which can build bridges among multi-culture/faith communities based on sound understanding of finance and *Shari'ah*. It presents a case study of La Trobe University's pioneering Master of Islamic Banking and Finance (MIBF) degree, and on line Islamic Finance Professional Development (IFPD) jointly with Ethica Institute in UAE. The course is then linked with other degrees; like Masters' in professional accounting (MPA), financial analysis (MFA), and MBA (restricted to electives only) and professional bodies; CFA, GARP and then extension to Ph.D. level education in IF. This model creates a general mould in this teaching practice that can integrate IF and CF. The chapter addresses various aspects of IF education such as the significance of the knowledge, curriculum design, and procedures in acquiring support from the university academic community and challenges in marketing the course. It also reviews some illustrating statistics to support the need for the course in Australia.

The structure of the rest of this chapter is as follows. The next section presents the motivation for IF education globally as well as in Australia. It demonstrates that the increase in Muslim population and the demand in IF is the driving force behind the growth of IF experts. It explains about the structure of the course. Section 3 concentrates on the rationale, marketing as aspects, and curricula design of various IF and Islamic Banking (IB) courses being offered at La Trobe. Section 4 explains the recruitment of students and their classroom experience, graduation process and then finally job seeking internships and career development in various areas of finance. The final section of the paper contains some concluding remarks.

Contemporary Islamic Finance in the world

The concept of IF has arisen from a requirement for interest-free finance in the 1940s in Malaysia and the late 1950s in Pakistan. The first officially accredited IF institution, the Muslim Pilgrims Savings Corporation, was founded in Malaysia in 1963. That was followed by a series of institutional and banking establishments in the Middle East, Africa and Southeast Asia. Significant milestones in IF history took place when Muslim countries established the Organization of the Islamic Conference (OIC)[3] and the Islamic Development Bank (IDB).[4] These are seen as the official international associations to govern and foster IF transactions around the world. These organizations have contributed to the success of the IF industry to its current level of growth. However, the total assets of the 10 largest Muslim nations are only equivalent to approximately 2.7 per cent of global GDP.[5] It is still a minuscule figure which indicates the infant status of the IF industry. The modern challenges for IF are the shortage of standardization in international law and in practice not only between Western-styled finance countries and Muslim-styled finance countries, but also between the Islamic countries themselves with their different interpretations of *Shari'ah* principles. Moreover, the isolation of investors around the globe who have been familiar with only CF for a long time is also a considerable obstacle.

All of the reasons previous illustrate an essential demand for a basic and complete academy about IF which can raise awareness among investors and bring standardization to the world financial picture in which IF services and products have emerged to contribute to the diversification of investments.

Islamic Finance in Australia

In Australia, the Muslim community is expanding with the second fastest growth rate of 40.2 per cent compared to Christianity. Muslims number over 480,000 individuals across approximately 100,000 households. The majority of the community are young with 49.5 per cent below the age of 24. This growth creates a crucial need for a financial industry which is based on Islamic principles. A bright instance is the Muslim Community Corporation of Australia (MCCA), which has been on the road to becoming the first Australian Islamic bank. According to *MCCA News* (No. 1, 2012), MCCA will achieve $1 billion in Islamic financing by 2015 . Meanwhile, all over the world, Western conventional banks – such as HSBC, Lloyds TSB, Citibank, ABN AMRO, Deutsche Bank, Standard Chartered, JP Morgan – have established IB subsidiaries called 'Islamic windows'. In Australia, in the last few years, there has been the establishment of: the Kuwait Finance House in Melbourne; Westpac's commodity-trading facility Crescent Wealth, which launched the first *Shari'ah*-compliant equity fund; ANZ's investment in AmBank; NAB's operation in *sukuk* and the stated intentions of HSBC Amanah to compete down under.[6] In light of this activity, an official authority has been established by the Australian Financial Markets Association (AFMA) as an IB and IF working group that operates closely with the Treasury to facilitate these sectors in Australia. The Australian Government can see the additive advantages of IF in various industries (such as agriculture, mineral resources and infrastructure advances), and the IF products related to commodities can flourish and reinforce the position of Australia as a global leader and innovator in public and private infrastructure complex financing. Moreover, continued growth in major Asian economies will result in a need to develop resources-related services and infrastructure, which are ideal assets for some forms of IF, such as *sukuk, mudaraba, murabaha* and *ijarah*.[7] Australia is well positioned to structure and offer such instruments as part of financing packages for resources-related development. That is also a crucial plank in the national strategy to advance Australia's ambition to be an Asia-Pacific financial centre. However, to be successful Australia must train and produce a generation of IF scholars who are able to comprehend the *Shari'ah*-compliant products and have an intensive knowledge about current global finance.

The industry requires a standardized and well-established IF education system in the world and especially in Australia.

Islamic finance education

In response to the significant growth of IB and IF, some educational training courses and degree programmes have been designed by various agencies and the universities in the US and UK, GCC and Asia-Pacific regions to supply a basic knowledge for investors and students. However, there are still no internationally standardized curricula for these programmes. To date, academic training in IF has been delivered by mixed offering, face-to-face and distance learning modes. These can be based on short courses (diplomas, professional qualifications) and degrees (undergraduate and postgraduate).[8]

The first two result in a wide range of certificates and postgraduate diplomas. The online programme is usually based on four modules that cover Islamic Economics, IF instruments, IB and *takaful*. In addition, there are many short courses related to contract law in Islam and Islamic law including Australian Centre for Islamic Finances (AusCif) short courses and IFPD.

Research degree programmes dominate the landscape in Australia (La Trobe only), Europe and North America. The Harvard IF Project, the establishment of a chair in IF at Rice University, the Master's degree in Islamic Economics and Finance at Loughborough University, Leicester, UK, the MA and MSc in Islamic Finance at Durham University, UK, and the MA in Islamic Management, Banking and Finance at Markfield Institute of Higher Education, Leicester, UK are all examples of a growing emphasis on intellectual rigor. This category is rounded out by the Islamic Economics Research Centre at King Abdulaziz University in Jeddah and the Master's programmes with Islamic orientation at the International Islamic University in Bangladesh, Malaysia, Pakistan and Sudan.

However, there is a lack of uniform curriculum at international standards in these programmes. Academic standardization needs to be established and accepted to generate degrees which can be recognized and accepted by industry and academia worldwide.

In Australia, the education services sector is a significant contributor to the GDP and was Australia's third largest export between 2006 and 2008. The latest ranking of Australia's top exports of goods and services shows education services ranked fourth in 2008–9, followed by coal, iron and gold. In spite of being home to less than 1 per cent of the world's population, Australia attracts 7.5 per cent of the world's foreign students.[9] The majority of these students are from Asia including China, the Indian subcontinent, Malaysia, Hong Kong, Vietnam, Singapore and the Middle East and North Africa's oil-rich countries.

Australia has the opportunity to combine its ambition to be a strategic financial hub in the Asia-Pacific region with its reputation as a significant player in the world education services sector to develop its financial-services education capacity and its educational partnerships with the region to set the standard and provide the human resources required for an IF industry in Australia and in the region. In light of this, La Trobe University launched MIBF course on 6 July 2009. The event marked the first time a course in Australia had been dedicated to training in IB and IF. Since 2009, the course has provided students with postgraduate training in the technical skills demanded by global Islamic capital markets and institutions. The Master's curriculum is created to appeal to the international students around the world and especially from Asia-Pacific and Middle Eastern regions (who would like to acquire IF training in English) and local students who are keen to develop their careers in this industry.

In addition, an online course, namely the IFPD was designed and launched in January 2011 to satisfy the interest of students and other audiences who want to stay current with developments in the banking industry and especially the development of IF. This chapter aims to describe the La Trobe programme in terms of good educational practice that establishes a standard in Australia and around the world for the provision of expert knowledge on the operation of IF globally.

Islamic finance courses at La Trobe

Master of Islamic Banking and Finance

Rationale of the MIBF course

The MIBF is an unprecedented full-time, course-work Master's programme in Australia. It is designed to cater for the demand of postgraduates with academic knowledge and practical skills in a variety of subjects such as Islamic Banking, Insurance, Commercial Law, and Capital Markets of IF industry. The course has been designed to be suitable for international students as well as local students who are interested in learning and developing the existing IF industry. As stated by the IF programme's director,[10] 'the most attractive and advanced quality of MIBF is integration of IF with CF and banking perspectives which is consistent with Shari'ah principles as set out in Qur'an'. The academic quality of the programme is further enhanced by its ties to the Chartered Financial Analysis (CFA) programme. This allows participants of the course to be well prepared as new financial products related to IF emerge in the CF markets. Through this programme, La Trobe University seeks to bridge a shortage in the IF academy to provide well-equipped experts and technical professionals in Australia. The course supports the national strategy to foster and develop IF in Australia and is one element of the goal of making the country a financial hub in the Asia-Pacific region.

The academy of the course has been recognized by the International Centre of Education in Islamic Finance (INCEIF) based in Malaysia. Malaysia with LTU and INCEIF joint MOU between 2008–2012. Graduates who achieved MIBF from LTU may be entitled for partial exemptions in Chartered Islamic Finance Professional (CIFP)[11] Part 1 subject to passing their requirements. It is a globally recognized certificate to work in the industry of the Middle East, Southeast Asia, GCC, Malaysia and Indonesia where there is still an academic gap in IF service training.

The strength of MIBF is its curriculum, which is industry-driven through the consultancy of industry experts as well as renowned academic staff. In addition, the course puts a strong emphasis on foundation units focusing on economics, finance, quantitative analysis methods and accounting that result in multidimensional understanding about the theory of IF and its operation in practice.

Target audience

There are currently more than 300 IF institutions[12] around the world with three organizations based in Melbourne. These institutions serve a growing Muslim population, and their continued growth depends on academic and technical human resources which can cover principles, operation and mechanism of the currently dynamic Islamic capital market and IF industry.

MIBF provides graduates with an understanding of various products and processes in the IF industry along with accreditation and linkages with the CFA, CIFP and Ethica, Dubai. The audiences for the course can be put into three categories.

- Financiers and bankers who seek specialized knowledge of a newly rising market and academic recognition for their own professional development. As specialists in IF in Western banks, this groups enhances their career opportunities.
- Academic researchers and CF experts who wish to achieve advanced IF knowledge and study new aspects of the phenomenon.
- Investors who wish to enhance their awareness about a rising market in order to improve portfolio diversification with modern IF products.

Curricular design

Due to the needs of the various target audiences, the curriculum of the course is a mix between discipline-specific lectures and class activities, which provide academic understanding about techniques and operation in IF. The course provides opportunities for internship activities and incorporates guest speakers from both CF and IF, which bring practical experience regarding industry mechanisms. The curriculum in MIBF was created with the objective of developing an advanced knowledge in the field of economics, finance and complicated working mechanism of IF including its legal and regulatory framework and *Shari'ah* compliancy process in Australia and abroad. Throughout the course, students are exposed to the five key principles Figure 10.1 which underlie IF:

Since the initial launch in July 2009, the course has been structured as a combination of two or three modules (foundation, core and elective modules) depending on the background of applicants.

In 2011, the curriculum Table 10.1 was restructured to make it better align with the curriculum of the Master's in Financial Analysis (MFA) by the inclusion of compulsory subjects in order to create more opportunity for the students to obtain a double degree in MIBF and MFA. That characteristic of the course potentially attracts more international students with an international accreditation and collaboration of IF with INCEIF's CIFP, Ethica Dubai, CFA and Global Association of Risk Professional (GARP) linkage.

The curriculum changes of MIBF Table 10.2 resulted from the input and advice of the Course Advisory Board. That is a group of academic professionals and industrial experts such as David Kingsley, director from Kuwait Finance House (KFH). Other members of the committee are director of National Australia Bank (NAB), the MCCA and other commercial banks. They all contributed to the main unique feature of the course which integrates perspectives on IF with CF.

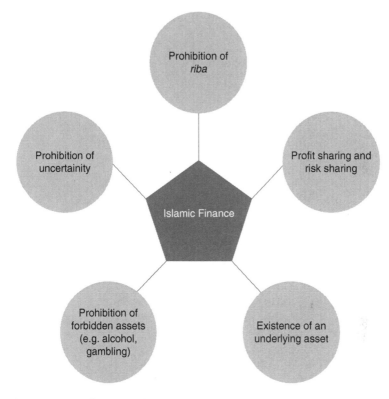

Figure 10.1   Five key principles

Table 10.1   Master of Islamic Banking and Finance – old curriculum

Part 1	Part 2	
Foundation module	Core module	Elective module
Principles of Finance [FIN5POF]	Islamic Jurisprudence [LAW5IJL]	Islamic Commercial Law [LAW5CLI]
Principles of Economics [ECO5POE]	Islamic Capital Markets [FIN5CAP]	Islamic Banking [FIN5BNK]
Accounting for Managers [ACC5AFM]	Islamic Insurance [FIN5INS]	Elective Unit from Master of Financial Analysis (MFA) or approved by School
Statistics for Business and Finance [ECO5SBF]	Elective Unit from LMFA or approved by School	Elective Unit from LMFA or approved by School

Table 10.2   Master of Islamic Banking and Finance (MIBF) – new curriculum

Part 1	Part 2	
Foundation module	Core module	Elective module
Principles of Finance [FIN5POF]	Islamic Banking [FIN5BNK]	Elective Unit from Master of Financial Analysis (LMFA) or approved by School
Principles of Economics [ECO5POE]	Islamic Capital Markets [FIN5CAP]	Elective Unit from LMFA or approved by School
Accounting for Managers [ACC5AFM]	Islamic Commercial Law [LAW5CLI]	Elective Unit from LMFA or approved by School
Statistics for Business & Finance [ECO5SBF]	Islamic Insurance [FIN5INS]	Elective Unit from LMFA or approved by School

During the last class of each main topic, professional representatives are invited to give a professional talk to MIBF students. It serves as a good opportunity for students to learn from real-life experience and ask questions about today's Islamic market. Approximately 60 per cent of the guest speakers have been from financial institutions including the four major banks, 30 per cent from government bodies and *Shari'ah* experts in IF (KFH, MCCA), and 10 per cent from international corporations. These guest speakers provide authentic learning experiences for students and choose qualified graduates for their internship programme which helps students transfer theory into practice and consolidate learning which later leads to jobs for our graduates.

Students who have a Bachelor's degree and 6.5 IELTS or an equivalent level of the Test of English as a Foreign Language (TOEFL) are eligible to apply for the course.

Duration of the course depends on the prior learning and experience of the student Table 10.3.

Procedure for acquiring approval from faculty

Marketing image

MIFB of La Trobe University can be considered as an unprecedented Master's course in Australia with a full programme consistent with

Table 10.3 Prior learning and experience

Prior learning and experience	Required modules	Duration
Three-year Bachelor's degree in an area other than Finance, Accounting or Economics	Foundation module and Core module	18 months
Three-year Bachelor's degree in Finance, Accounting or Economics	Core module and elective module	18 months
Three-year Bachelor's degree in relevant area and two years' relevant experience, advanced standing granted for elective module	Core module	12 months
Four-year Bachelor's degree with honours in Finance, Accounting or Economics or completion of LMFA, advanced standing granted for elective module	Core module	12 months

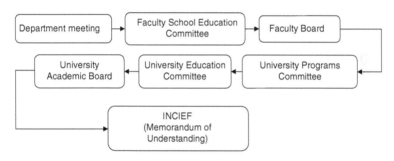

Figure 10.2 Procedure for acquiring approval from faculty

Shari'ah-compliant principles which are stated in the *Qur'an*. It is advertised with the unique statement: 'An international Master degree for students wanting to study for an internationally recognized qualification in IF'.

Due to a shortage of academic human capital in the industry in Muslim countries, MIBF targets students from GCC, Malaysia, Indonesia, second-generation Australian Muslims, and the Western-financial experts who are going to seek a global recognition to capitalize on IF. The course and related course are increased in value due to accreditation form well-known Islamic academic organization such as AAOIFI (Accounting and Auditing Organization for Islamic Financial Institutions) and INCEIF Malaysia Figure 10.2. That results in undergraduates receiving a globally recognized certificate in IF.

Tireless efforts of academic staff and straightforward strategy have been contributing to the success of the unique MIBF marketing campaign. With the key words 'Master of Islamic Banking and Finance, La Trobe University', more than 19,900 results can be found in Google window. One of the most noticeable qualities in the launch of MIBF has been the application of new communication technology. iTune University has been used to record many of the talks presented by professional guest speakers.

Islamic Finance Professional Development course

Rationale of the course

An online course has been structured to meet the demand of audiences who simply want to know the core nature and operation of IF. In light of that, the audience can be international students who are searching for an appropriate course in the industry or local members of the business community who would like to obtain a primary awareness of IF to make business decisions about this new sector of the world finance structure.

Online course

As stated, IFPD can be considered as an introductory course for MIBF. By finishing the online course, graduates are equipped with comprehensive principles of IF. From that experience, a decision to start further academic study in the sector can be made.

The course covers the key principles underlying IF: modes of IF such as: Islamic leasing (*ijarah*); Islamic investment (*mudarabah*); cost-plus financing (*murabaha*); partnerships (*musharakah*); Islamic forward selling and manufacturing contracts (*salam* and *istisna'*); and Islamic securitization (*sukuk*). Other topics include: global development of IF; challenges for Islamic financial providers; opportunities in Australia (government policies and tax reforms); Islamic capital markets; Islamic insurance (*takaful*); and IB products.

The curriculum of the IFPD course is designed to follow the standards of AAOIFI and is accredited by Ethica Institute of IF – the world's most recognized IF certifier – delivering standardized e-learning IF training and certification to professionals and students around the world. After finishing the course by sitting in a standardized online exam, the graduates are granted a certificate from Ethica CIFE™. The structure of the IFPD course is appended in this chapter.

Proposed pathway to obtain MIBF with existing course

Due to the flexibility of the MIBF curriculum's design and its consistency with the MFA, students with finance and business backgrounds can be offered different combinations between the courses to continue their academic studies. This property of the curriculum's design results in a remarkable benefit in time-saving for students as well as a qualified degree. The number of students involved in the course is projected to grow in future.

For applicants with an undergraduate university degree

Students who have already completed a university degree may enrol in the six-week IFPD course. Those who choose to continue into the Master of Islamic Banking and Finance at La Trobe University receive one elective subject exemption Figure 10.3.

For existing postgraduates with Master of Financial Analysis degree

Students in the MFA course (or students who have already completed the course) are completely able to apply for an additional degree of Master of Islamic Banking and Finance resulting in a double degree Figure 10.4.

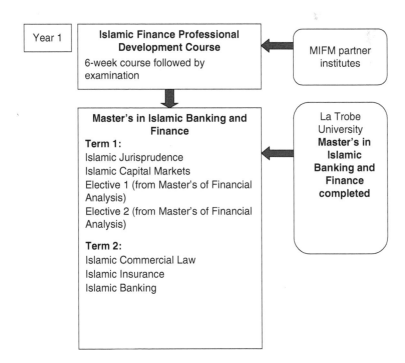

Figure 10.3 Applicants with an undergraduate university degree

Term 1	Four foundation subjects based on principles of finance, economics, accounting and quantitative analysis methods	
Term 2	*Core subjects*	*Elective subjects*
	Debt Securities Econometrics	2 units from LMFA or approved by School
Term 3	*Core subjects*	*Elective subjects*
	Derivative Securities Portfolio Management	2 Units from LMFA or approved by School
Term 4	*Core subjects of Master's in Islamic Banking and Finance*	
	Islamic Commercial Law Islamic Insurance Islamic Banking Islamic Capital Markets	

Master's in Financial Analysis finished ⬅

Master's in Islamic Banking and Finance completed ⬅

Figure 10.4   For existing postgraduates with Master of Financial Analysis degree

For existing postgraduates with Master of Accounting and Financial Management (MAFM) Degree

Students who are enrolled in La Trobe's Master's in Accounting and Financial Management are eligible to continue one addition term to achieve a second Master's degree in IB and IF Figure 10.5.

This pathway enriches accounting postgraduates' knowledge of the principles and operation of the new sector of finance. Students will be exposed to integration between the concepts of CF and accounting with IF. This represents a great opportunity for accounting students who can obtain an international accreditation from reliable global Islamic academic institutes as well as skills and techniques to work with new financial products emerging.

The development of Islamic Finance education at La Trobe University

With the successful launch of the Master Islamic Banking and Finance (MIBF) degree in 2009, La Trobe University has been a pioneer in developing the education for a special industry in Australia. That degree has continued to contribute to development of the academic foundation for IF and will continue to enhance the marketing of Australia as a financial hub in the Asia-Pacific region. Following this success, a series of combination courses has been implemented which are designed to lead to a gradual increase in number of student enrolments.

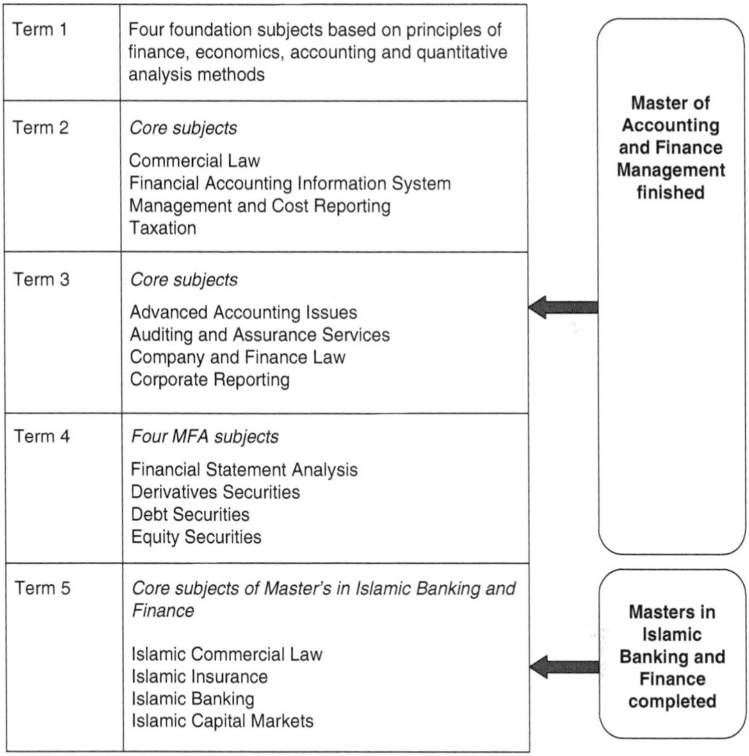

Term 1	Four foundation subjects based on principles of finance, economics, accounting and quantitative analysis methods	**Master of Accounting and Finance Management finished**
Term 2	*Core subjects* Commercial Law Financial Accounting Information System Management and Cost Reporting Taxation	
Term 3	*Core subjects* Advanced Accounting Issues Auditing and Assurance Services Company and Finance Law Corporate Reporting	
Term 4	*Four MFA subjects* Financial Statement Analysis Derivatives Securities Debt Securities Equity Securities	
Term 5	*Core subjects of Master's in Islamic Banking and Finance* Islamic Commercial Law Islamic Insurance Islamic Banking Islamic Capital Markets	**Masters in Islamic Banking and Finance completed**

Figure 10.5 For existing postgraduates with Master of Accounting and Financial Management degree

At the time of reporting, the number of enrolments in 2012 is incomplete. We can expect an addition to the figure of 2012 Figure 10.6. In line with this, the figure in 2009 was just collected for the second semester. Over four years, La Trobe University has an average of approximately 28 students enrolled into IF study with a standard change of nine students from the average number per year.

Moreover, throughout the years, an approximate growth of 37.78 per cent can be observed.[13] Especially in 2010 and 2011, there were significant increases of 130 per cent and 23.3 per cent respectively. These are understandable because of full-year recognition of 2010 and 2011 student enrolments. They signify a sustainable growth in the need of academia for the industry as long as the marketing campaign is effective and quality in education is maintained.

| ■ Master of Financial Analysis/Master of Islamic Banking and Finance | ■ Master of Islamic Banking and Finance | ▨ Master of Financial Analysis (Islamic Finance) |

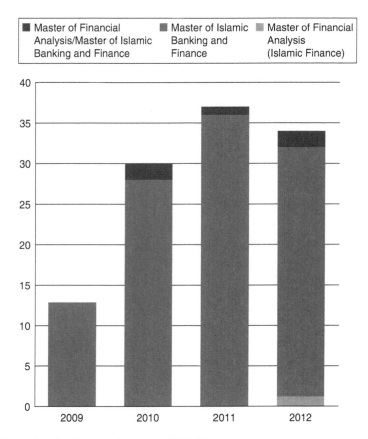

Figure 10.6   Student enrolments in 2009–12

Figure 10.7 illustrates the average weights of a variety of IF courses. This shows a growing diversification in course choice and a flexible combination between related courses. La Trobe offers three different Master level courses. MIBF, MFA and the joint double master degree MIBF/MFA. The MIBF still plays an important role which accounts for 91% in the total number of IF masters students followed by MFA and the joint Double Master degree. When the data is separated between domestic and international students the pattern of the number of students in MIBF enrolment dominate. However, domestics students are declining due to lesser job opportunities in Australia as there are Islamic banks and financial institutions due to lack of IF regulation and taxation issues. The international students are still increasing in MIBF.

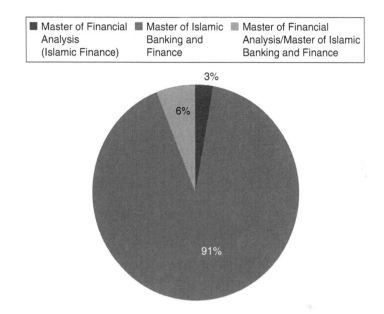

Figure 10.7 Average weights of Islamic Finance courses in La Trobe University

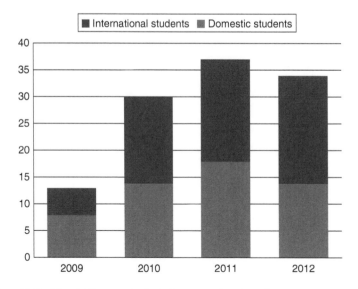

Figure 10.8 Islamic Finance students in terms of nationality

From this experience we learn that the students like to have more pure IF education preferring MIBF over rest of the combinations; MFA in IF or MIBF/MFA double degrees. This may have greater policy making effects on rest of the institutions in structuring curriculum for Islamic Banking and Finance education in Australia and/or elsewhere.

Along with an increase in the number of students, there is a growth in the international segment. However, as shown in Figure 10.8, the number of domestic students still outweighs the number of international ones. The average number of students as observed from 2009–2012 is almost 14 for the domestic segment and 15 for the international one Figures 10.9 and 10.10. However, coefficient of variation in given figures shows that volatility in enrolment is 26.44 per cent in the domestic segment and 39.72 per cent in the international one Table 10.4. This demonstrates a more stable increase in the need of domestic graduates for IF study. Nonetheless, with an annually growing increase in international enrolments, it can be projected that there will be an increasing interest and demand from overseas countries with a robust internationally based marketing campaign.

The attraction of the course is also illustrated by the gender structure of participants Figure 10.11. In the first half of 2012, 30 per cent were female, whereas this figure was 70 per cent for males. The structure

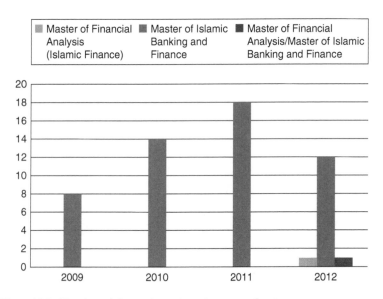

Figure 10.9 Number of domestic students in terms of unit

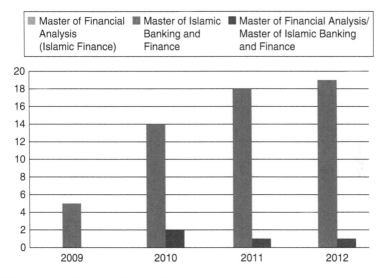

Figure 10.10 Number of international students in terms of unit

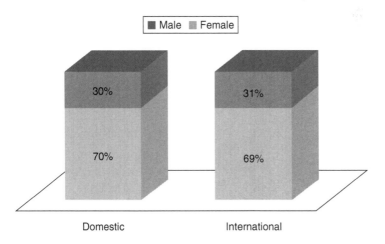

Figure 10.11 Gender group of MIBF graduates (2012)

stays the same for both the domestic and international segments. It reflects the increasing interest of both genders in the rising finance sector. Moreover, it signifies the desired involvement of women in IB and IF, where men still play a dominant role. Therefore, a special marketing campaign should be taken into account to encourage the participation of females to improve gender equality.

In terms of age groups Figures 10.12 and 10.13, 70 per cent of the participants are 20–9 years old. That is a good signal for the course as well as the industry. Notably, 92 per cent of international students fall within this age range. The majority of the age groups suggests young people's interest in enhancing their academic knowledge of IF. Accordingly, it can be claimed that an active human capital with professional skills and expert understanding has been prepared for the official launch of the IF

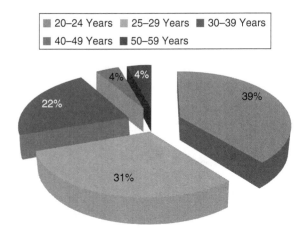

Figure 10.12   Age group of MIBF graduates (2012)

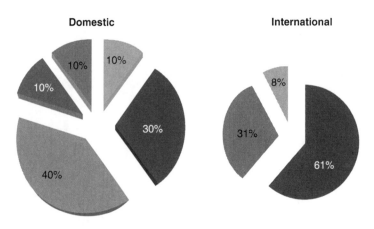

Figure 10.13   Domestic vs international graduates

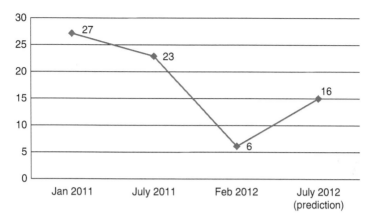

Figure 10.14 Islamic Finance Professional Development course

industry in Australia. It serves the national strategy to develop an Islamic capital market for commodities and infrastructure, and import capital from Pacific regions such as ASEAN, APEC and Middle East countries.

IFPD was officially launched in 2011 with the initial purpose of providing students and graduates with a fundamental basis in IF and its principles within a 6-week course. In January 2011, there were 27 students enrolled. This was followed by July 2011 training session –2 with 23 students and February 2012 session –, only 6 students enrolled Figure 10.14. These disappointment figures were shocking for us because IFPD was the first ever on line short course in IF in Australia. We discuss this with our IF academic quality assurance board and LTU's marketing department and realize we may need to run one more session if the numbers go above 15 then we may continue otherwise we may stop or restructure online course. One opinion was that the fall may be due to the common effect of the decrease in number of international student enrolments in 2010–11 as reported by the Australian Bureau of Statistics (2011).[14]

It is noticeable that 60 per cent of the audience is local and the remaining 40 per cent comes from overseas. That suggests that there should be a robust marketing campaign to raise a strong awareness about the course in the international segment. It can improve the number of student enrolments in coming period of time. The number of participants in IFPD courses plays an important role to expansion of MIBF.

Academic achievement

Over the four years, La Trobe academic staff in IF education have achieved many precious experiences in developing teaching techniques, curricular design and materials. This is reflected in the academic results of students from four core subjects: Islamic Banking (FIN5BNK), Islamic Capital Market (FIN5CAP), Islamic Commercial Law (LST5CLI) and Islamic Insurance (FIN5INS).

It is reported that 96 per cent of graduates pass the subjects with approximately 60 per cent categorized as achieving A and B ratings. Only about 4 per cent failed Figure 10.15. (This may be due to the new exposure of students to the concept.) Noticeably, 100 per cent of the graduates who were involved in the IB subject are reported as passing, with approximately 64 per cent achieving A and B ratings. Moreover, this subject has been also attracting more students because it is classified as an elective subject in the curriculum of the MFA degree. This is a flexible combination with the CF degree, giving students accreditation in IF as well as a shortcut to achieving a double degree.

After its launch in 2009, five graduates completed Master's degrees in Islamic Banking and Finance in 2010. This figure was 17 in 2011 Figure 10.16. The average mark was 70.29 per cent in 2010 and 64.61 per cent in 2011 Figure 10.17. The decrease in the mark of 2011 may be due to a drop in the quality of domestic graduates, as can be observed

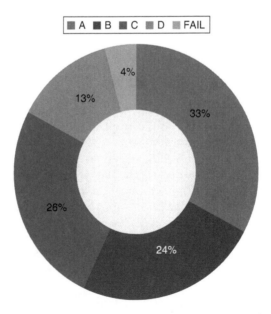

Figure 10.15   Average academic record for Islamic Finance core subjects

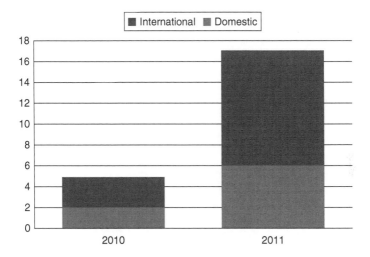

Figure 10.16   MIBF graduates

Figure 10.17   Weighted average mark of MIBF

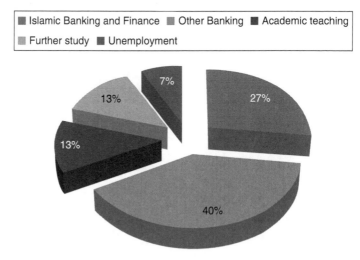

Figure 10.18 Career outcomes of MIBF graduates

in the graph further. However, the quality of international students has increased slightly from 65.08 per cent to 66.29 per cent. These results are an encouraging sign of the suitable quality of curricula in IF education for international training.

Industry feedback

The career outcomes for a sample of 15 students who graduated from MIBF in current years is demonstrated in Figure 10.18.

Approximately 67 per cent of the graduates are involved in the finance industry and nearly 27 per cent are working for IF banks and institution in overseas countries, especially in Malaysia and the Middle East. This suggests that the banking and finance industries may prefer graduate students who took the MIBF course at La Trobe University.

However, 7 per cent of the graduates remain unemployed. This figure indicates that there is less unemployment for IF graduates because IF is relatively far smaller than the CF industry.

IF in Australia has been under discussion at government levels for a number of years. An official launch is anticipated when legal regulations are available. There will probably be more demand for human capital in the IF to build up the industry, which will serve the national strategy to be a capital-importing country.

Table 10.4 Regression model summary[b]

Model	R	R Square	Adjusted R Square	Std. error of the estimate	Change Statistics					Durbin-Watson
					R Square change	F change	df1	df2	Sig. F change	
1	.843[a]	.710	.565	7.07107	.710	4.900	1	2	.157	2.000

Note:
a. Predictors: (Constant), date.
b. Dependent Variable: enrolment.

Model	Unstandardized coefficients		Standardized coefficients	t	Sig.	95.0% Confidence interval for B	
	B	Std. error	Beta			Lower bound	Upper bound
1 (Constant)	11.000	8.660		1.270	.332	−26.262	48.262
Date	7.000	3.162	.843	2.214	.157	−6.606	20.606

Residuals statistics[a]

	Minimum	Maximum	Mean	Std. deviation	N
Predicted value	18.0000	39.0000	28.5000	9.03696	4
Residual	−5.00000	5.00000	.00000	5.77350	4
std. Predicted Value	−1.162	1.162	.000	1.000	4
std. Residual	−.707	.707	.000	.816	4

Note:
a. Dependent variable: enrolment.

Forecasting enrolments

To predict students' enrolments for the next period, a regression model between year and historical record has been built up. The statistics are calculated based on statistical packages for social sciences (SPSS) as follows:
   The regression model can be written as:

Future enrolment = 11 + 7 * i-th Year

Based on the regression model, we can estimate the number of upcoming IF students in 2013, 2014, 2015, 2016:

2013: 11 + 7*5 = 46
2014: 11 + 7*6 = 53
2015: 11 + 7*7 = 60
2016: 11 + 7*8 = 67

However, at the moment, the course is still in its infancy. Therefore, because of the lack of observations, the prediction cannot avoid a big deviation from the true observation. This regression can be revised in the later when there are more observations and more independent variables identified.

Conclusion and remarks

The world has witnessed an increasing growth in the IF industry since its establishment during the 1940s in Malaysia. Although the industry has accounted for approximately 2.7 per cent of global financial transactions, it is believed that the continual growth will be 10–15 per cent.[15] Due to the nature of the industry – which has positively contributed to real economic activities, commodities markets and public infrastructure construction – central government is discussing the formation of an official legislative frame to apply and develop IF in Australia. This framework will support the objective of making Australia a financial hub in the Asia-Pacific region. There is an essential demand for academic and technical training in this emerging sector. However, lack of consistency in standardized regulations between Islamic countries may create some obstacles to the expansion of IF globally. Establishing standardized criteria in IF education could be a solution to these concerns. There needs to be a focus on developing a generation of Islamic scholars who have a comprehensive and complete knowledge of global finance as well as IB and IF. This could lead to the generation of a united framework for global IF standards. La Trobe University can be seen an unprecedented pioneer in this industry's education in Australia with the launch of its Master's in Islamic Banking and Finance in 2009. The success at the first stage is continued with an improvement process contributed by academic staff and industrial professionals. Its advantage in curricular design has played an important role in the success of the course. Its curricular uniqueness is that it integrates the perspectives of CF and IF. La Trobe University can become the first IF academic institution in Australia. Such a centre would allow industry professionals to update and enhance IF industry standards in Australia and the rest of the world.

The true success of the course is the development of a generation of industry experts who will actively contribute to the national strategy and the development of global IF.

Notes

1. Kearney (2006).
2. Perry and Rehman (2011).
3. OIC is an inter-governmental organization grouping 57 States. They decided to pool their resources together, combine their efforts and speak with one voice to safeguard the interest and ensure the progress and well-being of their peoples and those of other Muslims in the world over. It was established in Rabat, Morocco, on 25 September 1969. Member countries are; Afghanistan, Albania, Algeria, Azerbaijan, Bahrain, Bangladesh, Benin, Brunei, Burkina-Faso, Cameroon, Chad, Comoros, Cote d'Ivoire, Djibouti, Egypt, Gabon, Gambia, Guinea, Guinea-Bissau, Guyana, Indonesia, Iran, Iraq, Jordan, Kazakhstan, Kuwait, Kyrgyzstan, Lebanon, Libya, Malaysia, Maldives, Mali, Mauritania, Morocco, Mozambique, Niger, Nigeria, Oman, Pakistan, Palestine, Qatar, Saudi Arabia, Senegal, Sierra Leone, Somalia, Sudan, Suriname, Syria, Tajikistan, Togo, Tunisia, Turkey, Turkmenistan, Uganda, United Arab Emirates, Uzbekistan, and Yemen.
4. IDB is an international financial institution established in December 1973. Its main purpose is to foster the economic development and social progress of 57 member countries of OIC and Muslim communities individually as well as jointly in accordance with the principles of *Shari'ah* (i.e. Islamic Law). The functions of the IDB are to participate in equity capital, grant loans for productive projects and enterprises besides providing financial assistance to member countries for economic and social development. The Bank is authorized to accept deposits and to mobilize financial resources through *Shari'ah*-compatible modes (source: http://www.isdb.org/).
5. World Bank Data (2006).
6. Colan (2012). He graduated from La Trobe in 2011, is an advisor to MCCA and the founder of AusCif (Australian centre for Islamic Finance). He also teaches Islamic Finance Professional Development (IFPD) course at La Trobe.
7. Austrade, Islamic Finance (2010).

8. Chowdhry (2010).
9. Kocer (2009).
10. Dr M. Ishaq Bhati: Associate Professor in the Department of Finance, La Trobe Business School, at La Trobe University, Melbourne, Australia.
11. INCEIF's CIFP is industry-based certificate initiated by Malaysian Central Bank and Bank Negara Malaysia.
12. *Global Finance* (2011).
13. The number is calculated by Geometric mean.
14. Australian Bureau of Statistics 4102.0 (2011).
15. Cihak and Hesse (2008).

References

Australian Bureau of Statistics 4102.0 (2011) Australian Social Trends, December.
Austrade, Islamic Finance (2010) http://www.austrade.gov.au/search.aspx?articl eid=4345&moduleid=8367&keywords=islamic%20finance&sitesection=&sites ectiondescr=
Chowdhry, S. (2010) 'An introductory review of the major centers and initiatives for Islamic finance education around the world', *Dinar Standard*, June, http://www.dinarstandard.com/finance/finance_instit120604.htm
Cihak, M. and Hesse, H. (2008) 'Islamic Banks and Financial Stability: An Empirical Analysis', IMF Working Paper, p. 5, http://www.imf.org/external/pubs/ft/wp/2008/wp0816.pdf
Colan, A. (2012) 'Principles of Islamic Finance', *MCCA News*, No. 1, March.
Global Finance (2011) *World Best Islamic Financial Institutions*, http://www.gfmag.com/tools/best-banks/11198-worlds-best-islamic-financial-institutions-2011.html#axzz1vO6LR3a2
Kearney, A. T. (2006) 'Booming Islamic banking will need 30,000 jobs in the Gulf in 10 years', *AMEinfo*, 20 December, http://www.ameinfo.com/106063.html
Kocer, K. (2009) 'The global financial crisis and international migration: Policy implications for Australia', Lowy Institute for International Policy, July, p. 4.
Perry, F. and Rehman, S. (2011) 'Globalization of Islamic finance: Myth or reality?' *International Journal of Humanities and Social Science*, 1, 9 (December), pp. 107–19.
World Bank Data (2006) World Development Indicators, Washington, DC.

11
Islamic Finance in Reims Management School

Ghassen Bouslama

Islamic Finance (IF) has experienced phenomenal growth in the last decade, particularly in the Middle East and North Africa, Southeast Asia and recently in the West. It has become an important alternative banking and financing method all over the world. More than 300 IF institutions are operating in more than 70 countries. Their combined assets exceed $500 billion with an annual growth rate of 12–15 per cent. The continued growth of this industry even during the financial crisis raises the problem of a shortage of specialists.

Furthermore, the growing interest in Europe, and particularly in France, in the development of this system of finance was also a strong reason behind the choice of Reims Management School (RMS) to offer training in this area, which has become part of the financial landscape. Over the last five years a number of regulatory advances have been made in France, and several IF products are now marketable. Similarly, with the largest Muslim population in Europe, the potential for development in the French market is by far the greatest on the Continent. In the medium term this will require the training of experts in this field or specialists who are familiar with the techniques of IF. Interest in this alternative form of finance in Luxembourg and the United Kingdom was also a determining factor in our decision to offer courses in IF. Apart from Paris, these two countries are far and away the favourite destinations for RMS graduates who choose to specialize in the finance or auditing professions, particularly in IF.

Finally, beyond the desire of RMS to respond to the needs of the finance industry in terms of skills in this field, the offer of this type of course is also a reflection of the school's desire to offer its students the possibility of studying other economic models, and financial techniques different from those habitually taught in top higher educational establishments. It is part of our policy of openness towards other alternative, responsible, ethical or faith-based forms of finance, which we believe will develop students' sense of critical analysis and their natural curiosity.

So, to respond to the shortage of expertise in this field and with the desire to remain open to other forms of finance, RMS has offered an elective in Islamic Banking and Finance since the academic year 2008–9, and a Certificate in Islamic Banking and Finance in cooperation with the International Centre for Education in Islamic Finance (INCEIF) since 2011–12. So our range of courses takes the form of two programmes which differ in terms of teaching time and target students, and which each respond to different specific needs.

Islamic Banking and Finance elective

This specialized elective is open to Master's students on the Sup de Co Reims programme. The course is delivered entirely in English, and is programmed twice a year with 45 hours of classes spread over three weeks. The course therefore targets students of all nationalities, both domestic students and those from abroad following an exchange programme.

The creation of the elective enhanced the original structure of the RMS Master's programme, which had been developed to be flexible and reactive, so as to respond rapidly to the demands of professionals in terms of training. For more than 15 years now, the 'Grande Ecole' (High School) programme Sup de Co Reims has been based on modular courses, giving students the possibility of putting together their programme of study according to their personal aspirations. As they pursue their studies they continually make choices. In particular, in the second and third years they select the specialized electives they wish to follow. They have the choice of nearly 100 electives, including Islamic Banking and Finance.

The course aims to give the students an understanding of the foundations of IF and of its most recent applications. Students are introduced to the economics and law of Islamic contracts. The course also covers how IF institutions operate, in particular Islamic Banking (IB) and insurance institutions. Another part of the course presents the principles on which Islamic capital markets operate Islamic investment funds and the principal Islamic financial instruments such as the *sukuk*.

The course is delivered by academics but also by professionals. Among the course speakers are expert jurists in the field who have taken part in several IF projects in France and elsewhere. Associates of the most prestigious audit companies and leaders in the audit of Islamic banks also contribute to the course to explain the accounting principles that are applied in Islamic banks. Investment fund managers and asset management experts also take part; they explain how capital markets and their principal financial instruments operate. Leading European consultants in the field also contribute to the course, to explain *Shari'ah* auditing, the role of *Shari'ah* boards in IF institutions and *'takaful'* Islamic insurance. This mix of academics and professionals makes it possible to keep students up to date with the latest progress in both research and practices in the field.

Islamic Banking and Finance certificate

The reasons behind the launch of this certificate programme are essentially the same as those mentioned for the Islamic Banking and Finance elective. However, the target and the type of participants are not the same. The choice of a certificate format can be explained by the nature of the job market in this sector. At the moment, employment opportunities in France and Europe remain limited, and do not justify the opening of a specialized Master's course in IF with an appropriately high volume of classes. However, people who are already working, or students who are interested in working in the sector, can obtain additional specialization in the field by adding to their initial qualifications a certificate representing 180 hours of classes.

For the moment, the French and European markets are still in their infancy and there are not yet sufficient opportunities for students who are looking to specialize in IF. Advertised positions are often reserved for senior managers who already have some years of experience, even in conventional fields. However, there are more opportunities in the Gulf region and since the Arab spring the RMS can foresee interesting developments in the Maghreb and the rest of North Africa also.

Thus, this certificate is fully taught in English and planned over a period of four months, which represents 180 hours, the equivalent of half a Master of Science. It has four courses of 45 hours each which cover *Shar'iah* rules in financial transactions, Islamic economics, deposit and financing operations of Islamic banks and Islamic capital markets. The certificate is intended for practitioners, bankers, financiers, and lawyers with a solid educational background; and for students with at least a Bachelor's degree or equivalent from a recognized educational institution.

The certificate is jointly taught with the Malaysian university INCEIF and complies with the Chartered Islamic Finance Professional (CIFP) Part 1 delivered by INCEIF. The partnership with an expert in the field offers our students an excellent learning experience that draws on the research and industry experience of Reims Management School and INCEIF academic staff. Courses are taught jointly by professors of RMS and INCEIF. Interventions are also provided by European practitioners (lawyers, consultants, financiers) who come from Paris, London and Luxembourg.

Another specificity of the certificate is that it offers the possibility to access a wider qualification for students wishing to further specialize in the field. As such, the degree covers four modules of the CIFP Part 1. In addition, students who successfully complete these four modules are eligible to apply for exemptions to the equivalent CIFP modules from INCEIF. They are qualified to enrol in the CIFP programme, or other equivalent programmes at INCEIF. Students who complete the certificate programme are entitled, upon the exemptions being granted, to apply for student membership of the Association of Chartered Islamic Finance Professionals (ACIFP). The CIFP is a collaboration of academia and industry knowledge and skills intended to bridge the supply–demand gap for the IF services industry. All course modules are designed to provide a platform for participants to exchange ideas and experiences with academics and industry experts. This gives participants a better insight into worldwide and cross-cultural perspectives for a robust IF industry.

The Islamic Banking and Finance Certificate is also one of the options in the MSc in Finance and International Banking at RMS. To be awarded this full MSc degree, students must obtain the Certificate of Finance and the specialized certificate in either Islamic Banking and Finance or International Banking. This full-time, 12-month programme, taught in English at RMS campus, aims at delivering knowledge in both conventional finance (CF) and IB and IF industries. The academic programme includes over 400 learning hours, between October and May.

Perspectives for Islamic finance

Since courses in IF were launched at RMS, many students have already had the opportunity to follow them and some have been able to obtain internships or jobs in this field. Some students, for example, have been able to enhance their knowledge in the area and to get work in project finance for the finance departments of international companies established in the Gulf States. A number have found internships, for example, in one of the ratings agencies specializing in rating IF institutions, while others have found work in Islamic banks in the United Arab Emirates. Some have even had the opportunity, after a time, of being given auditing missions in Islamic investment funds in Luxembourg for the Big 4 or of moving into Islamic Asset Management in London.

The position occupied today by IF in the international financial landscape calls for appropriate, accessible training to be offered for all finance professionals. Therefore, apart from the aforementioned programmes, several seminars have also been programmed as part of our Master of Science courses, such as the MSc in International Financial Analysis, delivered in French and the MSc in Finance and International Banking delivered in English. This demonstrates once again RMS's interest in developing this form of finance and in making it accessible to many candidates who hope to make their career in banking and finance in general and IF in particular.

The current range of programmes at RMS aims to respond to today's job market in the sector of IF. However, nothing excludes the possibility that in the near future RMS may develop a specialized Master's programme in IF, if the sector continues to develop in Europe and particularly in France. For the moment, students who really want to work in this sector often look to the Gulf States and North Africa, and to a lesser degree to the United Kingdom. The French IF sector is as yet underdeveloped and is not significant enough to absorb all the candidates who aim to work in this field. Of course, if the sector continues to develop in France, RMS would be able to develop more specialized training programmes with a greater volume of teaching hours.

The development of IF in the West will require the involvement of many different actors: regulatory bodies, professionals, consumer and educational institutions. The latter have a very important role to play both upstream and downstream of the process of development. Downstream, top educational institutions have a vital task in responding to the skills needs of professionals, in a sector where there is a great lack of experts. Upstream, educational institutions also have a role to play in training the people who will stimulate and develop a market which is still in its infancy in Europe and more particularly in France.

More than elsewhere, the Western higher education institutions have a role to play in this field. They will provide training in the necessary skills and deliver cutting-edge training in finance. However, training in IF has not historically had much of a place in these institutions. The programmes they offer must therefore be developed initially in conjunction with other experts in the field, as RMS chose to do when it launched the Certificate in Islamic Banking and Finance with INCEIF. Other joint projects in terms of research also need to be developed so as to offer academic skills in this field and to create synergies by bringing together the experience and expertise of recognized Western academics from the worlds of CF and IF.

12
Islamic Finance at Newcastle University

Abdul Karim Aldohni

Introduction

Growth in the Islamic Banking (IB) and Islamic Finance (IF) sectors has attracted a significant level of academic interest, one of the manifestations of this being the rise in the number of academic courses, particularly at the postgraduate level, that aim to provide a better understating of the operations of the IF sector. Further, in the wake of the financial crisis, there has been a growing global awareness of IF and rising interest in analysing the currently used IF products in order to evaluate the higher level of resilience that IF institutions have demonstrated throughout the crisis.

Many universities across the UK – such as the University of London, Reading University, Durham University – have introduced different courses in IB and IF.

This chapter highlights the experience of Newcastle University in the United Kingdom in this context, which is quite different to other academic institutions in the Northeast of England for a number of reasons which the chapter highlights. The chapter provides an insight into the University's experience in this field, the nature of the IF courses it currently offers, the teaching and learning methods used, and the importance of these courses to the interdisciplinary strategy of Newcastle University.

Introducing Islamic Finance to the legal education domain

The commercial aspect of Islamic law has always been considered as a difficult subject that requires a number of designated modules. This is mainly due to the nature of this topic, which lends itself to economics, law and theology. Stressing the importance of Islamic law in the commercial context, New York Law School's Professor Sadiq Reza said that 'for 30 years [a knowledge of this area] has been necessary for commercial and business purposes ... it is a very important body of law practically and academically'.[1]

The principles of IB and IF lie in Islamic commercial law, as they represent a rather unique and substantial feature of this subject. Therefore, it can be suggested that the main introduction of Islamic commercial law to legal education has been through IB and IF courses.

Legal education has always been influenced by the surrounding economic circumstances.[2] Taking into account the shifts in the financial markets and the growth in the IB and IF industry, there is most certainly a need for qualified individuals who have the required level of understanding not only for the structure of IF products but also for their legal application.

It has been suggested that the legal job market is not limited to law firms but also includes corporate legal departments.[3] In relation to the latter, IF institutions seem to lack those individuals who have the required level of expertise to operate these departments effectively. One of the ways of dealing with this challenge is to promote the role that higher education institutions can play in this context. Teaching and research at university level have a profound effect in shaping the structure of the legal profession since legal educators have a critical role as the architects of this structure.[4] This equally applies in the context of IB and IF business especially as the legal aspect of the business is emerging as a challenging topic and requires a lot of attention from legal educators.

In order to ensure the success of their mission, legal educators should carefully consider the following fact. As a part of Islamic commercial law, IF principles cannot be taught successfully without explaining the economic theory that influences their substratum.

Therefore, the design of the MSc programme 'Finance and Law with Islamic Finance', which Newcastle University started offering in 2009–10, has reflected a clear consideration of this fact.

The programme represents an interdisciplinary collaboration between Newcastle University Business School (NUBS) and Newcastle Law School, which means that it is destined to have an economic angle. Islamic Finance and Islamic Economics (taught in the first semester) and The Legal and Regulatory Aspects of Islamic Banking and Finance (taught in the second semester) provide the compulsory specialist core modules. It must be noted that these two modules are also available as optional ones (with the same mentioned order ,and the first module is a prerequisite for the second module) to the students of the other collaborative MSc programme on Finance and Financial Regulation with the Law School.

The relevance of the two Islamic finance modules to the UK legal higher education field

Modules in Islamic Finance and Islamic Economics, and The Legal and Regulatory Aspects of Islamic Banking and Finance, both have a significant relevance to the development process of UK legal higher education.

On the one hand, competitiveness and employability are two key elements that should be carefully considered by higher education institutions regarding the offering of their degrees, especially at the postgraduate level. In this regard, it has been argued that the concept of internationalizing higher education degrees is rather important in this day and age. This objective can be achieved by integrating an international dimension into the current degrees which allows them to keep up with the current challenges brought by globalization.[5] Therefore, the introduction of IF to the UK legal higher education field, one way or another, serves the internationalization objective.

At Newcastle University, the MSc programme Finance and Law with Islamic Finance clearly has the internationalization issue as one its main concerns. By including the two IF modules the students are not only learning about new financial products which are used in different international financial markets but also they are being introduced to, first, a new legal system that represents the genesis of these financial products and applies in a number of jurisdictions, and, second, to the economic theory that is the result of this legal system.

On the other hand, it can be argued that higher education, to a certain extent, might have an impact on the way individuals practise their business, which can be used in the long run to positively influence their conduct.

The recent banking and financial crisis has exposed an element of the financial services business that has been neglected, namely the ethical dimension of the business. With hindsight, the ethical aspect has proved to be rather essential; the irresponsible practices, to say the least, of those who were involved in the financial sector have contributed significantly to the scale and impact of the recent problem. In other words, the ethical behaviour of the participants in the banking and financial industry is a key factor of the stability of the business that should be carefully considered. Therefore, it has been argued that the development of the moral compass in the financial business is a process that starts with the teaching of financial law. Accordingly, this does not require having a separate module that teaches these ethical principles but rather that students should learn how ethical principles apply in the financial and banking sector and why they matter.[6] In this regard, first, The Islamic Finance and Islamic Economics module, to a certain extent, serves the same objectives. It provides students with a theory under which moral and ethical commitments play a greater role in relation to the conduct of the business. Second, The Legal and Regulatory Aspects of Islamic Banking and Finance module advances this argument as it expands on the legal rules that safeguard the ethical aspects of IF products. Further, it examines the application of these financial products, which are ethically oriented, within the conventional legal and regulatory framework. Finally, it highlights some of the key benefits of using these products in the financial services sector.

Locating the two Islamic Finance modules

As the title Finance and Law with Islamic Finance suggests, this MSc programme is designed to introduce students to more than IF alone. Among the other compulsory modules, students will learn about the legal and regulatory systems in the UK, financial theory and corporate policy, and research methods in international economics and finance.

However, IF is still the programme's main focus since writing a dissertation on IF is a compulsory component for the students on this programme. The suggested topics for the dissertation module are mainly based on the subjects that have been examined over the year in Islamic Finance and Islamic Economics and The Legal and Regulatory Aspects of Islamic Banking and Finance modules. These two courses have an imperative role in providing the programme with the required IF substance.

The first module, Islamic Finance and Islamic Economics, is a necessary introduction of the subject of IF in general as it deals with the genesis of its principles from legal and economic perspectives. It primarily introduces the core principles of IF – the prohibition of *riba* and *gharar* – by explaining, first, the legal authority of this prohibition and then its application in the context of banking and finance. Further, the module examines some of the key concepts of Islamic economic theory in the light of the other conventional economic theories (capitalism, socialism and social market theory).

The Legal and Regulatory Aspects of Islamic Banking and Finance module is an interdisciplinary one that has certain legal components and yet is still designed to be studied by a wider range of students. The course primarily examines some of the main governance challenges in relation to the structure of IF institutions and some of their products. The course considers the UK legal and regulatory framework and some of the internationally established standards in this context. This module is designed to achieve two aims at the programme's level: first, to present students with the legal components that are related to the subject of IB and IF; and second, to develop students' legal skills particularly in relation to IB and IF.

These two modules are rather essential to meet the expectations of the students who have registered for the MSc programme Finance and Law with Islamic Finance, and to broaden their understating beyond conventional banking and finance.

It must be noted that since this programme is offered by NUBS, it not only targets law graduates, but is designed for students from different related backgrounds, such as economics and politics. Also, work experience is an important factor to consider in the admission process. The programme was first fully run in 2010–11 when we had a mix of EU, UK and international graduates from law, politics and business. It is worth observing that the majority of registered students over the last two years have been international ones.

More importantly, the two IF courses in the 2010–11 academic year were taken as optional modules by a relatively large number of students from the other MSc programme in Finance and Financial Regulation (two UK, five from China, and one each from Italy, Ireland and Germany).

The final issue to mention in this context is the composition of the teaching staff. Due to the nature of the programme the two core IF courses are delivered by one member of staff from Newcastle Law School: myself, where I am in charge of the lectures and seminars for these two modules. Also, I supervise the dissertation module that allows the students to present a comprehensive piece of research on a particular issue in IF.

Despite its effectiveness, the current teaching staff composition carries certain risks; for example, the University could not run the programme for 2011–12 when I was on research leave. However, on my return the Islamic Finance and Islamic Economics module was offered as an option in Semester 2 and was taken by students from the MSc programme Finance and Financial Regulation. One of the students who took the module is from Malawi, and his employer and sponsor there (the Central Bank) requested him to take this course.

Intended learning outcomes of the two Islamic Finance courses

Identifying the learning outcomes is a crucial part of the delivery process of these two courses as it influences the methods of teaching that are used.

Students by the end of these modules are supposed to have the ability to:

- Recognize the core principles of IF and their legal and theological genesis.
- Critically analyse the different interpretations that Islamic economic theory provides for some of the key economic concepts such as money, market, profits, equality, and economic justice.
- Identify the practical aspect of IF principles which students were introduced to in Semester 1 in the Islamic Finance and Islamic Economics module.
- Recognize the main IF products and explain the structure of these products and their origins in Islamic economic theory.
- Critically analyse the differences between conventional banking products and their Islamic counterparts.
- Review the application of the IF products within the UK conventional legal and regulatory framework.
- Debate the main pressing legal issues regarding the practice of Islamic banking and examine the recent legal development in this respect.
- Develop 'transferable skills' (referring to the level of competence in understanding the Islamic and English legal systems) and acquire cultural awareness.[7]
- Develop the required skills for those who are interested in joining the IB industry.

Achieving the intended outcomes: Activities involved in the programme

When designing these two courses a special consideration was given to how the delivery could achieve effective teaching which enriches the learning process. In defining what effective teaching is, there is a consensus on three factors: systemic, stimulating and caring. However, it must be kept in mind that the emphasis on these factors is not the same across all academic disciplines and subjects.[8]

To achieve the previously listed outcomes the two modules employ a number of teaching/learning practices which are used specifically in the legal education. These methods are used effectively throughout the topics of these modules. Also, the structure of the two modules is designed to facilitate and support the application of these methods. Each module is taught over 14 hours of lectures and four hours of seminars. The lectures and seminars both allow the application of various teaching methods in order to create an effective teaching and learning process. Finally, the assessment of the modules is also designed to advance this process, as will be explained shortly.

I personally understand and appreciate the importance of the teaching and learning environment, and therefore, while designing these modules, special attention was paid to some of the key issues that help to create it. Stress is one of the key issues that the literature has identified as an element that hinders students' ability to learn. It has been suggested that stress prevents students from receiving and processing information.[9] The design of the courses focuses mainly on one of the key elements that causes stress which is workload, and takes this issue into consideration. The issue of workload is particularly relevant to the seminars. Therefore, the seminar handouts are designed to include a manageable reading list, where one or two sources are nominated as 'essential reading', and four others as 'recommended reading'. I believe achieving this balance is rather important to create a productive teaching and learning environment. Then, if the students are capable of managing their preparation, this eventually helps create cooperative learning in the seminars which itself – cooperative learning – is one of the main identified methods of maintaining an effective learning and teaching environment.[10]

The discussion in the following sections reflects on how the design of the modules is set to achieve the three factors of effective teaching (systemic, stimulating and caring)[11] in the context of IF. It also addresses how the design supports the learning experience to achieve the intended learning outcomes. Finally, it highlights the role of assessment in this process.

Lectures

Legal education has moved from the concept of passive learning to active learning which requires the involvement of the learners in the process,[12] which in a sense shows that teaching and learning are two integrated parts of the same process. One of the methods used in these courses is the Socratic method. It has been suggested by Friedland that the'Socratic approach' remains firmly entrenched in legal education'.[13] This method is based on the idea of exploring concepts through posing questions to students which clearly advance the process of active learning.[14] This is primarily used regarding the topics that concern the application of IB and IF within the UK conventional legal and regulatory framework. Students are able to engage with these questions as they have studied these regulations throughout the MSc programme. The use of this method in this context stimulates students' critical thinking as they need to merge the regulatory issues with the key concepts of IF which they have learned in Semester 1 (Islamic Finance and Islamic Economics) in order to address the legal implications.

The other method that has been included in the modules design to promote active learning is experiential learning. It brings real-life experiences into the class which assist students to integrate theory with practice. There are certain tools that can be used to provide experiential learning such as actual legal documents, videos and speakers.[15] I usually aim to invite guest speakers to give a couple of lectures (per module) in each semester. The speakers will not only provide the students with an insight into the industry through their personal experience, but they will also illustrate how in reality the IF products are structured. This helps achieve the intended learning outcomes. The use of experiential learning provides the student with the critical understanding of the differences between the conventional financial products and their Islamic counterparts, especially since most of the speakers have previous experience in the conventional banking sector. Further, experiential learning can also have certain benefits for students: it broadens their understanding of the topic; it increases their interest (and speakers' practical experience can have a major role in motivating students); and finally it helps them to develop the knowledge, skills and values that they need to join the industry.[16]

It must be noted that experiential learning is a complementary method to the Socratic approach whereas the Socratic method is necessary to establish a robust foundation upon which 'experiential learning' can be used.

Seminars

As explained before, these two courses consist of both lectures and seminars. The previous section demonstrated, in alliance with the literature, the key methods that are used in the lectures to create an effective teaching and learning process, and serve the intended learning outcomes. In relation to the seminars, they are designed to complement the topics that are taught in the lectures, as they focus on some of the most challenging issues in the two courses. Therefore, they can be described as a way of identifying students' needs. Both courses – Islamic Finance and Islamic Economics and The Legal and Regulatory Aspects of Islamic Banking and Finance – are new topics which bring certain challenges not only to the students but also to the lecturer (in terms of the best way of delivering them). Also, seminars are used in these courses as a feedback technique that helps to show students where they failed to learn,[17] assists them in overcoming these challenges, and corrects any misconception that they have obtained from the lectures.

Additionally, seminars have an imperative role in achieving the intended learning outcomes. This can be explained as follows:

- Seminars allow the use of the 'case method' where students are required to read a number of the lead cases in relation to IF contracts. This helps them to understand the legal challenges imposed by these financial products. Using case method would assist the students to learn more effectively.[18] Students would have a better appreciation of the difficulties that IF faces when it is applied within a conventional legal and regulatory framework.
- Seminars present a great platform for a planned discussion where the prepared handouts identify the goals, materials and questions. This allows students to discover new ideas, which eventually deepens their learning.[19] Therefore, seminars give students the opportunity to perform the two aspects of critical thinking which are 'reasonable and reflective thinking'.[20] This presumption can be mainly supported by the fact that seminars consist of a smaller number of students which makes them more specific and positively intense.[21] The use of these discussion groups has proved to be extremely popular and effective at the same time in most of the empirical research.[22]
- Seminars contribute profoundly to cooperative learning among the students. There are countless benefits of cooperative learning among the students such as: developing students' performance in general, aiding them to develop their problem-solving skills, promoting their attitude towards the subject, improve their tolerance of diverse perspectives.[23] And finally – most importantly from my point of view – it allows the students to cooperate with each other to develop their 'transferable skills', especially since the members of each seminar group come from different backgrounds.

It must be noted that the intended effective use of seminars has been associated with devoting the required financial resources to develop the library collection on Islamic economics and the legal and regulatory aspects of IF. A large part of the required references are made available as e-resources which offer easier access to all students. Both Newcastle Law School and NUBS contribute towards the finance of these resources.

Assessment

During the design process of these courses, the assessment form was a matter of great concern. There were a number of issues that have been taken into account before deciding the assessment model for these courses:

- the very new nature of these topics
- amount of credit attached to these modules (ten credits each)
- impact of assessment on the learning process
- my views of assessment as part of 'caring' which is required in an effective teaching process.

These factors have influenced our choice between the two main types of assessment used in higher education: formative assessment and summative assessment. The formative model of assessment was found to be more suitable for these courses for a number of reasons. It is worth noting that formative assessment can take different forms, such as undertaking a class presentation or writing an essay;[24] in relation to these two modules, students are required only to write one essay for each module (of 3,000 words each).

Deciding on the formative model of assessment, and particularly writing essays, can be justified on the following grounds:

- As the topics of the two courses are very new and different from what students learned before, it is rather essential to measure the students' interaction with the main issues studied throughout each semester. Formative assessment allows identification of students' strength and the areas that can be improved, thus eventually shaping the students' ongoing learning.[25] Therefore, formative assessment can be described as a learning experience in its own right.[26] Accordingly, the use of written essays as the assessment method would give the opportunity to effectively and efficiently address the difficulties that students are encountering, and respond to them through the feedback that is provided on the essay's feedback sheet. Further, it assists with the ongoing development process of the two modules and the MSc programme as a whole.

- The role of assessment in the learning process is significant. It has been suggested that students' learning is guided by assessment and that they learn what they believe to be the subject of their assessment. This effect is called 'backwash'.[27] In this respect, there can be a negative 'backwash' which is mostly associated with the summative model of assessment, particularly in an examination-orientated system. In such cases, students diverge from perusing the substance of the topics to developing the suitable strategy to pass the exam.[28] In other words, assessment becomes an end itself instead of being a means to better and more effective learning. On the other hand, the 'backwash' effect can be used positively when the assessment is aligned with the intended learning outcomes.[29] Therefore, in these two courses, the essay questions are designed to address the intended learning outcomes of the modules. For example, one of the key intended learning outcomes for The Legal and Regulatory Aspects of Islamic Banking and Finance is to develop the students' level of competence in understanding the two legal systems and achieving cultural awareness (referred to in the intended learning outcomes as 'transferable skills'). Therefore, the essay question will not be relevant to just one particular jurisdiction. In another example, Islamic Finance and Islamic Economics intends to provide the students with critical understanding of a range of economic theories, and therefore the essay question always aims to ensure that students must refer to other economic theories in order to answer it.

Finally, it is worth mentioning that the assessment method of these courses is one of the issues that will be subject to continuous reexamination just to ensure that it is still delivering what it was intended to achieve.

Islamic Finance research at Newcastle University

At present, the research of IF at Newcastle University has two distinctive features. First, it is mainly doctrinal; and second, it is mainly concerned with the UK. The research is mostly focused on the legal and regulatory aspects of IB and IF within the legal and regulatory framework of the UK with reference to the EU when it is relevant. However, although the research is mainly doctrinal, it still has an empirical edge. In 2009–10 I secured the *ifs* School of Finance/Henry Grunfeld Foundation Research Fellowship (£18,000) which allowed me to conduct interview-based empirical research. The fellowship project examined mainly the possibility of reaching an agreement on a soft law (code of practice) that governs some of the products that are mainly used by IF institutions in the UK market.

Further, the future research plan at the University is to widen the scope of IF research over the next few years. Over the last two years there have been a number of attempts to collaborate with colleagues from the Economics Department at NUBS to look at IF from a quantitative angle. This expansion in the IF research at the University will have a positive impact on the number of IF modules that we offer on the MSc programme 'Finance and Law with Islamic Finance, especially since all of our current offering of IF modules is research-led. For instance, some of the topics of the Legal and Regulatory Aspects of Islamic Banking and Finance course have been subject to various updates over the last couple of years in order to keep up with the recent published research that has been done in this area at the national and international levels.

Finally, since the research agenda of IF in the University is mainly law-orientated, Newcastle Law School since 2008 has welcomed Ph.D. applications in the field of IB and IF with a clear legal focus and we have had a successful completion in early 2011. Also, we welcome Ph.D. applications in the area of IF that require joined supervision with the Economics Department at NUBS.

Concluding remarks

The decision to provide an MSc programme that has the subject of IF as a major component of it has, no doubt, positioned Newcastle University alongside the other UK leading higher education institutions in this field. Yet the Newcastle MSc programme distinguishes itself from its other counterparts by having a clear legal and regulatory focus in relation to IF.

Providing these courses shows that the University is aware of the changes that are taking place in the financial market and is capable of responding accordingly.

The design of this MSc programme shows that it is not intended to target a particular group of students, rather it is structured to widen the scope of students' participation.

There are a number of key issues that must be considered in order to develop this programme further and make it more capable of corresponding to the students' and the industry's expectations.

One of the key issues is the University's links with the industry. It is important for the University to strengthen its links with some of the major players in the UK IB market such as HSBC Amaanah. Advancing the University's connections with the industry might allow the students to have placements in IF institutions, which would provide them with the practical experience that is very difficult to provide through any academic programme.

The other issue that can be mentioned in this context is the students' feedback. Over the last two years we have received very positive feedback on the MSc programme Finance and Law with Islamic Finance in general but more importantly on the two core IF courses. Students who took the courses seem to have been very satisfied with the level of Islamic law context that had been provided by the Islamic Finance and Islamic Economics module.

Finally, it is fair to say that IF will continue to be a subject of great importance to higher education in the UK as long as IF is a significant part of the finance and banking industry nationally and internationally.

Notes

1. Goldberg (2003: 20).
2. Thies (2010: 598).
3. Thies (2010: 607).
4. Edwards (1988: 286).
5. Bosch (2009: 285).
6. Yeoh (2010: 62–3).
7. It must be noted that this term was used in the context of the European legal systems. However, this does not change the fact that such skill is not only limited to European legal systems but also includes non-European legal system such as the Islamic one (see Bosch, 2009: 290).
8. Brown and Atkins (1988: 5).
9. Hess (2002: 78, 80).
10. Hess (2002: 94).
11. Brown and Atkins (1988: 5).
12. Richmond (1996: 943).
13. Friedland (1996: 28).
14. Hess (1999: 406).
15. Hess (1999: 413).
16. Hess (1999: 414).
17. Laurillard (2002: 187, 189).
18. Richmond (1996: 946).

19. Hess (1999: 407).
20. Friedland (1996: 7).
21. Ibid.: 25.
22. Hartwell and Hartwell (1990: 521).
23. Hess (2002: 94).
24. UK Centre for Legal Education (2010a).
25. Carless, Joughin, Liu and associates (2006: 9).
26. UK Centre for Legal Education (2010a). See also UK Centre for Legal Education (2010b).
27. Elton and Johnstone (2002: 6, 30).
28. Biggs and Tang (2007: 169).
29. Ibid.: 169.

References

Articles

Bosch, G. S. (2009) 'The internationalisation of law degrees and enhancement of graduate employability: European dual qualification degrees in law', *The Law Teacher*, 43, 3, pp. 284–96.

Edwards, H. T. (1988) 'The role of legal education in shaping the profession', *Journal of Legal Education*, 38, pp. 285–93.

Friedland, S. I. (1996) 'How we teach: A survey of teaching techniques in American law school', *Seattle University Law Review*, 20, pp. 1–44.

Goldberg, S. B. (2003) 'Islamic law comes to the classroom', *Student Lawyer* 32 (September), pp. 19–21.

Hartwell, S. and Hartwell, S. L. (1990) 'Teaching law: Some things Socrates did not try', *Journal of Legal Education*, 40, pp. 509–23.

Hess, G. F. (1999) 'Principle 3: Good practice encourages active leaning', *Journal of Legal Education*, 49, 3, pp. 401–17.

—— (2002) 'Heads and hearts: The teaching and learning environment in law school', *Journal of Legal Education*, 52, pp. 75–111.

Richmond, M. L. (1996) 'Teaching law to passive learners: The contemporary dilemma of legal educations', *Cumb Law Review*, 26, pp. 943–59.

Thies, D. (2010) 'Rethinking legal education in hard times: The recession, practical legal education and new job market' *Journal of Legal Education*, 29, 4, pp. 598–622.

Yeoh, P. (2010) 'Teaching ethics in financial services law', *The Law Teacher*, 44, 1, pp. 59–74.

Websites

UK Centre for Legal Education (2010a) 'Summative v Formative', 22 August, http://www.ukcle.ac.uk/resources/assessment-and-feedback/formative/ 15/05/102

—— (2010b) 'Effective Assessment in Law', 22 August, http://www.ukcle.ac.uk/resources/assessment-and-feedback/effective/15/05/12

Books

Biggs, J. and Tang, C. (2007) *Teaching for Quality Learning at University* (Maidenhead, Berkshire: McGraw Hill and Open University Press).

Brown, G. and Atkins, M. (1988) *Effective Teaching in Higher Education* (Routledge).

Carless, D., Joughin, G., Liu, N-F. and associates (2006) *How Assessment Support Learning: Learning Orientated Assessment in Action* (Aberdeen, Hong Kong: Hong Kong University Press).

Elton, L. and Johnstone, B. (2002) *Assessment in Universities: A Critical Review of Research*, January (London and New York: LTSN generic centre).

Laurillard, D. (2002) *Rethinking University Teaching* (London and New York: Routledge).

13
Islamic Finance at Bangor University

Philip Molyneux

Introduction

Bangor University has had a long tradition as being one of the leaders in banking teaching and research in the UK. As such it is no surprise that it has been one of the first universities to embrace the study of Islamic Banking (IB) and Islamic Finance (IF). Bangor University was the first UK university to offer an MSc in Banking and Finance commencing in 1973, and the array of courses on offer has grown now to encompass a broad array of financial economics Bachelor's and Master's programmes. The Bangor Business School was assessed as the top in research in Accounting and Finance in the 2008 UK Government's Research Assessment Exercise (RAE), and much of the assessed work was in the banking area.

Interest in the study of IB and IF began in the late 1980s when Dr Abdelkader Chachi completed his Ph.D. thesis on IB under the supervision of Professor Ted Gardener. A few years later I took on two Ph.D. students to supervise. The first – Idris Al-Jarrah – came from the Jordanian Central Bank and had completed his Master's. He then commenced his thesis on 'Efficiency in Arabian Banking' which he successfully completed in 2002. At the same time I was also supervising Sari Al-Shammari from Saudi Arabia, who was investigating bank performance and efficiency in the Gulf Cooperation Council (GCC) region. Both theses used parametric modelling approaches (typically stochastic cost and profit frontier models with underlying translog and Fourier flexible functional form technologies) to derive efficiency estimates for conventional and Islamic banks operating in the respective countries under study. Part of the research focused on comparing technology differences between Islamic and conventional banks – this was particularly interesting as both Ph.D.s found Islamic banks (while smaller in size) were typically found to be more efficient (see Al-Jarrah and Molyneux, 2005). This led to my interest in studying IF issues in more detail, examining differences in the production features between the two types of banks. My research eventually culminated in the publications of two texts, Molyneux and Iqbal (2005) and Iqbal and Molyneux (2005), both of which covered, to varying degrees, the evolution of IF in various countries as well as the performance of banks. Since then I have had an ongoing interest in IB and IF issues as witnessed by recent work on 'Risk and Islamic Banking' (with Amnine Tarazi and Pejman Abedifar from Limoges University, France) being presented at the European Central Bank's Workshop on Islamic Finance and Financial Stability in January 2012 and finishing off the supervision of John Yip's Doctor of Business Administration (DBA) on Islamic bank diversification in April 2012.

The combination of Bangor's long track-record in banking research, combined with interest in the IB and IF field, made it almost inevitable that the Business School would offer programmes in IF sooner than later. Both MBA and MSc courses in Islamic Banking and Finance were introduced in 2008–9, and in 2011 the MBA Islamic Banking and Finance programme was made available through Bangor Business School's London campus. In 2011, Bangor appointed Professor Muhammed-Shahid Ebrahim as professor of Islamic Banking and Finance at the Bangor Business School. His broad interests lie in the area of financial sector development (Ebrahim, 2009) as well as asset pricing and financial contracting as applied to Islamic Banking and Finance (as well as other areas).

Starting from the beginning

Almost all courses on IB and IF have to put the area into context illustrating the evolution of such activity. Most banking courses emphasize that IB that started on a modest scale in the 1960s has shown exceptional growth. We all know that what started as a small rural banking experiment in the remote villages of Egypt has now reached a level where many global banks now offer IB and IF products. The practice of IB spread from East to West all the way from Indonesia and Malaysia towards Europe and the Americas. Forty years ago, it was considered not much more than wishful thinking but now it is a reality. It has been shown to be both feasible and viable and can operate just as efficiently and productively as Western-style financial intermediation. The successful operation of these institutions and the experiences in Saudi Arabia, Pakistan, Iran, Malaysia, Bahrain and throughout the Islamic world demonstrate that this alternative is a both viable and successful alternative to Western commercial banking and finance. The fact that many conventional banks are also using IB and IF techniques is further proof of the viability of the Islamic alternative. Even though Islamic banks emerged in response to the needs of Muslim clients, they are not religious institutions. Like any other types of bank, they are profit-seeking institutions. However, substantial attention when teaching IF issues focuses on the different model of financial intermediation.

Specific aspects of Islamic Finance

IF is based on *Shar'iah* principles which forbid payment or receipt of *riba*. This is a feature of IF that typically is discussed in detail in our courses. *Riba* means an excess to be returned on money lending.[1] The Islamic terminology for such a kind of lending is *qard-alhasan*. It is interesting to note that *Shar'iah* recognizes the time value of money, since according to Islamic rules the price of a good to be sold on a deferred payment basis can be different from its current value. Interest reflects the time value of money and the interest rate is an exchange rate across time. While *Shar'iah* recognizes interest in business, it prohibits interest on lending.

IF has evolved on the basis of the Islamic rules on transactions, *fiqh al-muamalat*, and it can mainly be categorized as follows (1) Debt-based financing: the financier purchases or has the underlying assets constructed or purchased and then sells it to the client. The sale would be on a deferred-payment basis with one or several instalments. (2) Lease-based financing: the financier purchases or has the underlying assets constructed or purchased and then rents it to the client. At the end of the rental period or proportionate to the rentals, the ownership would be transferred wholly or partially to the client. (3) Profit and loss sharing (PLS) financing: the financier is the partner of the client and the realized profit or loss would be shared according to the pre-agreed proportion. The first two IF methods are called collectively the Non-Profit and Loss Sharing ('Non-PLS') Method. Besides restrictions on *riba*, *Shar'iah* has some other prohibitions which should be taken into account. For instance, according to the *Shar'iah* all contracts should be free from excessive uncertainty (*gharar*), hence Islamic financial institutions face some restrictions on application of financial derivatives and insurance policies.

Islamic versus conventional banks

A feature of IF on our banking courses emphasizes the different balance-sheet structures of Islamic banks compared to conventional ones, as well as the different risks these institutions face.

Islamic banks are authorized to receive deposits mainly in the following two forms. The first constitutes current accounts that bear no interest, where Islamic banks are obliged to pay principal amounts to the holders on demand, The second form is composed of investment accounts. While the holders of saving (investment) accounts in conventional banks are debt-holders, Islamic banks are agents or partners of such depositors for mobilization of their funds in profitable projects. Islamic banks may announce a preliminary profit rate to depositors. Such rates may be adjusted according to the realized profit or even loss which can then be shared between the Islamic bank and the investment account holders. This feature of IB can create a layer of protection against adverse economic conditions, as depositor returns can be reduced in economic downturns and boosted in upturns (pro-cyclical deposit returns). This contrasts with conventional banking where deposit returns can be countercyclical (higher rates paid in downturns and lower returns in upturns). It can also have some impact on the asset portfolio of Islamic banks.

Due to the obligations towards depositors as debt-holders, conventional banks try to allocate a considerable part of their funds to loans, which position them as debt-holders and senior to the shareholders of companies. In other words, conventional banks endeavour to decrease the volatility and uncertainty of their revenue to be able to meet their obligations towards depositors. However, Islamic banks have more flexibility, since they can consider depositors more similar to equity holders.

Islamic banking asset quality and risk

The special relationship with investment account holders may have a differential impact on Islamic bank behaviour. It might weaken their incentives to put enough effort in due diligence and loan monitoring – a typical moral hazard. Alternatively, the special relationship can discipline Islamic banks more effectively as compared to conventional banks, since investment accounts holders have more incentives than depositors of conventional banks to closely monitor Islamic banks and shift their funds across them. Hence, (deposit) withdrawal risk can discipline Islamic banks to monitor their loan and investment activities carefully and encourage them to prudentially manage their balance sheets.

Sharing the realized profit or loss with investment account holders may make Islamic banks risky. On the upside, high payoffs to investment accounts enhance demand for putting new funds at the bank, and consequently equity holders should increase their share capital to keep capital ratios unchanged so as to prevent dilution. On the downside, the situation would be reversed. This could make Islamic banks relatively unstable.

Deviation of Islamic banks from the principles in practice

Islamic banks, in practice, tend to deviate from traditional PLS principles and can operate similarly to conventional banks. Withdrawal risk may persuade management to deviate from Islamic principles by paying competitive market returns to investment accounts regardless of the realized performance. Chong and Liu (2009), using Malaysian data, show that investment deposit rates of Islamic banks are closely linked to conventional banks' deposit interest rates. One explanation is that the competition pressure of conventional banks constrains the actual implementation of IB. Such a deviation is made in the downside scenario, especially when the Islamic bank incurs losses. However, in case the whole banking system is hit by a financial crisis, in the absence of competitive pressure from conventional banks or other Islamic banks, management may share the realized loss with the investment account holders to avoid insolvency. Hence, in such a case, Islamic banks have more capacity to resist loss as compared to conventional banks. In the upside scenario, Islamic banks may partly adjust the rate of returns payable to investment account holders, exploit a part of their rights, in the absence of supportive regulations on the account holders' rights. This would restrain expectations of investment account holders in the next period. Such a policy can help to decrease the volatility of funds supplied by investment account holders over time, which can be treated as another motivation for the deviations.

Where management does not face any upside or downside scenario, withdrawal risk cannot be the motivation for the deviation, since adjustment in rates of return are unlikely to be large enough to convince investment account holders to withdraw funds, taking into account the switching cost of moving from one bank to another. Therefore, managements tend to deviate because they might intend to avoid the active monitoring of investment account holders. In fact, strictly sharing realized profit or loss means that management have to explain their performance not only to the equity holders but also to investment account holders.

Implicitly, investment account holders own a bond, a long position on a call option and a short position on a put option. The strike price of the call, however, is determined arbitrarily by Islamic banks, in the absence of supportive regulations on the account holders' rights. The strike price of the put is determined based on the degree of market competitive pressures, level of incurred loss and the capital ratio of Islamic banks. Islamic banks, in practice, tend to apply the non-PLS paradigm, possibly due to the risks associated with the PLS method. Mills and Presley (1999) also indicate that PLS is marginally practised in other countries, such as Bangladesh, Egypt, Iran, Pakistan, the Philippines and Sudan.

Complexity of Islamic modes of finance

IF agreements (even for non-PLS methods) are often less straightforward than conventional loan contracts. Generally, in debt-based or lease-based finance, such as *murabaha,* Islamic banks arrange the goods/projects to be purchased/implemented and then sell or rent these to the client. For purchase/implementation of the goods/projects, Islamic banks normally appoint the client as their agent. Such a framework is somewhat complicated compared to conventional loan contracts. The specific risks attached to some non-PLS methods, such as *salam* and *ijara,* are particularly complex. In the former, Islamic banks are exposed to both credit and commodity price risks; in the latter, unlike conventional lease contracts, Islamic banks cannot transfer ownership and thus are associated with the risk of the project during the lease period.

Some Islamic banks do not charge default penalties as they are believed to not be authorized by *Shar'iah*, and as a consequence they use rebates instead. First they charge clients with a mark-up, which implicitly covers the interest rate and the default penalty rate, and then in case of fulfilling the obligation the client will receive the rebate. While default interest rates are calculated over the delayed period in conventional banking, some Islamic banks might collect the delayed penalty over the whole financing period. Islamic banks might also face some restrictions regarding collateral; for instance, they are not allowed to use interest-based assets, like bonds, as collateral.

Investment limitations and risk taking

Banks allocate a part of their assets to investments as well as loans. Such investments normally include the purchase of bonds of different types, yields to maturity and durations to cover associated portfolio risks. However, Islamic banks may have relatively limited options for such investments, since they are not authorized to invest in bonds except *sukuk*. This limitation, to a certain extent, has been weakened due to the expansion of IF markets over time. Nevertheless, Islamic banks typically are restricted to behave more conservatively in their asset management activities compared to conventional banks.

Taking into account the foregoing characteristics of Islamic banks, we might question whether they are riskier than conventional banks. In the absence of a specific framework, Islamic banks should be riskier than conventional banks due to their special relationship with investment account holders. To avoid such a risk, Islamic banks may deviate from the IF principles and operate similarly to conventional banks. Given the limited investment opportunities, they may be forced to hold more liquid assets than conventional banks, and potentially greater withdrawal risk may also force Islamic banks to hold more liquid assets. Retained earnings, and therefore capital strength may also be greater in Islamic banks. Interestingly, recent studies that examine asset quality (Beck, Demirgüç-Kunt and Merrouche, 2010) stability (Čihák and Hesse, 2010; Abedifar, Molyneux and Tarazi, 2012) and other risk dimensions including loan default rates (Baele, Farooq and Ongena, 2010) find no difference between Islamic and conventional banks.

Courses in Islamic banking and finance at Bangor

Much of the discussion outlined previously underpins the teaching of IB and IF at Bangor. Initially, prior to developing full degree programmes, the Business School introduced a postgraduate optional module in the subject area – available to all the Master's students. In the first year the module had 30 students, and around half had practical IB experience – mainly from Saudi Arabia, other GCC countries and Sudan.

The following year we first offered the MBA in Islamic Banking and Finance. The programme was designed to equip executives with the specialist knowledge required for professional development in the international finance sector. The programme followed many of the same core modules as the Banking and Finance MBA, providing rigorous training in the theory and practice of mainstream financial services management and strategy. Specialist modules in Islamic Banking and Finance provide a particular focus on the theoretical foundations, products, performance, financial instruments and risk management issues of what is by now the preferred way of banking for one-fifth of the world's population. Teaching staff are active in their research work, allowing students to benefit from an education that reflects contemporary, cutting-edge issues and developments that can be applied in the work-place from the outset.

The compulsory modules on the Islamic Banking & Finance MBA in 2012 are as follows:

- *Organizations and People:* This module examines key issues arising from contemporary research in organizational behaviour (OB) and human resource management (HRM). It provides an integrated analysis of management, organizations and people, developing the conceptual, strategic and practical skills necessary for managers in complex, global organizational contexts.
- *Management Research:* This module analyses the philosophical basis for research in the management sciences, and examines a number of key methodological issues and approaches. Research designs for both quantitative and qualitative research methodologies are developed, including interviews, case studies, focus groups, surveys and experiments.
- *Islamic Finance:* This course provides an insight into topical issues relating to Islamic financial instruments and related risk management issues. The first part of the course examines issues relating to financial contracting, instruments and various intermediation issues. The second part of the course focuses on the role of the capital market in providing IF and highlights financial engineering issues and well as risk management features of this type of business.
- *Islamic Banking:* This module provides an insight into the key features of IB business. The first part of the course outlines the theoretical foundations and development of IB practices. In particular, the main characteristics of various types of IB products are discussed. The second part of the course examines the operational features of Islamic banks, focusing on their performance and how they compete with conventional interest-based banks. The final part of the course outlines contemporary challenges to IB business.
- *International banking:* This module examines the origins of international banking, the activities of international banks, the markets in which they participate, and the sources of risk. Students investigate the determinants of the efficiency of international banks, and evaluate the implications for banks' strategic decision-making.

Students have to choose three optional modules from the following:

- *Strategic management:* This module analyses strategic decision making within business. Students develop a critical understanding of the strategic processes of business management, the interconnections with the functional domains of marketing, human resource management and corporate finance, and the management of knowledge systems.

- *Marketing financial services:* This module critically evaluates the contributions of various schools of thought in marketing, and examines the relevant analytical models and management practices, with emphasis on the strategic importance of marketing to all organizations.
- *Banking and development:* This module critically evaluates the theory underlying the policy of financial liberalization, and examines its implementation, primarily in developing countries. The impact of financial liberalization on the financial systems of developing countries is analysed in depth.
- *International financial management:* In this module, the financial management of multinational companies and the influence of macroeconomic, fiscal, currency and political environments on business and financial decision making are examined in an international and global context.
- *Bank financial management:* This module provides a grounding in the nature, strategic context and managerial functions of financial management in banks and other financial services firms. Three key themes are: identification and management of the trade-off between risk and return; improvement of a bank's value using market models; and external market-based tests of bank performance.
- *Financial institutions' strategic management:* This module examines the main theoretical and practical issues concerning banking business. Students develop a critical awareness of the theory of the banking firm, the motives for international banking, and regulatory and structural issues impacting on bank behaviour.

The course is designed for candidates with degrees or relevant business backgrounds who wish to develop their expertise and further their professional careers in the international finance industry. The course is of particular interest to:

- Graduates who have professional experience in the financial sector;
- Managers and accountants in public and private organizations who wish to develop their financial management skills;
- Managers employed in the financial services industry;
- Graduates contemplating a career in the banking and financial services industry;
- Graduates who have relevant practical experience and wish to enhance their skills in the areas of banking and finance;

- Finance professionals (like corporate treasurers and accountants) who deal with the financial services industry;
- Finance professionals who work in institutions that transact banking business on Islamic principles.

In addition to the MBA in Islamic Banking and Finance, Bangor University also offers an MSc in Islamic Banking and Finance geared more to new graduates. The course has a higher quantitative methods component than the MBA, and students are required to study Financial Econometrics and Research Methods. The IF components are similar although students on the MSc also have an option to cover a whole module on Islamic Insurance. We also offer an MA Islamic Banking and Finance course which has a lesser quantitative component. For all our Master's, students can choose to do a dissertation over the summer or courses – depending on their own choice.

Conclusion

Bangor Business School is a unique school striving to be a leader of education in the field of IB and IF as well as mainstream banking and finance. Our faculty members are well published scholars in the field as reflected in the highest ranking achieved of any UK university department in the UK Government's Research Assessment Exercise. The School offers a variety of banking and financial programmes, including MBAs, MScs and MAs in Islamic Banking and Finance. In 2011, the School opened a City of London campus at Broadgate Tower (next to Liverpool Street station) offering a variety of courses including the MBA in Islamic Banking and Finance. Given the School's expertise and unrivalled track record in banking and financial sector research and teaching, we aim to continue to be among the leaders in the IB and IF field for the foreseeable future.

Note

1. Editors' note: This is only one apparent and dominating form of *riba* in today's financial practices, or even in the pre-Islamic era. The author is familiar with these issues and was just keeping the discussion brief.

References

Abedifar, P., Molyneux, P. and Tarazi, A. (2012) 'Risk in Islamic banking', paper presented at the European Central Bank's Workshop on Islamic Finance and Financial Stability, January, Frankfurt.

Al-Jarrah, I. and Molyneux, P. (2005) 'Efficiency in Arabian banking', in M. Iqbal and R. Wilson (eds) *Islamic Perspectives on Wealth Creation* (Edinburgh: Edinburgh University Press), 97–117.

Baele, L., Farooq, M. and Ongena, S. (2010) 'Of religion and redemption: Evidence from default on Islamic loans', CentER Discussion Paper Series No. 2010-136; European Banking Center Discussion Paper No. 2010-32, available at SSRN: http://ssrn.com/abstract=1740452 or doi:10.2139/ssrn.1740452.

Beck, T., Demirgüç-Kunt, A. and Merrouche, O. (2010) 'Islamic vs. conventional banking: Business model, efficiency and stability', World Bank Policy Research Working Paper Series No. 5446, Washington, DC, the World Bank.

Chong, B. S. and Liu, M. H. (2009) 'Islamic banking: Interest-free or interest-based?' *Journal of Pacific-Basin Finance*, 17, 1, pp. 125–44.

Čihák, M. and Hesse, H. (2010) 'Islamic banks and financial stability: An empirical analysis', *Journal of Financial Services Research*, 38, 2, pp. 95–113.

Ebrahim, S. (2009) 'Can an Islamic model of housing finance cooperative elevate the economic status of the underprivileged?' *Journal of Economic Behavior & Organization*, 72, 3, pp. 864–83.

Iqbal, M. and Molyneux, P. (2005) *Thirty Years of Islamic Banking* (Basingstoke: Palgrave Macmillan).

Mills, P. S. and Presley, J. R. (1999) *Islamic Finance: Theory and Practice* (London: Macmillan).

Molyneux, P. and Iqbal, M. (2005) *Banking and Financial Systems in the Arab World* (Basingstoke: Palgrave Macmillan).

14

Islamic Finance at Markfield Institute of Higher Education

Toseef Azid and Tariq Saeed

Introduction

The beginning of the twentieth century witnessed a number of Muslim countries emerge as independent states around the globe. Although, even during the colonial period, the Muslim masses had tried to follow Islamic teachings, after their independence there was, more or less everywhere, a thirst for the implementation of *Shari'ah* laws in all spheres of their social lives.

Most of the Muslim populations were eager to see the implementation of these principles and laws at the state level. For example, the Muslim world has seen these movements (implicitly and explicitly) on a massive scale in Iran, Algeria, Sudan, Pakistan and likewise in many other Muslim countries. Most of the emphasis was placed on the radical change in their political and economic systems, which were previously heavily based on Western conventional philosophy. It was demanded by *Shari'ah* scholars and by the masses who wished that their economic system especially should be based on *Shari'ah* that interest-free economy and business activities be joint ventures (*mudarabah* and *musharakah*).

In addition to this, there was a great demand from different sections of society that the system of *zakat* should be channelled through state agencies in a proper way in order to reduce the level of poverty in Muslim societies. Historically, it was observed that *zakat* as a fiscal instrument played a significant role in the elimination of poverty in Muslim states.[1] At the same time, *Shari'ah* scholars were also emphasizing the importance of the *waqf* system.[2] A consensus emerged that the target of welfare should be achieved through the implementation of *Shari'ah*.[3]

Current Developments in Islamic economic teaching

In 1973, the Islamic Foundation, Leicester, UK was established with the objective of serving and protecting the interests of the Muslim communities in the UK and Europe especially and the Muslim *ummah* generally. In 1976, it established its Islamic Economics Unit as perhaps the first Islamic economics research centre in the world soon after the organization of the First International Conference in Islamic Economics by King Abdulaziz University at Makkah Al-Mukaramah in 1976. The founder and chairman of the Islamic Foundation, UK, Professor Khurshid Ahmad, played a great role in the organization of the conference and was one of the main organizers.

The Islamic Economics Unit of the Islamic Foundation, UK published the English proceedings of the First Conference under the title *Studies in Islamic Economics*. This was edited by Professor Khurshid Ahmad and jointly published with the International Centre for Research in Islamic Economics that was established in 1977 by King Abdulaziz University in Jeddah. It later became the Islamic Economics Research Centre (IERC) and recently changed its name to the Islamic Economics Institute (IEI). Thereafter, it published a number of books on Islamic Economics (IE), Islamic Banking (IB) and Islamic Finance (IF) by pioneers such as Dr Nejatullah Siddiqi and Dr Umer Chapra.

In 1995, the Islamic Foundation, UK succeeded in promoting the teaching of the disciplines of IE, IB and IF by negotiating a deal with a leading British university, Loughborough University to teach them at the postgraduate level. This was a real breakthrough, as for the first time a Western university agreed to teach the subject, while the Islamic Foundation not only sponsored the salary of the research fellow appointed to do research and to teach at Loughborough University, but also provided a grant to the library so that it could acquire the necessary books and teaching materials. This agreement lasted for five years until it established its own institute, the Markfield Institute of Higher Education (MIHE).

The Islamic Foundation, UK also organized a number of annual seminars and orientation courses on the subjects for university teachers, researches and students, in collaboration with the Islamic Research and Training Institute (IRTI) of the Islamic Development Bank (IDB) and Loughborough University.

In the year 2000, the Islamic Foundation, UK established the MIHE to develop and promote teaching of IE and IF. MIHE made consistent efforts to develop conventional tools of economic analysis and their implementation in the field of IE.

In 1975 the IDB was established to foster the economic development and the social progress of the Organization of the Islamic Conference (OIC) member countries and Muslim communities individually as well as jointly in accordance with the principles of *Shari'ah*. In order to provide intellectual support to the demand for a *Shari'ah*-compliant economic system, the IDB organized a number of conferences in different parts of the world.

In 1980, the IRTI was established as the knowledge arm of the IDB. IRTI's strength lies in its specialization in IE and IF. IRTI's contributions are expected to be primarily in two areas; comprehensive human development; and the Islamic financial services industry development. IRTI is the focal point for knowledge-based services and for capacity building offered by the IDB to member countries in the areas of IE and IF. IRTI is also aiming to contribute in the other strategic thrust areas depending on its existing competencies.

In 1977, King Abdulaziz University in Jeddah, Saudi Arabia established a research centre, the International Centre for Research in Islamic Economics, later named the Islamic Economics Research Centre (IERC), and since 2011 the Centre has been upgraded to an Institute; Islamic Economics Institute (IEI). It published a large number of publications on the different aspects of Islamic economics, banking and finance in addition to a regular journal on IE since 1980.

In 1984, the International Association for Islamic Economics (IAIE) was established. The organization was established to promote the study and application of IE, IB and IF. It involves the reconstruction of economics and finance – both in theory and practice – in the light of the Islamic principles. The IAIE thus aims to develop an integrated approach to economics while welding together the material aspects of economic life with Islamic values and norms. Membership is open to academics, professional financiers and bankers, and students who are interested and involved in IE, IB and IF and who agree with the aims and objectives of the Association.

The Islamic Development Bank, Jeddah; the Islamic Research and Training Institute, Jeddah; the International Association of Islamic Economics, UK; Umm Al-Qura University, Mekkah; Imam Muhammad Bin Saud University, Riyadh; the International Islamic University, Malaysia; the International Islamic University Islamabad; and the Central Bank of Indonesia and other organizations and universities organized many conferences and seminars around the world to develop intellectual models to promote teaching and research in the field of IE and IF. These conferences and seminars provided general awareness for the theoretical background of an interest-free banking system. Observing the inclination of the majority of the Muslim populations towards an interest-free system, quite a large number of financial institutions have been established all over the world that are dealing with the *Shari'ah*-compliant products. In addition, most of the financial institutions have opened their Islamic windows or launched separate independent branches having their own independent *Shari'ah* board of governors in most parts of the world.

In the light of the previous background, policymakers and *Shari'ah* scholars in many Muslim countries have jointly made some efforts and initiated different programmes in many disciplines of higher educations. Consequently, three international Islamic universities were established: Gombak (Malaysia), Islamabad (Pakistan) and Khartoum (Sudan). Iran also established a fully-fledged Islamic university: Imam Sadiq University, Tehran.

It is worthwhile to note that the main emphasis of the aforementioned universities and research institutes is on teaching and research of IE. IRTI, the IEI and the Islamic Foundation provided marvellous services towards the publication of literature on IE. IRTI and the IEI published a large number of books and academic papers. Moreover, both institutes have regularly published journals on IE. Likewise, one cannot ignore the role and services of the Islamic Foundation, Leicester, UK in the promotion of IE. The Islamic Foundation has published a reasonable number of original works on IE, IB and IF and is currently jointly publishing the *Review of Islamic Economics* in collaboration with the IAIE.

As a result of the aforementioned activities, IE has now become one of the offered subjects in several institutes and universities of the Muslim as well as the Western world.

Since the year 2000, many other higher education institutions have dabbled in IB education. However, MIHE is one of those institutes which offer a wide range of curricula to promote the subjects of IE, IB and IF based on the *maqasid al-Shari'ah* (objectives of the Islamic Law). The academic infrastructure of MIHE (i.e. the programme specification, the framework of quality of higher education, the subject benchmark and the code of practice) fully follows the objectives of *Shari'ah* and serving society in the UK and elsewhere. All the programmes which are developed in this institution from its form and substance/essence are fully matched with its objective.

Section I

Learning and teaching approaches in higher education

Generally, for the teaching of any subject (including IE) two types of approach prevail in academic circles:

1. **Commodification**
   The proponents of this approach aim to produce students according to the requirements of the market. In this way, they can benefit from multinational corporations, the world of financial institutions and the market economy. Through this mode they can develop different dimensions of the subject theoretically as well as practically (Thomas, 2004).
2. **Originality and inventing new paradigms**
   Members of the other group raise the objection that commodification endangers academic freedom and minimizes the role of university education in society. In their opinion, new subjects will develop only if we give less attention to the market dimensions and place more emphasis on the development of original ideas.

Two approaches also exist related to the mode of learning at higher education level; that is, the deep learning approach and the surface learning approach. The first approach argues that all topics should be covered in detail in the prescribed module (so much time is required). This should be based on three layers: presage, process and output. The second approach proposes that more topics should be covered within a given time period and students can later on apply this knowledge in their practical life (Guest and Vecchio, 2003).

MIHE institutional history and context

Prior to establishing the first campus to teach IE and IF in the West, the Islamic Foundation, Leicester, UK had been engaged in research and academic activities since the inception of its Islamic Economics Unit in 1976. The Islamic Foundation had gained a national and international reputation as a research and publication centre in the field of IE, with a number of journals and other publications to its credit. The Islamic Foundation developed research facilities (including a library and video conferencing suite) as well as organized seminars and conferences. The Islamic Economics Unit, as a pioneer initiative, helped many students of IE and IF, especially in early years of the 1980s and 1990s. The UK academic infrastructure is an embedded reference point at MIHE.

The reputation gained by the Islamic Foundation, UK has been corroborated by the fact that the first IDB Prize in Islamic Economics was conferred on its founder and chairman Professor Khurshid Ahmad in 1988 in his own capacity as one of the pioneers of IE, and on the Islamic Foundation in 2011 for the services it had rendered to promote IE worldwide.

MIHE was established by the Islamic foundation, UK in the year 2000 to fulfil the growing need for systematic academic establishment, within the Western academic conventions and pedagogies, to develop human capital resources in line with Islamic ethics. MIHE is committed to provide an education service consistent with the themes outlined in the Quality Assurance Agency (QAA) for Higher Education code of practice, which espoused, among other things, the establishment of consistent standards in education and training, the promotion of quality, increasing access, transfer and progression opportunities, and the ability to understand and compare qualifications at home and abroad.[4]

MIHE is a partner college of University of Gloucestershire (UoG). All MIHE awards are conferred by UoG. Quality Assurance Agency (QAA's) charter defines such arrangements as 'educational provision leading to an award, or to specific credit toward an award, of an awarding institution delivered and/or supported and/or assessed through an arrangement with a partner institution'.[5]

The objectives of the teaching programmes related to IE in the different universities are given by Azid (2009, p. 167) as follows:

> The basic purpose of the module of all these programmes is to educate students in conventional economics as well as teaching them economics from *Shari'ah* perspective to allow competitive discussions between the two, and to explain how IE can be applied to provide alternative solutions to modern economic problem. After a period of thirty years, it is now appropriate to analyse the problems and challenges faced by the institutes teaching IE and to understand the future prospects of this discipline.

Islamic Finance at Markfield Institute of Higher Education

At present MIHE has launched an MA programme in Islamic Banking, Finance and Management. In this programme, five modules cover different aspects of IE and IF (see Table 14.1).

The MA degree requires research into a specialist area of economics, banking or management, with special reference to the Islamic system, of the student's choice and submission of a dissertation of 15,000–18,000 words.

Table 14.1 Modules of Islamic Finance at MIHE

Mandatory:

Module name	Credits
Foundations of Islamic Economics	15
Islamic Banking, Theory and Practice	15
Research Methodologies	15
Islamic Financial Instruments	15

Optional:

Module name	Credits
International Management	15
Financial Systems: Markets And Institutions	15
Regulation and Governance of Islamic Finance	15
Takaful and Re-*Takaful*: Principles and Operations	15
Islamic Law	30
Quantitative Financial Methods	30
Human Resource Management	15
Organizational Behaviour	15

Except for the Foundations of Islamic Economics, all others start with the conventional economics and then discuss the concepts with reference to Muslim countries and in the light of IE. During the development of these courses the institute considered the following basic points:

1. Use topical issues particularly those involving policy implications to illustrate a range of ideas.
2. Provide some empirical grounds for theoretical model in the modules.
3. Make sure that students know something about the Islamic economic history especially the first two centuries (*hijrah*) and the importance of IE institutions.
4. Take advantage of advances in computer technology to enable students to use interacting agent-based models wherever possible.

The model is based on the deep learning approach and simultaneously also applies the principle of commodification.

Issues

1. At the initial stages of development, the lack of structured curriculum and pedagogy restricted the development of the IE and IF modules.
2. That issue which has been observed is the difficulty in presenting the IE and IF theories, as it is a developing discipline; Most of the issues

remain to be discoursed rather than being some tested facts and realities. This makes the entire exercise terribly difficult for those students who would like to see IE and IF beyond fancily designed discourses. In other words, theorization is missing; also because much of the efforts go to IF issues, IE has not been granted proper attention. For instance, for economic growth, IE has not come up with a theoretical framework to demonstrate how economic growth can be achieved in an IE system. Another example is development economics. While it is true that many criticisms of the capitalist system are presented, the IE approach remains very discursive and does not even provide a concrete theoretical formulation and therefore consists of only poverty-oriented policy suggestions. This is an important issue, as some of the books on IE and IF suggest policy recommendations which are not substantially different from the neo-classical approach. Therefore, it is not surprising that a number of students write their assignments on the critics of IE development discourse. Thus, the discipline has not evolved enough to provide the relevant material and as a result it causes students' disappointment with IE and IF courses.

3. However, as far as IF is concerned, students may find it more relevant and more easily handled, as IF heavily relies upon the neo-classical economic way of understanding finance. Thus, students coming from conventional finance background can easily handle the IF, despite its *Shari'ah* injunctions.

4. The difficulty in IF teaching is that students tend to expect too many practical dimensions of IF. They complain that the course is mostly theoretical and that the financing modes and their practicality are not clear. This is troubling, as most of the students come to the course expecting jobs in the IF sector after completing their Master's degree. However, the IF institutions prefer to employ people who have degrees in conventional finance. Thus, this creates problems between supply and demand and, as a result, students feel that they should learn more practical aspects of IF. However, this is also due to the fact that the IF sector is far ahead of academia in the field of IF engineering. This is something that students feel and realize as well. Consequently, in order to satisfy the market conditions, IE, IB and IF courses include a number of modules on conventional economics and finance to substantiate students' understanding of the subjects and prepare them for better futures in terms of their professional career.

5. In addition to the previous subject-related issues, it should also be mentioned that the variations in students' backgrounds can be a

difficulty as well. This is because of the fact that students are drawn either from traditional *Shari'ah* backgrounds or modern economics and finance backgrounds. While they take the same modules, the variation in their background can create problems in how much in detail or advance one can go in covering the subject material.

6. At MIHE, one of the difficulties is human resources in terms of teaching the Islamic Economics, Banking and Finance Master's degree. If the resources were available, then it would have been possible to breakdown Islamic Economics, Banking and Finance subjects into more detailed modules. This would have resulted in a number of optional modules and provided different specialization areas. However, in addition to the lack of teaching resources, this currently is not an economically viable option either since MIHE has about 20–3 students, and hence MIHE cannot offer many optional modules for such a small number of students.

However, since this is a compact programme, so far more emphasis has been placed on finance rather than on management. Students seem to be emotionally motivated and they have the curiosity of finding out how the Islamic instruments will be applied in the real world. They also have some confusion about the different instruments like *murabahah*, other fix-return modes and *tawarruq*. They have the opinion that the policy of compromises is not the best one. In their opinion they have good exposure of IE and IF, however, less emphasis is placed on Islamic jurisprudence so a balance should be made in the syllabus. MIHE are also starting a distance learning programme of IE and IF.

Section II

A general outlook

Some common problems which were observed during the study are presented next:

1. *Lack of literature and experts*: In practice, generally, the main problem is a lack of literature; almost all of the institutions lack the full literature that covers all the aspects of IE. Especially, students in general need a textbook but no particular comprehensive example is available. Furthermore, most of the literature is on interest-free banking and finance. It shows that more emphasis is placed on IF rather than IE. Moreover, there is a lack of experts having

knowledge of both traditional and Islamic economics since most tutors are trained in traditional economic concepts but only a few are in IE and IF.

2. *Opinion of the senior faculty members in the institutions*: Another considerable enigma being faced in introducing IE and IF at universities relates to the opinions of the senior faculty members. They believe that the discipline has not been able to develop the kind of rigour that would justify a fully-fledged postgraduate course under that title. It is possible that the opinion is a little biased; however, it does suggest that the experts of mainstream economics have not as yet been introduced to the subject effectively.

3. *Important queries:* Tutors of IE have the following typical queries that are still not clear to them.

   • Technically, what are the dominating behavioural values or ethos assumed in this discipline?
   • Is competition the unique, positive driving force of our economic activities?
   • What makes an economy work?
   • How scientific can we be in studying the economy in an Islamic framework?
   • Can we know about the future economy with a stress on history?

4. *Differences between conventional and IE and IF*: We have to understand what is the difference between greed, materialism, individuality, and rationality according to Islamic injunctions. We also need to examine the ethics, the methodology, the history, the institutions and the policy formulations and how these are different from the secular systems. It is important to know what is the basic difference between the Islamic and secular systems; and what are the basic foundations of these two systems.

5. *Internal inconsistencies*: Due to ideological commitments, IE and IF have not been able to progress the way they could have. The subject is in its transitory phase, so one can find differences of opinion in *fatawa* and practices. However, the differences on these matters should not lead to 'heresy'. It is worth noting that the AAOIFI and IFSB are international standard-setting organizations whose objectives are to promote and enhance the soundness and stability of the IF services industry by issuing global prudential standards and guiding principles for the industry, but still more work needs to be done.

Some recommendations

After reviewing the teaching systems of IE and IF by the institutions under study and collecting the opinions of experts, the following suggestions may be made:

1. *Provision of resources for research*: It has been felt that in order to overcome the difficulties facing the teaching of IE and IF, it is important that more research should be conducted in the field. This requires considerable resources, but unless such resources are found, developments in the discipline will be very small and the gap between academic endeavours and the professional IF sector will widen. It is already the case that professionals have a very dismissive attitude towards academics in this subject area.

2. *Empirical research*: There is a tremendous demand for more work on the empirical aspects of IE and IF theory. Those works should be presented in the academic conferences and the knowledge, problems and experiences should be shared. There is a need for empirical studies, especially in Muslim countries which should involve more people in the research. Theoretical models taught in the IE and IF courses need empirical grounding if they are to be persuasive. Probably there is no other way out but to publish more and more articles in academic journals of high repute on IE as well as in the well-regarded Western academic journals. Simultaneously, standard textbooks need to be developed having a sound base of theory with empirical evidence. We also need to put more effort into the classic works written by Muslim scholars, which are full of original ideas and could be compared favourably with modern concepts and theories of economics. There are several intellectuals who cannot visualize the existence of an IE and IF system that can meet the needs of modern society and compete favourably with the dominant economic/financial system. So we need to develop the durable foundations and practices of IE to satisfy those intellectuals.

3. *Highlighting the essential difference between conventional and Islamic economics*: In mainstream economics it is taught that economic agents respond to price mechanism or behave rationality. Students frequently ask how these concepts differ from Islamic injunctions. It forces academics to address the issues constructively. IE makes a real and substantial difference in how economic affairs are understood and how economics is taught; that is, we have to teach this subject with the moral and ethical attitude. And we need to emphasize how the concept of rationality differs in an Islamic framework.

4. *Training of IE and IF tutors*: A university or a college is only as good as its faculty (Dressel, 1981), which is an institution's most valuable resource. The faculty determines the structure and quality of the curriculum, controls the quality of instruction, positions the institution relative to creativity and scholarship, and implements the institution's service linkages and relationships. Apart from the physical plant, the faculty is the institution's greatest investment (Jennings, Barlar and Bartling, 1991). Orientation, education, training and development of tutors of IE is a principal thrust. Periodic training programmes for tutors should be arranged offering alternative economic contents to the mainstream but also changing the way we as tutors conceptualize the learning process. Tutors should have the ability to predict the knowledge expansion in this field and have the ability to design the curricula accordingly. Tutors should know the present challenging realities in attaining the goal of an effective and relevant curriculum and they also should have the command to develop the research needs, priorities and their management. The teaching should follow the following criteria:

- *Philosophical criteria:* Theoretical, methodological, and value position of the curricula, to enhance the intellectual development of the students (include the technicalities).
- *Psychological criteria:* Develop high level skills, reasoning, problem solving, critical thinking and creativity, and relate to the process of activity (papers, case studies and exercise).
- *Practical criteria:* Articles based on the empirical evidences.
- *Student criteria:* Relevant, interesting and contemporary.

5. *Module development*: Tutors should know the extrinsic and intrinsic needs of the subject whereas students should know all the important aspects of the chosen field. At the time of module development, some priorities should be established and these three questions should always be asked: what, how and how far, knowing how and knowing what is the most important. More effort should be made on the durable concepts rather than the transitory ones. More emphasis should be placed on the application and the practical value of the contents.

6. *Balanced approach*: There should be a dynamic balance between the culture of IE and conventional economics. In this present scenario, every branch of academia has local and global dimensions; keeping this in view, experts should be very careful in generation,

production and then distribution of IE and IF knowledge. Questions about the diversity or uniformity of both the cultures should be clear to the tutors as well as to the students.

7. *Interaction among institutions*: There is a vacuum in the area of academic interaction in this field. It seems that there are a large number of institutions providing education and training in IE and IF, but a lack of communication between these institutions. It is felt that a closer relationship would improve educational and research work conducted in each of these institutions. So some level of twinning partnership and other forms of close academic exchange are recommended. It is also suggested that interaction among the tutors of IE should be continued or started. Strong and efficient networking is required among institutions of higher education offering IE and IF, industry, marketing and financial institutions, commercial multinational organizations and international bodies such as the IDB.

8. *Problem-solving approach*: Students should be better equipped to meet the challenge of the age of super complexity. They should be aware of global and international issues and also be able to face challenges both now and in the future. They should be encouraged to pursue sound critical, innovative and creative thinking, active participation, and apply what they have learned. The strong impact of IE education should also be observed on their character (reflecting their own cultural needs and values). The following points are suggested for the development of students. A course on IE should:

- have a content that is relevant to contemporary world issues
- encourage students to question the theoretical content and its practical relevance
- stimulate students' analytical thought
- engage and inspire students' minds
- encourage a high level of interaction between students (recognizable interaction and exchange of knowledge, skills and attitude).

Term papers: Each student should write an essay on any of the topic related to the IE and present it in the class and submit it after presentation. Then a discussion to improve the paper and presentation may follow.

9. *Emerging domains of knowledge*: In this present age of globalization, internal and external variables affect the academic environment in

every society. The internal variables are related to the culture of the society. Nowadays, a new domain of knowledge is emerging; that is, aesthetic, normative and spiritual knowledge. So in this scenario the importance of IE is growing since it discusses a significant portion of the normative economics. A comparative economic/financial theory and international relations theory are also required.

10. *Emphasis on deep-learning approach*: No doubt the main emphasis should be on traditional economics, but universities (especially in Muslim countries) have to introduce some basic courses in IE and IF, such as Fundamental/Doctrine of IE and IF and Current Issues etc. For teaching, the deep-learning approach will be more useful than the surface-learning one. Because every topic has its own externalities, the deep-learning approach gives more insight into the subject. There should be a process of teaching whereby first we have the presage, then the process of learning and then product. This is a natural phenomenon. The model should be market-oriented as well as provoking original thought.

11. *Concerted efforts to promote the subject*: Aggressive propagation is required from the international institutes such as IRTI for the development of this subject. Significant finances are required for setting up new departments in different parts of the world and also some chairs for IE and IF may also be announced in other institutions.[6] Sufficient research projects should be announced through IDB, and young and new scholars should be encouraged. In this way we can benefit from their abilities in a proper way to promote the subject.

Recapitulations

Based on the previous review of MIHE provided in the first section of this chapter, it is clear that the teaching of IE and IF is still passing through a transitory phase and requires some sound and durable ground. Through teaching we can produce the dedicated and good students who will be able to develop this subject. However, our suggestion hinges on striking a trade-off between the idealistic and pragmatic, and the less attainable and more attainable: all within the constraints of cost, accessibility, staff and time.

Notes

Professor of Islamic Economics and Finance, MIHE, Leicestershire, UK, LE67 9SY.
Visiting Lecturer, MIHE, Leicestershire, UK, LE67 9SY.

1. Sirageldin (2000).
2. Cizakca (1998).
3. Azid and Asutay (2007).
4. MIHE has been approved as a Highly Trusted Sponsor by the UK Borders Agency. For reference, see http://www.ukba.homeoffice.gov.uk/sitecontent/documents/ employersandsponsors/pointsbasedsystem/registerofsponsorseducation, The Association of Business Practitioners, which is a UK-recognized body for professional qualifications, has now advertised the MIHE programme on its website; follow the link here: http://www.abp.org.uk/qualifications/index. php?option=com_content&view=article&id=25
5. QAA Code of Practice, Part 2, paragraph 14, p. 3.
6. Brunei Islamic Bank has announced a Chair for Islamic Finance in the faculty of Economics and Business in the University of Brunei Darussalam.

References

Azid, T. (2009) 'Anthology of Islamic economics', *Review of Islamic Economics*, 13, 2, pp. 165–94.

Azid, T. and Asutay, M. (2007) 'Does ethico-moral coalition complement to economic coalition? A response in the periphery of Islamic economics', *Humanomics*, 23, 3, pp. 153–73.

Cizakca, M. (1998) 'Awqaf in history and its implications for modern Islamic economies', *Islamic Economic Studies*, 6, 1, pp. 43–70.

Dressel, G. A. (1981) 'The professional staff: Two accounts of addressing the challenge', *Journal of College of Personal Association*, 32, 1, pp. 22–9.

Guest, O. and Vecchio, N. (2003) 'Are there learning spillovers in introductory macroeconomics?' *International Review of Economics Education*, 1, 1, pp. 36–60

Jennings, C. M., Barlar, A. D. and Bartling, C. A. (1991) 'Trend in colleges' and universities' faculty development programmes', *Journal of Staff Programme & Organizational Development*, 9, 3, pp. 147–54.

Sirageldin, I. (2000) 'Elimination of poverty: Challenges and Islamic strategies', *Islamic Economic Studies*, 8, 1, pp. 1–16.

Thomas, E. (2004) 'Knowledge cultures and higher education: Achieving balance in the context of globalization', Institute of Education, University of London.

15
Islamic Finance at Strasbourg University

Ibrahim Zeyyad Cekici

After the first conference on Islamic Finance (IF) at Strasbourg University,[1] the decision to enhance the research and education there was taken in January 2008. The Faculty of Law and the Business School worked together in order to establish the new areas of research and education.

In June 2008, the French National Research Agency (ANR) financed our university for four years, and the Business School EM Strasbourg[2] decided to launch the first IF Master's Degree.[3]

Islamic Finance research at Strasbourg University

Our main objective being to become a research centre recognized at international level in the field of IF, we aim to attract young Ph.D. students and economic actors willing to work on the various aspects of the subject area.

The research centres of the Economics and Management Laboratory (LARGE) and the Corporate Law Centre (CDE) have worked together since 1 January 2008. They set up the Strasbourg Finance Institute (IFS) which aims to ensure the complementarity of the researches in finance and law, and to allow the development of interdisciplinary education between 11 Master's connected with this institute.

Thanks to our research, we share and diffuse our knowledge and our expertise in the direction of the political and economic institutions, also to the public and naturally in the direction of universities.

The CDE – supervised by Professor Michel Storck – examines Islamic and conventional juridical and financial mechanisms and instruments, all types of Islamic credit, criminal law and IF, project financing and

Islamic capital markets, screening of securities, Islamic mutual funds, private equity, money laundering and Islamic securitization.

LARGE, supervised by Professor Laurent Weill, examines the influence of IF on the economic development, the Islamic economic system, Islamic prudential ratios, standardization and harmonization of the accounting of IF institutions, risk and liquidity management, auditing of IF institutions.

Strasbourg University and EM Strasbourg Business School, with the collaboration of many organizations (like the Islamic Research and Training Institute, Islamic Development Bank) organized more than ten conferences, symposia and seminars in four years.

Moreover, we have published a journal called *Les Cahiers de la Finance Islamique* which has so far published three issues.[4]

At the moment, there are in Strasbourg University nine researchers and lecturers who have already published more than 20 papers in different research areas. They have also contributed to chapters in jointly authored books and participate in many symposia, conferences and seminars.

Islamic Finance Education at Strasbourg University

In the area of Education, the Business School launched a university degree in IF, equivalent to a Master's, in 2009 and IF became an elective course in two others Master's degrees.

University degree in Islamic Finance at EM Strasbourg Business School

The EM Strasbourg Business School has been part of Strasbourg University since January 2009, after the merger of three universities in the city.

The previous director of the School decided to launch the university degree in IF after a meeting with Professors Michel Storck and Laurent Weill. Their joint team was joined by Ibrahim Zeyyad Cekici, who was in charge of the programme and the management of the degree. The project of the university degree was presented to the board of directors at EM Strasbourg Business School and the University in May 2008. After their agreement, we started to contact teachers and lecturers.

The objectives of the degree are to diversify types of knowledge, know-how and self-management skills. The learners acquire technical skills in finance, law and management adapted to the needs of international companies, law firms and banking institutions in a variety of strategic contexts. They have to develop critical analysis through practical courses (i.e. case studies, simulations, trading rooms) and to develop awareness of the importance of specific self-management skills and knowledge bases in connection with the development model of Islamic Banking (IB) and IF in the countries where these are growing (the Gulf countries, Southeast Asia and Europe).

There are more than 30 teachers for 270 hours of course. They come from the UK, USA and the Middle East and North Africa. The course is divided into 12 units:

1. *Introduction to Islam.* It contains theological, sociological and ethical approaches.
2. *Introduction to Islamic Economics.* This concerns Islam's history, vision and objectives. The unit points up the difference between conventional and Islamic Economics, (IE) and presents the IF system's concepts of currency and monetary policy. Then, it compares the interest-rate theory and the profit-and-loss-sharing theory. Of course, study of business ethics is important in order to understand IF, including *zakat* (the purification of income) and *waqf* (pious foundation).
3. *Sources of Islamic Law.* Included in this are the methodology of the analogical reasoning (*qiyas*) and the purposes of *Shari'ah* (*maqasid Shari'ah*) compared Business Law in order to explain the criteria of the lawful and the unlawful in Islam. Hence, students learn the legal status of the prohibitions on *riba* (interest), *gharar* (alea) and *maysir* (gambling).
4. *Islamic contracts structuring Islamic banking and financial products*: partnership agreements (*moudaraba, mousharaka*), contracts of sale (*mourabaha, moussawama, bay mouajjal, salam, istisna, inah,* etc.). Study of these allows students to distinguish between authorized and forbidden sales.
5. *Islamic Banking Law.* The difference between conventional and Islamic banks, the regulation of banking activities. Students come to understand Islamic accounts, deposits, credit and payment instruments, bank guarantees and bankers' liability.
6. *Islamic capital market.* This covers regulation of IF in different countries, financial markets opened to IF, the transactions on exchange, bonds and money markets. Of course, it teaches structuring IF securities like *sukuk* securities, and how the Islamic derivatives (options, futures, swap), the Islamic investment funds and asset management work. It also explains the issue, negotiation and selection of

Islamic securities, listing of securities, Islamic hedging and Islamic indexes.

7. *Management and governance of organization*, teaching the governance of Islamic banks through the existence of the *Shari'ah* board.
8. *Banking management.* This concerns the principles of financial decision making, financial analysis, risk and liquidity management, the prudential ratios of the Basel Committee, the Islamic Accounting and Auditing standards (IFRS, AAOIFI).
9. *Others matters*, including bank syndication, project financing, structured finance, financial engineering, mergers/acquisitions, Islamic securitization, equity capital and leveraged buyouts, Islamic microcredit, *waqf* and monetary funds.
10. *Taxation.* It is important to know how different countries establish taxation for IB transactions. This unit is also dedicated to *zakat*, an Islamic form of taxation.
11. *Elective unit* teaching socially responsible investment, capital laundering, credit rating, *halal* market, Islamic insurance (*takaful*).
12. *Front office training.* This teaches the pricing and the trading of securities, stock and bond management, simulations and case studies.

This Master's degree is currently open only for professionals. For this reason, two other Master's degrees at the University proposed an elective matter on this subject area.

Islamic Finance in other Master's degrees

Many students from the Master's degree in IB and IF and the Master's degree in Islamology have chosen an elective course in IF. They receive around 20 hours of course focused mainly on contract law.

The University received the official approval of the Ministry of Education for the establishment of an LLM (Master of Laws) in Islamic Banking and Finance at the Strasbourg Faculty of Law.

Notes

1. http://www.unistra.fr/index.php?id=accueil
2. http://www.em-strasbourg.eu/
3. http://www.em-strasbourg.eu/formations/du-finance-islamique
4. http://www.em-strasbourg.eu/docs/dufi/cahiers_fi_01.pdf; http://www.em-strasbourg.eu/docs/dufi/cahiers_fi_02.pdf

16
Islamic Finance at Leuven University

Reza Zain Jaufeerally

History of Leuven University

Situated at the heart of Western Europe, the Katholieke Universiteit Leuven[1] (The Catholic University of Leuven) has been a centre of knowledge for almost six centuries. Founded in 1425 by Pope Martin V, it is the oldest Catholic university anywhere and the oldest university in the Low Countries.[2] Initially modelled on the universities of Paris, Cologne and Vienna, Leuven University quickly became one of the leading universities in Europe. Amongst the leading scholars that it attracted were:

- Desiderius Erasmus (the sixteenth century humanist), who lectured at Leuven University and in 1517 founded the Collegium Trilingue, for the study of Hebrew, Latin and Greek, the first course of its kind.
- Adriaan Cardinal Florensz of Utrecht, who was tutor to the young Emperor Charles V and a professor in Leuven University before being elected pope in 1522.

Other prominent scholars have included the mathematician Gemma Frisius, the cartographer Gerard Mercator, the botanist Rembert Dodoens, the father of modern anatomy Andreas Vesalius and the Leuven theologian Cornelius Jansenius. The philologist, legal scholar and historian Justus Lipsius taught for years in Leuven, helping to build the foundations of modern science and tutoring many famous scientists. His influence on economic thought is pervasive even to this day. In the seventeenth and eighteenth centuries, Leuven University was an important educational centre for Roman Catholic intellectuals from Protestant countries. In the nineteenth century, at the instigation of Pope Leo XIII, Leuven University became an important centre of Neo-Thomist philosophy.

The University's long history was far from being blissful. Most recently, the two World Wars deeply scarred it. In 1914, University Hall with its precious library was set in flames by German troops and 300,000 books were reduced to ashes. Afterwards, an international solidarity campaign with a major American contribution helped construct a new library in 1928: the Monseigneur Ladeuzeplein. Unfortunately, this library was burned down in 1940 during the war. Only 15,000 of its 900,000 volumes were saved. Since then, the University library, and in fact the entire University, has undergone a thorough reconstruction.

The University is located in Flanders, which is the Dutch-speaking (northern) part of Belgium. In 1968, with the renewed prominence of the Dutch language, the University was split into two new universities. The French-speaking Université catholique de Louvain moved to the newly built campus in Louvain-la-Neuvein Wallonia, in the southern part of Belgium. The Dutch-speaking Katholieke Universiteit Leuvenhas remained in the historic town of Leuven.

One of the most important economic thinkers of Louvain University remains Leonard Lessius, a Flemish Jesuit and theologian. He was born in Brecht, in the province of Antwerp, on 1 October 1554 and died in Leuven on 15 January 1623. An orphan from a modest background, Justus Lipsius was an intellectual prodigy; he was a doctor in philosophy at seventeen years old. In 1572, he entered the Society of Jesus He studied theology in Rome, where he had Francis Suarez as his professor for two years. In 1585 he returned to Leuven as professor of theology in the Jesuit College and held this chair for 15 years. Lessius was considered to be the legal and theological genius of his era.

De iustitia et iure (On justice and law), published 1605, is Lessius' masterwork on economic thought. An extremely influential book, it went through more than 20 editions in the seventeenth century alone. It is a moral and theological investigation of economic and financial questions. Far from being a purely theoretical book, *De iustitia et iure* is grounded in commercial reality. Lessius was consulted by Antwerp traders on matters of justice and travelled to Antwerp (already a major trading hub) to study the actual workings of business, banking and finance. Modern economists acknowledge the expertise of Lessius regarding the subtlety of business matters. This remarkable practical insight added credibility to his ethical solutions to moral questions dealing with commercial and financial matters. Lessius' major innovation was his novel treatment of interest; he considered that the stance proposed by Thomas Aquinas was not applicable to the sixteenth century and instead advocated a 'just price' approach.

Islamic Finance at the Centre for Economics and Ethics

The Centre for Economics and Ethics (CEE), part of the Faculty of Economics and Business, is where Islamic Finance (IF) research is conducted. Officially founded in 1987, the CEE's primary academic goal is to contribute to the integration of ethical considerations in economic research. This follows the recent developments in normative welfare economics and business ethics.

Vital to the CEE is interdisciplinary communication between economists, philosophers, theologians and scientists from other disciplines. There are regular seminars and colloquia arranged. In this area, the CEE works with many similar institutions and networks, in particular with the Centre of Ethics at Universitaire Faculteiten Sint-Ignatius Antwerpen (UFSIA), the Chair Hoover (Université catholique de Louvain) and the Network EBEN (European Business Ethics Network).

The CEE is the brainchild of Professor Luk Bouckaert. With his background in economics as well as in philosophy, Bouckaert gave the necessary impetus and drive to the Faculty of Economics and Business Administration to establish a centre that has served to focus on the interaction between economics and ethics. It began in 1987 as a public-private initiative, and in the 25 years since has become an integral part of the Faculty. Both education and research provide the fairly broad interface between economics and ethics. Themes such as the healthcare sector, the values of SMEs, the importance of cooperative entrepreneurship, historical studies on the role of interest, equity of income differences, the importance of corporate social responsibility; and – along the more philosophical side – Leonard Lessius, the place of sobriety in our society, the role of trust have been investigated.

A similar diversity is found in the doctorates originating from the CEE over the past 25 years. Themes have included the importance of autonomy, defining duties of distributive justice in a cosmopolitan world, the limits of rational choice theory, the role and significance of participation structures in companies, Nusbaum and Sen on capabilities, the delicate balance between equity and efficiency in health care and so forth. Additionally, the CEE has used a very wide range of research starting from pure philosophical reflection on empirical analysis to prosperity theoretical treatises. In this multitude of themes and subjects, the common thread has been a strong concern for the plight of the vulnerable in our society.

The CEE belongs to the vanguard of European research centres in applied ethics; tackling issues on the borderline between economics and ethics. It cofounded the EBEN, which today has more than 1,400 members in 40 countries. Professor Luc Van Liedekerke has acted as EBEN president; CEE remains active in the EBEN network.

Islamic Finance research

Regarding IF, our most important project is the forthcoming launch of a postgraduate course on Ethical and Islamic Finance in March 2013. The title of the postgraduate course is Finance and Ethics: Neoclassical, Islamic and CSR/SRI views. The objective is that in a period of ten weekends (Fridays and Saturdays, 14.5 hours per weekend), course participants will gain an in-depth knowledge of the increasingly important area of Finance and Ethics. We shall be exploring and comparing neoclassical finance with two rapidly growing areas of finance: Ethical Finance (EF) and IF. We endeavour to offer participants a holistic view of the evolving financial landscape and provide them with tools enabling them to adapt to the new environment. This course will be jointly organised with the University of Antwerp.

The postgraduate course will be very useful to a variety of stakeholders including:

- financial sector employees
- lawyers and accountants
- regulators
- members of EU institutions and international organizations
- fund managers

Regarding the contents and structure of the postgraduate course, we are using a common structure without electives. The contents are as follows:

1. *A Survey of neoclassical finance:* 45 contact hours. Portfolio theory: optimal diversification and investment performance analysis; capital budgeting and cost-benefit analysis. Corporate financing: debt vs

equity, and public versus private debt, including governance issues such as tax considerations, costs of financial distress, information issues and signalling. *Risk management:* hedging and insurance.

2. *Ethical and sustainable finance:* 45 contact hours. Why socially responsible investing (SRI)? History. SRI products and screening techniques. Challenges (e.g. micro-finance). Cost-benefit analysis and investment performance appraisal. Portfolio management.

3. *Islamic Finance:* 45 contact hours. Basic principles. The four legal traditions. Islamic capital markets and insurance. Governance issues. The role of finance in the corporation and in the economy.

4. *Research paper:* Assessment will take the form of a short research paper per module. Upon successful completion of the research papers, the participants will be issued with a certificate.

The Teaching Faculty for the postgraduate course will be composed of:

- A survey of neoclassical finance – Piet Sercu, FEB KU Leuven.
- Ethical and sustainable finance – Luc Van Liedekerke, FEB-CEE KU Leuven, Univeristy of Antwerp.
- Islamic Finance – Iqbal Asaria, Cass Business School; Reza Jaufeerally, CEE FEB KU Leuven.
- Numerous specialist lecturers on (including but not limited to) emerging markets, private equity, crowd-funding, angel investing and venture capital.

Recent publications of CEE on IF include:

- 'Islamic Finance: An informed guide for the non-specialist', by Professor Van Liedekerke and Reza Zain Jaufeerally in *Streven Tijdschrift – Cultureel Maatschappelijk Maandblad* (forthcoming 2012).
- 'A critical analysis of the obstacles to the alliance between SRI & Islamic Finance' by Professor Van Liedekerke and Reza Zain Jaufeerally, in *Harvard University Islamic Finance Project: Building Bridges Across Financial Communities* (27 and 28 March 2010).
- 'Some critical thoughts on a possible synergy between SRI and Islamic Finance' by Professor Van Liedekerke and Reza Zain Jaufeerally in *Finance and Ethics*, edited by A. Löhr and M. Valeva, published by Rainer-Hampp-Verlag (2010), pp. 43–59.
- 'Islamic Banking and responsible investment: Is a fusion possible?' by Reza Zain Jaufeerally in *Responsible Investment in Times of Turmoil*, published by Springer (2010), pp. 151–63.

- 'Insolvencies and asset recovery regarding Islamic Banking investments' by Reza Zain Jaufeerally and Nora Wouters in INSOL World – Fourth Quarter (2009).

International conferences

The CEE has organized two specialized international conferences on Islamic and EF:

- International Conference on 'Islamic and Ethical Banking and Finance' on 25–6 May 2009, Leuven. Present were numerous luminaries from both EF and IF. This event enabled a memorable dialogue between stalwarts from both sectors. The keynote speaker was Frans De Clerck, the cofounder of Triodos Bank, one of the world's leading sustainable banks, based in the Netherlands with branches in Belgium.
- A 'Moral Economy Forum' on 7 May 2011. This was held under Chatham House rules. It was a candid conversation between key players of IF, EF and CF. The keynote speaker was Dr Volker Nienhaus.

Greater Paris Investment Agency/Bain & Co. study and working group

From October 2011 to April 2012, Reza Zain Jaufeerally acted as expert for Bain & Company for their study and working group on IF. The study and working group were ordered by the Greater Paris Investment Agency to the Paris office of Bain & Co. This study constitutes the most in-depth practical study of how to establish Paris as the IF centre of Europe. The working group was composed of the key stakeholders and decisionmakers.

Forthcoming event

On Monday 15 October 2012, we are organizing a high-level seminar on 'Islamic Finance: A potential solution to the global financial crisis'. The audience to this invitation-only event will consist of academics and professionals. More information will be available on the CEE website.

Conclusion

According to the 2010 Pew Report,[3] 6 per cent of the Belgian population is Muslim (638,000). This compares with 7.5 per cent in France

(4,704,000), 5.5 per cent in Netherlands (914,000) and 5 per cent in Germany (4,119,000). While there is certainly a growing interest in IF in mainland Europe, there are numerous hurdles to its development. Many European finance ministers are interested in the foreign direct investments that IF could bring, especially considering the global financial crisis. Major European economies have expressed interest in developing capabilities to attract that flow of foreign capital. A number of European governments have announced that they want to be the IF centre in Europe. It is a fact that there are large amounts of funds available in the Muslim world.

The best service that universities can render is to demystify IF, enabling individuals to learn and decide for themselves. Our forthcoming postgraduate course will be the first time that such a programme has been taught in the Benelux (IF rather than EF or CF). From comparing and contrasting, participants should gain many valuable insights and be able to cut through the political noise to understand the true benefits of IF. Lastly, the University of Leuven does not possess a career centre directed towards student placements in IF institutions; access to such a career centre could prove invaluable to persuade promising young professionals to contemplate a career in that area. Perhaps, here is an opportunity to develop a common facility for mainland Europe.

Notes

1. Please note that Leuven is known as Louvain in French. In this article, we shall be using the Flemish name 'Leuven'.
2. Historically the Netherlands region included the current Netherlands, Belgium and Luxembourg.
3. http://en.wikipedia.org/wiki/List_of_countries_by_Muslim_population.

Reference

Gordon, B. T. (1975) *Economic Analysis before Adam Smith: Hesiod to Lessius* (London: Macmillan).

17
Islamic Finance at Liverpool Hope University

Adel Ahmed

Introduction and background

The roots of Liverpool Hope University in the UK date back to its first founding College of Education in 1844 in Warrington by the Church of England. Its second founding college was established in 1856 by the Sisters of Notre Dame. Its third college – Christ's College – opened in 1965. These three church colleges, Anglican and Catholic, form the foundation of what is now Liverpool Hope University, the only ecumenical foundation in higher education in Europe. This unique ecumenical achievement and its long tradition of scholarly ambition inform its commitment to openness, social justice and widening participation. The University's Mission and Values are firmly based in the Christian tradition and encourage the development of a university with a collegial heart. Liverpool Hope University seeks to nurture the creative coexistence of the arts, sciences and theology in the quest for meaning and purpose in human affairs.

The Mission and Values at Liverpool Hope University underpin the Islamic Finance (IF) education. For example, the Mission Statement of Liverpool Hope University is as an ecumenical Christian foundation which strives to:

- provide opportunities for the well-rounded personal development of Christians and students from other faiths and beliefs, educating the whole person in mind, body and spirit, irrespective of age, social or ethnic origins or physical capacity, including in particular those who might otherwise not have had an opportunity to enter higher education;

- be a national provider of a wide range of high-quality programmes responsive to the needs of students, including the education, training and professional development of teachers for Church and state schools;
- sustain an academic community, as a sign of hope, enriched by Christian values and worship, which supports teaching and learning, scholarship and research, encourages the understanding of Christian and other faiths and beliefs, and promotes religious and social harmony;
- contribute to the educational, religious, cultural, social and economic life of Liverpool, Merseyside, the Northwest and beyond.

IF/Islamic Banking (IB) is among the fastest growing mechanisms of global finance. The market potential of the sector has attracted actors in higher education to offer postgraduate degrees in this area. Expanding IF needs increasing education, research and training. Many universities around the world rushed to offer postgraduate programmes in IF and IB to respond to the growing interest in IF, which is evidenced by a continuous increase in IB services, Islamic investment and other financial services based on Islamic principles. Most of those higher insinuations do not offer a real IF/IB degree as the focus is not IB and Islamic Finance (IF) but covering financial/economic systems as a whole using combinations of some of existing modules and just adding on one or two modules about IF/IB. Programmes in IF were quickly drawn up to meet the expanding demand. This rapidity resulted in unsuitable curricular frames and course designs; much of the research tended to be confirmative. The shortage of competent tutors worsened the situation further; compromises on the quality of instructions had to be made.

Therefore, the PG Certificate Contemporary Islamic Finance and Organisation at Liverpool Hope University offers a postgraduate certificate not a Master's-level degree as there are not enough modules and staff to offer MSc or Ph.D. levels.

Programme specification

Basic programme description

Table 17.1 Basic programme description of Islamic Finance at Liverpool Hope University

Programme	PG Certificate Contemporary Islamic Finance and Organisation
Study mode(s) and max. period of registration	Full-time Part-time

(continued)

Table 17.1   Continued

Programme	PG Certificate Contemporary Islamic Finance and Organisation	
	Mode of study Full-time Part-time	**Duration of study** One semester Two semesters
Awarding body	Liverpool Hope University	
Teaching location(s)	Hope Park	
Final award(s), including any interim awards	PG Certificate Contemporary Islamic Finance and Organisation (60 credits)	
NQF level(s)	National Qualifications Framework (NQF)	Framework for Higher Education Qualifications (FHEQ)
	Level 7	M (master's) Master's degrees, postgraduate certificates and diplomas
Sponsoring faculty	Sciences and Social Sciences	
Frequency of intake	Annual; September/February intake	
Name of programme/ pathway co-ordinators	Dr Adel Ahmed (PG Certificate Contemporary Islamic Finance and Organisation)	

Programme details

Programme philosophy

Many national and global contexts cannot be understood without reference to the impact of religion on economic, political and social systems. This programme affirms that Islam is a significant factor in the understanding of economic and social capital in both the Muslim and non-Muslim worlds. It aims to provide students with the means to engage in business, management or other professions with an understanding of the cultural exchange required when engaging in cross-cultural systems that draw from both religious (Islamic) traditions and global economies. This is achieved within a framework of analytical understanding of the relations between Islam and the West. The degree offers a coherent programme of study at Master's level that will enable in-depth engagement with key issues connected to the role of Islam within global economies. It has been constructed to draw upon and make accessible the research interests of the teaching team. The PG Certificate in Contemporary Islamic Finance and Organisation will be a stand-alone programme wholly owned by Business Studies in the Faculty of Sciences and Social

Table 17.2 Programme details of Islamic Finance at Liverpool Hope University

Aims	1. To provide a postgraduate-level programme that will give students a thorough grounding in the study of topical and relevant issues of concern for Islam in the contemporary world, with an emphasis on IF and management in the context of cultural encounters between Muslims and the West, informed by the research interests of a team of nationally and internationally known scholars, and that will provide a sound basis for further research.
	2. To enable students to relate contemporary issues in IF and organizations management to broader trends in society.
	3. To enable students to consider certain key questions and themes pertinent to cultural exchanges between Islam and the West in depth and in context.
	4. To develop students' subject-specific and transferable skills to postgraduate award level.
Learning outcomes	Subject-specific:
	By the end of the relevant programme, students will be able to demonstrate:
	PG Certificate Contemporary Islamic Finance and Organisation
	1. Critical insight into key themes in the study of IF and organization management.
	2. Capacity to locate themes pertaining to Islam within their cultural and historic settings, and to offer critical evaluation of their significance in the light of contemporary questions and issues.
	3. Ability to analyse and critique the complex relation between religion and cultures.
	4. Ability to articulate, analyse and compare IF, economics, and management systems with corresponding institutions in the West.
	In addition to the aforesaid, students completing the PG Certificate Contemporary Islamic Finance and Organisation will demonstrate in-depth and extensive knowledge of a complex area of their own choosing (in consultation with and under supervision by a tutor who is an expert in the chosen field and subject to specific staff expertise in the area).
Learning outcomes (key generic and transferable skills)	By the end of the programmes, students will be able to:
	1. summarize and create articulate syntheses of complex positions
	2. present information effectively in writing, including the ability to present and justify positions held
	3. understand and critically assess positions taken by others, both in discussion and in writing

	4. enter empathetically into contexts other than the students' own, to aid academic understanding
	5. offer independently formed judgments, supported by appropriate argument and evidence
	6. collate information independently, including the ability to construct a full bibliography on a specific topic, using both traditional and electronic sources
	7. experience and build up a range of research methods and skills.
Teaching/learning and assessment methods	A wide spectrum of teaching and learning methodologies is incorporated into the courses. Students will have experience of a range of modes of learning: lecture input, participation in seminars, discussion with other students, and individual tutorials where appropriate. They will learn through library searches, internet searches, the use of the university's virtual learning environment (VLE) system, preparation of written and oral assignments and feedback on assignments.
	Assessment will be varied within the limits of 15 credit Master's courses delivered over a short period of time and covering a broad range of interdisciplinary topics. Consequently, formal essays form the backbone of the assessment regime. It is considered that too many assessments that involve field research, or generation of original material, would create difficulties for students who will often find themselves with only days between courses. However, variety is brought into the assessment package through case studies. Examination is kept to a minimum as Level 4 is the bridge to independent learning and research. Consequently, both dissertation and independent study provide opportunities for research and independent learning under supervision.
	Timely and transparently managed feedback will form an important part of the assessment strategy.
Curriculum diagrams	**PG Certificate Contemporary Islamic Finance and Organisation**
	Islamic Economics (15 credits)
	Islamic Finance and Banking (15 credits)
	Islamic Management and Organisation (15 credits) Structures
	Islam in the West (15 credits)

(continued)

Table 17.2 Continued

Special features	The **PG Certificate** is distinctive in that it offers students engagement with topical areas of personal, professional and academic interest in Islamic and Muslim finance, management and Islamic organization, and allows students the opportunity to engage with these issues alongside Finance issues, or to provide an overall knowledge and understanding of Muslims' relations with the West.
	This programme is an interdisciplinary PG Certificate taught at Business School and drawing on the expertise of scholars of international renown in their respective fields. Liverpool Hope University has cross-faculty expertise in Islamic fields of knowledge that are rare in most university departments, and permits the development of a Master's programme that is both vocational (Finance, Management) and cultural. The PG Certificate is focused on business studies only and offers a competitive stand-alone programme of study.

Sciences. It is envisaged that the Certificate can be offered independently to professionals in various areas of Business who may wish to familiarize themselves with Islamic attitudes to finance, management, banking and economics.

Background and rationale for the development

Primarily the proposal has been driven by various Higher Education Funding Council for England (HEFCE) documents that identify the study of Islam/Muslims as a strategic subject; for example, the Siddiqui report on Islam at Universities in England; the report on the trends and profiles of Islamic studies courses and students in the UK (HEFCE 2008/09); the report, 'International Approaches to Islamic Studies in Higher Education', and the two consultation events, seminar report on 'Islamic Studies: Current status and future prospects', November 2007 and the seminar report on 'Islamic Studies: The way forward in the UK', April 2008.

This is set against a background in which here is a growing demand for postgraduate taught degrees amongst the Muslim community in Britain and overseas (HEFCE). Competitors in the Russell Group universities have not yet been able to respond to the demands of Muslim students and their contemporary interests because of their historic philological interest in the Middle East. Competitors outside of the Russell Group rarely have the resources available to Liverpool Hope University in this field. The University is fortunate enough to have academic expertise in a number of areas of popular and significant interest to young Muslims; these include media and Islamic Economics (IE). The fields of IE, IB, marketing and management are a rapidly growing area of interest to young Muslim professionals, especially in the aftermath of the banking crisis in the West which has drawn attention to the ethics of banking in the non-Muslim world as compared to banking with Islamic ethical codes. Many young Muslims are finding their way into business, finance, management, including public service organizations and Third Sector, but also demanding knowledge of their own culture and religion and how it meets the demands of the modern world. In many cases they find their way into businesses that serve their own communities either in Britain or globally. A traditional philological approach to Islamic Studies does not necessarily provide the tools for engagement with the modern.

The PG Certificate in Contemporary Islamic Finance and Organisation provides the possibility for the University to engage existing staff expertise in an area of strategic importance with HEFCE whilst offering a parcel of courses that provide unique learning opportunities in the field of contemporary studies of Muslims/Islam. Liverpool Hope University has cross-Faculty expertise in Islamic fields of knowledge that are rare in most university departments (such as Theology and Religious Studies or Middle-Eastern Studies). The curriculum was designed to combine with the research ability and experience of the academic team to attract Ph.D. candidates in the respective areas of expertise taught on the Master's programme.

Evidence of demand and consultation process

Young Muslims in Britain are very interested in finance issues and the impact of Islam in the West. Both are areas that HEFCE wants to be emphasized on Islamic Studies programmes. Liverpool Hope University is ideally placed regionally to tap into large concentrations of Muslims locally (Liverpool Arab-origin communities and the Lancashire/Yorkshire South Asian origin communities). Our competitors in the area (Lancaster, University College London, Liverpool, John Moores, Manchester, Leeds, Bradford) either do not offer Islamic Studies or only have expertise in areas of traditional religious curricula (philology, history of religions, textual studies) that are not necessarily relevant to the needs of young Muslims in the contemporary world.

Relationship to equality scheme(s)

The operation of this programme will reflect fully the Equality Scheme of Liverpool Hope University. Students with learning disabilities will be supported carefully on the programme in line with University policy. A variety of groups will benefit from a postgraduate programme of this type, including Muslim students hoping to enhance their employability through academic engagement with issues of significance in cross-cultural exchange, and non-Muslim students who might be likely to engage with the Muslim world in their future work lives.

The study of contemporary Muslim issues and the ways in which Islam is represented by different interest groups and organisations will engage students in the analysis of issues of ethnicity, nationality, gender and equality in different cultural contexts. By studying the ways in which Muslims represent themselves in the civil, economic and public domains, students will be engaged in academic study which is consistent with a number of benchmarking statements in the arts and humanities which stresses the importance of developing knowledge and understanding of differing values, systems and societies. However, in engaging with Islamic economics, finance and management, gender and media, the programme will provide cultural sensitivities that should enhance employability for both Muslims and non-Muslims hoping to engage across cultural borders in the domain of business and marketing.

Special features

1. The new PG Certificate in Contemporary Islamic Finance and Organisation programme is underpinned by strong research of not only national, but international standing. Several of the teaching team are authors in their respective areas covered by the taught courses.
2. The focused nature of the PG Certificate programme provides a clear and coherent product which ensures that delivery matches applicants' expectations.
3. The PG Certificate is unique in Britain in that it draws upon inter-disciplinary expertise in IF and Management, and Muslim relations with the West as general.
4. The PG Certificate is created to produce a match with employment opportunities within the Muslim communities, in particular, but draws upon the requirements of business graduates to deepen their cultural and religious knowledge of the Muslim world.

Curriculum design and organization

Curriculum design overview

The design of the programme is based on four courses encompassing 15 credits each as follows:

1. *Islam in the West (15 credits)*: This course explores the history, development and contemporary location of Muslims in the West in the context of relations between Islam and the West, acknowledging that 'the West' is a symbolic construction where a set of cultures were established over the course of the last 200 years with more or less liberal and democratic regimes based upon 'sovereignty of the people'. Drawing upon case studies (e.g. Britain, France, Germany and the USA), the course will examine religion and public life, citizenship, the relation of the secular and the 'sacred', and pluralism in the context of the Muslim presence.
2. *Islamic Finance and Banking (15 credits)*: This course introduces the candidate to the fundamentals of IF and IB. It provides a detailed working knowledge of IB and IF operations, helping the student to understand from the beginning how the principles of IF differ from

those of conventional banking. The course starts with the overview of the key differences between conventional banking and IB. It then covers the distinguishing features of IF, understanding and explaining the concepts of operations of IB and understanding and explaining *takaful* as an alternative to conventional insurance. The course assumes no previous knowledge of Islamic studies.

3. *Islamic Economics (15 credits)*: This course introduces the candidate to the fundamentals of IE by considering the implications of the application of *Shari'ah* law for the economy. It provides a detailed working knowledge of scope of IE in relation to conventional economics, history of the Islamic economic system in various eras, contributions by Islamic economists, wealth creation and mobilization, and the concepts of money, risk and returns from an Islamic perspective. Students will gain an insight into how Islam can be considered as an economic system that can be applied to economic policies and business strategies. The course assumes no previous knowledge of Islamic studies.

4. *Islamic Management and Organisation Structures (15 credits)*: This course explores the evolution, background, social positioning and economic and organizational structures of Islamic management and organization. The course explains the central dimensions of Islamic organization such as the integral nature of business organization and ethical principles, the historical framework and evolution of Islamic scholarship about organization, management, leadership and motivation; and describes the leading schools of Islamic thought in historical context. There are case studies of some contemporary Islamic management and organizational structures. The linkages of Islamic organization and contemporary management concepts (such as learning organization) are explained based on research. The background and context of the growth of Islamic principles in international finance, banking and trade are explained. The course takes a critical perspective on the growth of Islamic organization, relating this to the socio-political and economic dimensions of contemporary global society.

Relationship to subject benchmark statement(s)

The published benchmark for Theology and Religious Studies refers only to Bachelor's degrees with Honours although the Subject Association is involved in developing taught postgraduate benchmarks in cooperation with HEFCE. Business Studies is benchmarked for postgraduate taught provision and has been used to develop the learning outcomes.

Learning, teaching and assessment strategy

Learning and teaching strategy

A wide spectrum of teaching and learning methodologies is incorporated into the courses. Students will have experience of a range of modes of learning: lecture input, participation in seminars, discussion with other students, and individual tutorials where appropriate. The University's VLE system will be used, in conjunction with appropriate training, to provide a dynamic online environment allowing for easy and reliable communication, ready dissemination of material and participative online possibilities. There will be field visits, outside speakers, engagement with Muslim communities informed by research. Overall, students will develop both subject-specific competencies and also transferable skills in critical reflection, self-expression (both oral and written), engagement with the ideas of others and presentation of written work.

The major emphasis is on encouraging independent learning, with the tutor providing appropriate support. All courses will require students to reflect on the issues involved, which may be through seminar debate or small-group discussion. Students will be encouraged to reflect critically on primary and secondary texts. They will be constantly required to discern the underpinning religious, philosophical, political, economic and historical contexts of the Muslim world views and to reflect on the implications of particular stances. These strategies reflect the aim of the programme to promote the development of transferable skills and a commitment to the students' continuing education.

Assessment strategy and assessment criteria

The assessment strategy enables students to demonstrate the acquisition, understanding, application, synthesis and evaluation of knowledge at the appropriate level, while also demonstrating subject-specific and transferable competencies and skills. Assessment is viewed holistically as an integral part of the learning and teaching strategy, intended to enhance learning as well as providing the means for verification of student achievement. A clear communication of expectations (chiefly through the course handbooks), and feedback to students on completed assessment, are pillars of the strategy. The following practices will be adopted to ensure that assessment is rigorous, transparent, equitable and valid: assessment will be varied within the limits of 15 credit courses delivered over a short period of time and covering a broad range of interdisciplinary topics. Consequently, formal essays form the backbone of the assessment regime. It is considered that too many assessments that involved field research, or generation of original material, would create difficulties for students who would often find themselves with only days between taught courses. However, variety is brought into the assessment package through case studies and research projects. Examination is kept to a minimum as Level 4 is the bridge to independent learning and research. Both dissertation and independent study provide opportunities for research and independent learning under supervision.

1. As part of the students' induction process, the following will be discussed:
   - the role and purpose of assessment within the PG programme
   - the grading system
   - the practicalities of submission
   - issues and opportunities around resubmission.

2. The following key aspects will be published to and discussed with students at the start of each course:

   - assessment details
   - marking criteria

3. The use of both internal and external moderation processes. All summative work is internally moderated. Depending upon cohort size and the teaching experience of the first marker, this will be either a sample or 100 per cent. A representative sample of assessments is sent to the external examiner for moderation, the sample size being agreed with the external examiner. All dissertations are both second marked and externally moderated.

4. Academic standards are maintained by a combination of the following:

   - the external examiner facilitates understanding of comparability with other institutions
   - members of the team, acting as external examiners in other institutions, foster discussions about comparability
   - new members of staff with recent experience of teaching elsewhere also bring enhanced understanding of comparability.

5. Feedback strategy: the provision of timely, effective and consistent feedback to students is an important element of the assessment strategy. It will be achieved by the following:

- notification to students of assignment due dates will also include notification of the expected return date and method
- first and second marking will be completed within the university timeframe – currently four term-time weeks
- the first marker will provide detailed feedback, reflecting the assessment criteria used. This, together with the appropriately annotated assignment, will be returned to the student with a reminder that until the external moderation process has been completed, the mark/grade is provisional only.
- The return of assignments will take place within class, where possible, to facilitate immediate further discussion if the student wishes or the tutor regards it as advisable. Where this is not possible, a suitable alternative method of feedback will be established, depending on individual circumstances.

6. Reassessment: students who fail any assignment will be given an opportunity to resit the assessment with a penalty, in that the mark will be capped to 40 per cent.

Programme management

Programme team

Responsibility for the day-to-day management and quality assurance of the programme is the primary responsibility of the programme team, headed by the programme coordinator. The teaching teams for the programmes of study will meet together at least once per term to hold minuted discussions of strategy, operational issues and plans for enhancement. In addition, each team will meet with its external examiner once a year at a board of examiners. The University operates more frequent university-wide boards of examiners at which the programme leaders will be present. These boards will be preceded by appropriate electronic communication with the external examiner. The University's normal annual monitoring procedures will take place in accordance with Quality Assurance Agency (QAE) guidelines.

Staff-student liaison

Representatives will be elected from the student body. They will comprise the joint Staff-Student Liaison Committee (SSLC), together with the programme coordinators. This committee will meet at least once each semester, and will follow the university norms. Minutes of the SSLC meetings – together with a formal response – will be made available to all students.

Each course will be evaluated at its end. Analysis of these evaluations will be fed into the annual monitoring process.

External examiner(s)

There will be two external examiners appointed to this programme. In view of the degree's interdisciplinarity, it would be appropriate for external examiners to scrutinize assessments from the respective subject areas. Two examiners will be appointed to deal respectively with IF and the cultural/religious elements of the degree.

Future development plan

This new programme will be carefully monitored, especially with regard to recruitment and close examination of markets abroad; the development of new courses; recruitment of MSc/Ph.D. students and organization of seminars/conferences/workshops.

Part III
Islamic Finance Higher Education in the West: Research and Other Initiatives

18
Islamic Finance at Harvard University

Nazim Ali

Historical perspective

Founded in 1636, Harvard University is America's oldest university and one of the most respected centres of higher education and research in the world. Harvard attracts an array of talented students and scholars. It houses the largest library collections of any academic institution in the world. Since the establishment of the Harvard Islamic Society in 1955, the University has continued to reemphasize its liberal attitude towards the study of Islam and other religions within a serene but academically challenging environment. In recent years, there has been an increasing interest in studying Islam. The Harvard Divinity School, Near Eastern Languages Civilization Department, Center for Middle Eastern Studies, the Islamic Legal Studies Program (ILSP), the Aga Khan Program for Islamic Architecture, the Islam in the West Program, and most recently, the Prince Alwaleed Bin Talal Islamic Studies Program demonstrate the breadth of coverage in these fields across the university's various schools and disciplines.

Meanwhile, the emergence of Islamic Finance (IF) services as a distinct field of inquiry is a welcome addition to this landscape. Harvard's first foray in this field was the Islamic Investment Study, which concluded with the 1998 publication of *Islamic Law and Finance: Religion, Risk, and Return* by Harvard professors Frank E. Vogel and Samuel Hayes III. The University's most significant investment in this area, however, has been the longstanding Islamic Finance Project (IFP), a research programme that emerged from the growing interest in IF among members of the Harvard community in the mid-1990s.

The IFP was founded by the Harvard University Centre for Middle Eastern Studies (CMES) in 1995. The IFP became part of the ILSP at

Harvard Law School in 2003. As the only Ivy League project of its kind, the IFP studies the field of IF from a legal perspective by analysing contemporary scholarship, encouraging collaboration among scholars within and outside of the Muslim world, and increasing the interaction between theory and practice in the IF industry.

The IFP is involved in the study of an interdisciplinary subject, drawing broadly from a variety of fields, and has relationships with professors and students at several Harvard institutions including the Harvard Law School, Harvard Business School, Harvard Divinity School, the Kennedy School of Government and the Faculty of Arts and Sciences. IFP organizes academic forums, bringing together scholars and experts in law, finance, economics, and traditional Islamic ethics and law (*fiqh*), to engage leading thinkers in a robust, interdisciplinary dialogue.

The IFP has become a leading research programme in the field of IF services. For scholars at Harvard and beyond, IFP serves as a research centre that collects and provides information on IF services that connects researchers to a network of resources in the field. For industry professionals, it offers a valuable platform to increase awareness on IF services, to stimulate research and development, and to manage debates about the future direction of the industry.

These ongoing efforts by the IFP underscore the fundamental need for continued exchange between academia and IF practitioners. Indeed, this dialogue has proven to be instrumental in the development of key areas in the field. The writings of Islamic economists in the 1950s and 1960s, for example, inspired the Organization of the Islamic Conference (OIC), while other intellectual visionaries transformed those ideas into practice by establishing what would lead to the current state of Islamic Banking (IB). The establishment of the first modern institutional Islamic bank, the Islamic Development Bank in 1975, was closely followed by that of the Dar Al Maal Islami Group, Dubai Islamic Bank, Al-Rajhi Investment Company, Dallah Albaraka Group, and Kuwait Finance House.

IF, however, remains overall a fairly niche industry. As it matures, it will undergo periods of change and self-reflection. This has certainly been the case in the process of business development, where some products offered by the industry have received criticism for departing from the *maqasid al Shari'ah* (*Shari'ah* objectives). Some products have been accused of being obsolete or irrelevant, or straying from the value-added goals of societal equity and fairness. These concerns emphasize the need to maintain, if not expand, the vital link between research and tangible developments in the field.

In this light, the purpose of this chapter is to present and discuss the activities that have emerged at Harvard institutions over the period of 17 years since the inception of the IFP, and to show the relevance of these initiatives to the broader understanding and research of the IF industry.

Objectives of the Islamic Finance project

Since its inception, the Project has grown larger in scope and has come to be recognized as one of the leading centres for the study of Islamic Economics (IE), IB and IF. As a multidimensional research project the IFP intends:

1. *To promote research and development in the field of Islamic Finance*: One of the missions of the IFP is to encourage the study of IF and IE across all of the schools and programmes within the University. Because of it is interdisciplinary nature, the study of IF brings together various Harvard departments and faculties. In conjunction with this goal, the IFP produces scholarly monographs and reports, including a compendium of the leading papers brought to its yearly conferences. The IFP produces both print publications and reports available as e-resources via the Project's website. The IFP works to assist researchers in their scholarly pursuits, including the development of theses, dissertations and other research reports.

2. *To develop the IFP DataBank, an electronic database on Islamic Finance*: The first of its kind, the DataBank has filled a niche role, serving as an online tool for the dissemination of bibliographic data in the field. The IFP contacts institutions that engage in IF research as well as researchers in the field to advance the acquisition and coordination of information. The DataBank's approach is encyclopaedic in scope, while striving to remain accessible to a general readership. In accordance with this mindset, the IFP is continually trying to create a more user-friendly interface in the layout of the DataBank. The DataBank aims to assist academics, researchers and professionals who require relevant academic information related to IE and IF and that pertains to *Shari'ah* rulings and sources.

3. *To foster an increased understanding of Islamic Finance between the Islamic and non-Islamic worlds as well as between industry and academia*: The IFP fosters dialogue and innovation in the field by organizing seminars, workshops, panel discussions, roundtables, and conferences. The Project monitors developments and emerging trends in

the IF industry and invites practitioners to discuss them in the form of seminars or workshops. The structured exchange of ideas between scholars and practitioners at the Harvard Forum and at private IFP workshops enables constructive debate and a longer-term view of the IF services industry. For industry professionals, it offers a valuable platform to increase awareness of IF services, to stimulate research and development, and to manage debates about the future direction of the industry.

4. *To foster faculty and student interest in the field by sponsoring workshops and courses on Islamic Finance in cooperation with other programmes*: As part of its mission, the IFP develops seminars, workshops and panel discussions to encourage faculty and student participation. The Project works with faculty in developing course material into which an IF and IE component could be introduced. The IFP works with various faculty members in developing case studies, projects and lectures pertaining to IF and IE. The IFP has assisted students with their theses and provided career-counselling services for students seeking to forge career paths in IF. IFP activities attract students and researchers who often turn to the IF industry for career opportunities in IF services.

5. *To assist governmental bodies seeking to understand the dynamics of this new global market and to create awareness and understanding of IF principles and trends*: The IFP has organized seminars and panel discussions to discuss IF regulation by inviting various regulatory bodies and IF providers to bridge the gap between industry and academia and create better understanding. The IFP has worked with the US Treasury, Federal Reserve Bank and other regulatory agencies to facilitate a better understanding of IF. Through its public lectures, newsletters, and other publications, the IFP seeks to disseminate information and create understanding of IF and IE within academia, industry, and the general readership.

An overview of major Islamic Finance Project initiatives

Over the last 17 years, the subject of IF has attracted growing interest among academics, students and professionals around the globe. In light of this interest, the IFP has undertaken numerous initiatives to meet the growing demand for information.

The DataBank project, one of the pioneering efforts of the IFP, was launched by the IFP in early 1995. It was closely followed by First Harvard University Forum on IF in 1997, an initiative that gained industry recognition as one of the most important conferences to discuss current issues in IF.

In 2006, the IFP began to host another initiative that focused on the contributions of two major players in the industry: *Shari'ah* scholars and Islamic economists. This event, which emerged as the Harvard-London School of Economics (LSE) workshop, has been held yearly in London since 2006 and serves as a forum to discuss methodological issues confronting the industry. The event includes several seminars, panel discussions and public lectures to address trends emerging from the industry, all of which are documented by active publications. The first book based on the LSE workshop was published in 1999 as *Proceedings of the Second Harvard University Forum on Islamic Finance*. Since then, the Project has published seven books and several papers and reports, including the famous monograph authored by Frank Vogel and Samuel Hayes titled *Islamic Law and Finance: Religion, risk and return*.

Lastly, a number of courses have been offered regularly at Harvard Law School dealing with Islamic contracts and other related areas.

1. *The IFP Databank*: Academic research often involves the dual task of data collection and systematic analysis. The Harvard Islamic Finance Information Program (HIFIP) has sought to further research in IF, IE and related *Shari'ah* issues at both ends of this process. The IFP's first major undertaking at Harvard was the development of the IFP DataBank, the then most comprehensive database of the IF services industry. The IFP continues to manage and develop the Publications, *Shari'ah* and Glossary components of this database, now as the IFP DataBank on the Project's website. Over 10,000 original records can be accessed free of charge by researchers from around the world.

   In the field of IF and investment, information is scattered across various sources and is not easily accessible. In fact, information is largely unavailable to most researchers because it comes from primary contacts in the industry and is published privately or obscurely. This difficulty hampered the Islamic Investment Study conducted during 1994–8 by Frank Vogel of Harvard Law School and Samuel L. Hayes III of Harvard Business School. The experience that emerged from this difficulty provided the driving idea behind the creation of the IFP DataBank in 1995: to provide a comprehensive resource that was universally accessible. In the 17 years of its existence, the IFP DataBank has become a well-established research tool and the largest source of information available to researchers worldwide on all aspects of IF.

A large proportion of IFP activity centres on the compilation, maintenance, and technical development of the IFP DataBank. Information in the DataBank is collected continuously by Harvard students who obtain primary and secondary sources of information on the field by scouring libraries, published government materials, Internet sources, and the 200 institutions in the IF field with which the IFP has contacts.

2. *Project website*: The IFP website (http://ifp.law.harvard.edu) is kept up-to-date with event notices and announcements. The website has been expanded to include summaries of and reports from important events such as the biannual Harvard University Forum on Islamic Finance, annual workshops, and specialized seminars, which can be downloaded from the website. The IFP is also in the process of providing access to full papers published from previous Forums.

Forums, seminars and other events

Harvard University Forum on Islamic Finance

The IFP has regularly organized and hosted the Harvard University Forum on Islamic Finance since 1997. It is unique among industry conferences for its academic aspect and its ability to bring together practitioners, academics and *Shari'ah* scholars in order to discuss and debate the direction of the industry.

The Harvard Forum grew during its ten conferences from a small one-day affair to a major multisession international conference that brings together the latest research in academia, contemporary developments in the industry, and leading analyses by academics and government officials. The IFP has published the proceedings from each Forum (with the exclusion of the first), serving as a resource for both scholars and professionals. As it has become more established, the Forum has also fostered a sense of community among researchers while promoting healthy debate and collaboration between academics, practitioners and institutions.

The Harvard Forum serves as a magnet for all types of individuals in the field of IF. Among the many attendees have been bankers, economists, *Shari'ah* scholars, financial analysts, attorneys, legal practitioners, management professionals, professors and students. On average, more than 200 people have attended each conference, with many others following the programme electronically and purchasing the proceedings.

The Forums, with their comprehensive approach to exploring the ideals, practice, and prospects of the industry, monitor the development of IF while analysing trends and future opportunities. The presentations have dealt with *Shari'ah* perspectives, investments and financial products, new opportunities and directions, and other aspects of economics, finance, and development. Forums have provided a broad range of resources including introductory programmes for newcomers and discussions of sensitive and critical issues such as Islamic jurisprudence, governmental regulation, product development, and ethics.

The IFP has remained committed to keeping the Forums as accessible as possible. The Forum has reduced registration fees for those with limited funds. A free and public presentation entitled 'Workshop on Islamic Finance for Newcomers' was also made available at the Fourth and Fifth Forums. The sessions aimed to introduce IF to those who had little or no prior exposure to the field. Beyond members of the Harvard community, other students and members of the Boston-area community have also been a significant presence at each Forum.

The Forum is also unique in devoting at least one entire session to *Shari'ah*, or Islamic law. Every year, jurists in *fiqh al-mu'amalat* (the branch of Islamic law dealing with economic and financial matters) have addressed the Forum audience and presented papers. Other sessions have covered IE, IF, and the practice of IF by financial institutions. In 2006, the Roundtable was established as a biannual event. The IFP has since introduced a specialized session on Current Academic Research in Islamic Finance, to further encourage graduate students to present papers based on a recently completed Doctoral or Master's thesis in IE and IF.

Previous forums are listed next and the details of these forums may be found online at http://ifp.law.harvard.edu/login/conference:

- Tenth Harvard University Forum on Islamic Finance: Islamic Finance and Development (2012)
- Ninth Harvard University Forum on Islamic Finance: Building Bridges Across Financial Communities (2010)
- Eighth Harvard University Forum on Islamic Finance: Innovation and Authenticity (2008)
- Seventh Harvard University Forum on Islamic Finance: Integrating Islamic Finance in the Mainstream – Regulation, Standardization and Transparency (2006)
- Sixth Harvard University Forum on Islamic Finance: Islamic Finance: Current Legal and Regulatory Issues (2004)
- Fifth Harvard University Forum on Islamic Finance: Islamic Finance: Dynamics and Development (2002)
- Fourth Harvard University Forum on Islamic Finance: Islamic Finance: The Task Ahead (2000)

- Third Harvard University Forum on Islamic Finance: Local Challenges, Global Opportunities (1999)
- Second Harvard University Forum on Islamic Finance: Islamic Finance into the 21st Century (1998)
- First Harvard University Forum on Islamic Finance: Islamic Finance in the Global Market (1997)

Harvard–London School of Economics Workshops

The IFP, in partnership with the LSE, has been organizing specialized workshops and public lectures on methodological issues confronting the IF industry on a yearly basis since 2007. The principal impetus for these workshops is to fill the conversational void between two of the professional groups integral to the evolution of IF: *Shari'ah* scholars and Islamic economists. The workshops also bring other partners, legal experts, regulators and industry leaders who are involved in day-to-day operations. Six workshops have been held in the past on a variety of issues: Islamic Financial Intermediation: Revisiting the Value Proposition Workshop (2012); Reappraising the Islamic Financial Sector (2011); Islamic Financial Ethics and Ethical Governance (2010); The Evolution of the Global Financial System from the Current Crisis (2009); Risk Management: Islamic Economic and Ethico-Legal Perspective on Risk Management (2009); Microfinance: Toward a Sustainable Islamic Finance Model (2008); Sukuk: Economic and Jurisprudential Perspectives (2008); and TAWARRUQ: A Methodological Issue in Shari'a-Compliant Finance (2007). Details of these workshops may also be found online at the IFP website (http:/ifp.law.harvard.edu/login/conference).

Public lectures

The LSE has hosted public lectures on IF with the IFP's assistance since 2007. The purpose of these public lectures is to create a better understanding of IF and to educate people about the misconceptions surrounding the IF industry. A total of six public lectures have been held on various topics, including Global Calls for Economic Justice: The Potential for Islamic Finance (2012); Building Bridges Across Financial Communities (2011); Global Perspective on Islamic Finance (2010); Islamic Finance in the United Kingdom: Current Initiatives and Challenges (2009); Advancements in Contemporary Islamic Finance: From Practice to Scholarship (2008); Islamic Finance: Relevance and Growth in the Modern Financial Age (2007); and Corporate Responsibility and Ethical Investment (2003). Detailed reports of these lectures may be found online at the IFP website (http:/ifp.law.harvard.edu/login/conference).

Information sessions with Islamic Finance student groups

Since 1998, the IFP has also organized one to two information sessions each year for members of the Harvard community interested in IB and finance in general and in the IFP in particular. At its office, the IFP holds informal discussions with students from Harvard College, the Graduate School of Arts and Sciences, the Business School, the Law School, and other Harvard institutions. As a resource for novices in IF, the IFP further organizes a workshop introducing newcomers to the basics of IF. This workshop has been traditionally offered during the IFP biannual Forum. This effort has expanded to provide more workshops focused on current academic research in IF.

Press services

The IFP has provided information on IF to the press, resolving misconceptions and raising awareness of developments in the industry. Media outlets with which the IFP has had contact over the years include *Fortune*, *Gulf Daily News*, *Islamic Banker*, National Public Radio, Reuters, and *The Wall Street Journal*.

Specialized courses on Islamic Finance and law

While no official degree or certification programmes for IF studies are currently available at Harvard, Harvard Law School (HLS) continues to offer a number of relevant courses. HLS has been at the cutting edge of IF research and teaching with a tradition of inquiry in the field spanning over a decade. The first course to mark this interest in IF at Harvard was offered in 1996 under the guidance of Professor Frank Vogel. The following courses have been offered throughout the years: Regulation of Islamic Finance; Islamic Contract Law; Introduction to Islamic Law; Comparative Law: The Islamic Legal System; Contemporary Islamic Legal Thought: Law, State, and World Order; Concept of Obligation in Islamic Law; Fatwas and Muftis; and Topics in Islamic Law.

The most recent addition to the list of courses offered at HLS has been Regulation of Islamic Finance, a seminar course focusing on the role of IF in the financial markets of nearly every country. In the first few weeks of the seminar, the course focuses on the Islamic legal rules at the heart of IF to understand how the twin prohibitions of *riba* (often translated as interest) and excessive risk serve as the foundations of the industry. After learning these basics, the course studies the place of IF in major markets worldwide, including in the US, England, France, and countries in the Middle East and Asia. The in-depth country-by-country approach of the course considers the details of each market, including the volume and types of products, the players on the demand and supply sides, and the regulatory framework. It also examines international IF standard-setting and regulatory bodies, as well as the crucial role of *Shari'ah* scholars.

Further, HLS has spearheaded efforts to offer seminars taught by visiting professors. Among the many classes available, a course on synthetic transactions was offered at HLS by Shaykh Nizami, Dars fi-Nawazil Fiqh al-Mu'amalat. The course focused on issues surrounding the legality of synthesizing financial transactions that have been debated by Muslim jurists (*fuqaha'*, singular *faqih*) throughout the history of Islamic law. Since *Shari'ah*-compliant financial institutions typically use alternative financial instruments that are combinations of themselves composition of simpler contracts (such as sales and leases), the legality of synthesizing (i.e. combining) financial transactions is of profound significance in application of contemporary IF law.

At the Harvard Business School (HBS), a seminar course was offered on the Principle of Islamic Finance. In this seminar, students were introduced to the theory and practice of IF, and the set of financial concepts, solutions and service providers that conform to the principles of IF ethics. Through discussions of the key concepts, techniques and institutions in the field as well as analysis of case studies of several important entities and transactions in the IF sector, students were able to acquire a sound foundation in the field as well as become well-prepared to pursue more advanced study of IF in the future, either as practitioners or informed observers.

In conjunction with various Harvard institutions, the IFP has also contributed to the development of IF curricula at other institutions of higher learning. At the Faculty of Arts and Sciences, the following courses containing a small IE component have been offered in the recent years: Ottoman Legal History; Islamic Legal Theory; Studies in Islamic Law: Early Sunni Legal Doctrine; Texts in Islamic Theology and Law; and Readings in Modernist Islamic Law.

Research and publications

Research

The IFP supports scholars at Harvard and beyond in their research on IF services. It also provides researchers and economists with access to its vast store of information. Researchers throughout the world are encouraged to contact the IFP to obtain resources. Financial professionals have also requested and received information from the IFP on matters ranging from *Shari'ah* issues to the engineering of financial services. The IFP director has served as an academic advisor to several student projects, and is the first point of contact for any number of research requests or media queries. The IFP has also hosted visiting scholars from outside institutions to support their research in the field.

Student researchers

The IFP has employed an average of about a dozen students a year, drawing mainly from the student body at Harvard College. Students from the Harvard graduate schools and neighbouring institutions such as Massachusetts Institute of Technology (MIT), Tufts University, Brandeis University, Northeastern University, and Boston University have also contributed. These students have carried out the task of compiling and updating the IFP DataBank and have been integral to the organization of each Forum. The IFP has also utilized volunteers from Harvard College, Harvard Business School, and HLS to compile and edit the proceedings that are issued following each Forum. Current and former IFP student associates form a network of academics and professionals within and without IF that strengthen the presence of the IFP in the field.

Islamic Investment Study

The Islamic Investment Study began in 1993 and culminated in the publication of *Islamic Law and Finance: Religion, Risk, and Return* by Frank Vogel and Samuel Hayes. This study was sponsored by several financial institutions including the National Commercial Bank (Saudi Arabia), the Islamic Development Bank (Saudi Arabia), Wellington Management Company (Boston), and Goldman Sachs (London). The study indicated increasing interest at Harvard in the study of IF. By attracting and centralizing resources, the IFP helped cultivate this surge in interest and has helped to establish Harvard as a leader in Islamic studies.

Visiting research scholars programme

The IFP supports research in IB and IF by providing visiting scholars access to Harvard University's vast resources, which include dozens of libraries, hundreds of periodicals, and millions of books. The Visiting Research Scholars Program invites prominent researchers in the field to Harvard under the IFP's auspices and provides them with the opportunity to complete their research. The IFP's first visiting scholar was Muhammed-Shahid Ebrahim, presently of Bangor University. While at the IFP during the summer of 1997, he published two papers on financial engineering in IF. As a visiting scholar at the ILSP in 1998, Gohar Bilal also conducted research at the IFP and helped organize the Second Harvard University Forum on Islamic Finance. She analysed Islamic tradable instruments and published an article titled 'Islamic Finance: Alternatives to the Western model' (1999). Finally, in 2001, Omar Kamal was a visiting researcher at the IFP while writing his Doctoral dissertation. S. Nazim Ali, director of the IFP, served as the external advisor for his thesis.

Harvard Business School

The IFP has assisted the Islamic Club at the HBS to organize several seminars since 2000. These seminars were intended to introduce IF as a subject of academic interest as well as to provide an opportunity for HBS students conducting research on IF and allied fields to network and share their ideas. Various case studies and research projects in the field of IF have been developed at the HBS. These research projects and case studies have explored a range of issues facing the industry. A list of these publications may be found in Appendix C. In the Winter 2010 term, a seminar course on IF Principle was offered. In this seminar students were introduced to the theory and practice of IF, including the set of financial concepts, solutions and service providers that conform to the principles of IF ethics.

Publications

Proceedings of the Harvard University Forum on Islamic Finance

In September 1999, the IFP published the proceedings of the Second Harvard University Forum on Islamic Finance, a landmark publication with over 30 original works covering IE, *Shari'ah*, IF, commercial products, and business models. The compilation of the proceedings was the work of IFP research associates, mostly students from Harvard University and especially Harvard College. This volume held the distinction of being the first complete proceedings of a conference on IF. Over the next few years, the IFP regularly published the proceedings of the Forum, adding scholarly introductions and an extensive index to the papers presented. Each volume has highlighted some of the most important developments in the field and served as a valuable resource for industry leaders as well as scholars. The academic papers presented at IFP events introduce some of the latest research in the field. A list of notable examples may be found in Appendix A.

Theses and dissertations at Harvard

Several students at Harvard Law School have written their Doctoral dissertations on topics related to IF. Four such students include Ayesha Khan, Kristin Smith, Walid Hegazy, Fatimah Iliasu and Aida Othman. A selected list of original contributions by Harvard affiliates at various departments at Harvard may be found in Appendix B.

Islamic Finance Project relationships

Harvard community support

Although the Project has never played a formal role in Harvard University's curriculum, it has assisted individual faculty members at the Faculty of Arts and Sciences, Law, Business, and Kennedy Schools with their research and teaching on an ad hoc basis. Faculty and students have used the Program's resources for their own research. It has also provided information access, informal advice, and guidance on thesis research to students from the Law and Business Schools and the Departments of Economics, Government, and History.

The Law School in particular has extended considerable support to the IFP. Under the auspices of the ILSP, the IFP has hosted fellows on a yearly basis who have consistently found the IFP to be a great resource in their research. In addition, the Law School a module in Islamic contracts since 1995 and, more recently, a fully-fledged seminar course on Islamic Finance Regulation. A number of students have completed research papers and theses on IF-related fields and have been supervised by senior Law School professors.

At the HBS, several faculty members have taken part in the biennial Islamic Finance Forum, especially Professor Emeritus Samuel L. Hayes, III. Several seminars have been sponsored and organized by the Business School Islamic Club on IF as a subject of academic interest and a field offering a number of career opportunities for MBA students.

At the Faculty of Arts and Sciences, students from the CMES and Departments of Near Eastern Languages and Civilizations, Economics and Government have found IFP resources to be helpful for their research.

Students at the Harvard Kennedy School have shown an interest in the IFP, especially with regard to policy, regulation, political economy and socially conscious investment. In the past, students have utilized the IFP for research on relevant public policy and governance issues.

At the Divinity School, a number of students and faculty members have had an interest in social, ethical, and faith-based investment.

The Project has also worked with various libraries including Langdell at HLS, Widener Library, and Baker Library in building their collections. These libraries have largely viewed the IFP DataBank as an invaluable research tool and have featured it as part of their research and information services.

Finally, the IFP has received continuous assistance from members of Harvard Islamic Society (HIS), who have helped in the organization of each Forum by providing logistical support. A number of undergraduate members of the Society have also taken an interest in the Project and often become student researchers during their college careers.

IFP and the regulators

The Project has worked to bridge the gap between institutions and governmental regulatory bodies by encouraging their engagement in the IF industry through various seminars and workshops. The Project has answered inquiries relating to IF from the US Treasury, and has in the past conducted two seminars at the Treasury for its staff, members of the executive branch, and Congressional staff. United States Treasury Undersecretary John Taylor was the keynote speaker of the Sixth Harvard University Forum on Islamic Finance in 2004 on 'Understanding and Supporting Islamic Finance: Product Differentiation and International Standards'.

The IFP has also hosted a workshop on the Supervision and Regulation of Islamic Finance Institutions in the United States that was held on 19 March 2005 at the Harvard Law School. This workshop was key in placing IF institutions face to face with relevant US regulators. The purpose of the seminar was to initiate discussions between IF institutions and regulators about the current and future supervision and regulation of the IF industry in the United States. There were over 40 representatives present from various government agencies such as the Securities and Exchange Commission (SEC), the Federal Deposit Insurance Corporation (FDIC), the Federal Reserve Board (FRB), and the Office of the Comptroller of the Currency (OCC), along with almost all institutions providing IF products and services in the US and abroad. A full report of the event may be found online at http://ifptest.law.harvard.edu/ifphtml/index.php?module=WorkshopReport01.

The IFP has also worked with the Federal Reserve Bank of New York (FRBNY) to organize an interagency forum on IB in the United States, held in March 2006. The purpose of this meeting was to advance the discussion of regulatory issues relating to IB.

IFP has also invited governors of several central banks to its biennial events to discuss relevant issues and regional advancement.

IFP and the Islamic Financial Industry

The IFP has taken a proactive role in collaborative research and industry-building efforts with other institutions. By educating regulators and connecting them to IF institutions, bringing together senior *Shari'ah* scholars and Muslim economists for a constructive engagement on critical issues, and cosponsoring events with other universities wherever possible, the IFP has sought to bring diverse constituencies and institutions closer together in the interest of the industry. One of the IFP's greatest assets has been the involvement and support it enjoys from individuals in the IF industry. The Program has further interacted with the IF community through its involvement with specific research projects, seminars, committee representations, the IFP Endowment drive, other IFP fundraising events, and the industry recruitment of Harvard students.

The Project maintains a balance between academic and industry-related interactions. Its links with the financial world have also increased the number of financial resources available to it. The IFP's position in the academic community has allowed the programme to participate in the creation of new products and services in the IF industry, while introducing the industry to original academic research.

Other institutions

The IFP has remained in contact with most Western institutions involved in research on IF. These have included departments and programmes within formal academic institutions, research and legal advisory departments of commercial financial institutions, and non-governmental organizations (NGOs) such as the Islamic Development Bank, Organization of Islamic Cooperation (OIC), Accounting and Auditing Organization for Islamic Financial Institutions (AAOIFI), the Islamic Finance Services Board (IFSB), the International Islamic Financial Market (IIFM), the International Monetary Fund (IMF), and the World Bank.

The IFP has sought to assemble the various research bodies and information service providers within the IF community at the International Research Roundtable in an effort to increase coordination, avoid duplication, and enhance the efficiency and synergy of the sector's research and development.

Internships

The IFP has organized internships and travel opportunities for its student researchers at numerous IF institutions and other firms, facilitating and furthering the education of its student staff. Several institutions have contacted the IFP in order to extend internship opportunities to IFP researchers.

Career opportunities

The IFP's extensive research network and industry-building efforts have positioned it as a key resource to help industry institutions identify promising candidates. In addition to informal career guidance, IFP has also organized career seminars at both HLS and HBS to cultivate interest in the field.

IFP affiliates have developed competence in a variety of relevant fields – business, corporate law and *Shari'ah* compliance – and have gone on to work with some of the most prominent institutions in the IF services industry, including the Islamic Development Bank, Al Baraka, HSBC Amanah, Citibank, ABN Amro and Deutsche Bank.

The future: Coordinating new developments

The IFP sees an especially important role for itself in the coordination of new initiatives in two areas: research and information technology. Although various research centres around the world are doing important work, no centralized registrar of novel developments exists, and there is much duplication of effort. The IF industry could benefit if developments in conventional economic and financial fields could be adapted and applied to IE and IF. The IFP is ideally placed to coordinate new research in IF and to serve as a contact nexus for researchers from around the world. The academic richness of Harvard affords the Project credibility that will be vital in convoking the disparate participants in IF research.

Training the leaders of the future

Every year, Harvard attracts many of the brightest students from around the world, a number of whom express interest in pursuing careers in IF. The Project has enabled many students to explore internship and recruitment opportunities in the IB sector, and has also placed several former associates in full-time positions in the industry.

The Project has held annual information sessions for students from the Faculty of Arts and Sciences, the Law School, and the Business School, at which attendees were introduced to the basics of IF, the workings and resources of the Project, and the latest developments in the field.

The IFP has sought to train future leaders in the field of IF. It has assumed the role of creating courses, internships, and fellowships centred around IF, at Harvard and beyond. The IFP has also sought to connect interested young students with scholars and practitioners to facilitate mentoring and guidance. The IFP's connections to the academic community of Harvard and the IF community around the world put it in a position to actualize these goals.

Friends of the IFP

The IFP has crossed paths with innumerable students and scholars, many of them affiliated with Harvard. After their departure from Harvard, many of these individuals have retained their interest in IF and have served as ambassadors of IFP in their later endeavours.

Many IFP student associates have continued to be involved with IFP activities after graduation. They have edited papers for the proceedings, suggested topics for the Forum, given advice on Project strategy, answered industry-related inquiries, collected information, and acted as liaisons between the Project and the IF industry at large. Regular communication and periodic face-to-face meetings have kept graduating students connected to the Project.

Conclusion

Rapid progress in the field of IE and IF services demands a critical look at the theory and mechanisms that have made *Shari'ah*-compliant economics possible. Such need for inquiry retains great importance within the field of IF at large, within both industry and academia. Through its intricate relationship with Islamic law and its quest to attain *Shari'ah* compliance, IF and its study traverse a number of spheres of intellectual discipline and scholarly thought. Founded in 1995, the IFP of Harvard University has played a significant role in the field of IF for over a decade. The Project does so in one of the richest settings for the study of IF and IE in the field, at a university with one of the highest numbers of scholars and programmes specializing in Islam and the Muslim world.

By promoting research and development in the field, developing the IFP DataBank, encouraging continued dialogue between the Islamic and non-Islamic worlds, fostering faculty and student interest by sponsoring conferences, workshops and courses on IF, and assisting governmental bodies seeking to understand the principles of IF, the IFP has played a key role in the field. HLS continues to be instrumental in inspiring discussions among the IF experts through its numerous forums, initiatives and workshops. The Project has further collaborated with the LSE and other Harvard institutions such as HLS and HBS to provide informative events for communities. The IFP considers the LSE Workshop in particular as a major forum for *Shari'ah* scholars and Islamic economists to come together to discuss the most pressing issues faced by the industry. Additionally, the Project aims to address IF issues by bringing Microfinance Providers and IF industry experts together so that individuals from both fields can learn and take advantage of each other's unique experiences. Finally, the IFP has placed a considerable emphasis on supporting students interested in the field. As one of the first programmes of its kind, IFP has sought to create a discursive space for IF academia and practitioners.

IF and IE remains a small portion of the broader financial industry and its impact is still relatively limited. Based on IFP's 17 years of experience, we believe that the lack of social relevance in the offering of IF products presents an immediate need. There remain valid concerns over the tangible advances IF has made towards societal equality in the economic system. These concerns highlight the need to close the gap between industry and academia. Through its efforts to coordinate new knowledge, host collaborative seminars, and shepherd the next generation of practitioners during their college careers, the IFP hopes to create a sustainable dialogue uniting disparate interests and efforts. We further aim to promote faith-based investing, socially responsible investing, and IF and hope that these three sectors can share their experiences and learn from each other. Ideally, such efforts will be replicated in other institutions of higher learning across the world and particularly in the West.

Appendix A: List of books

Balz, K. (2008) *Sharia Risk? How Islamic Finance has Transformed Islamic Contract Law*, 9, September (Occasional Publications).

Bilal, G. (1999) 'Islamic Finance: Alternatives to the Western model', *Fletcher Forum of World Affairs*, 23, 11, pp. 145–59.

Building Bridges across Financial Communities: The Global Financial Crisis, Social Responsibility, and Faith-Based Finance (Cambridge, MA: Harvard Law School, 2012).

Integrating Islamic Finance into the Mainstream: Regulation, Standardization, and Transparency (Cambridge, MA: Harvard Law School, Islamic Finance Project, 2007).

Islamic Finance: Current Legal and Regulatory Issues (Cambridge, MA: Harvard Law School, Islamic Finance Project, 2005).

Islamic Finance: Dynamics and Development: Proceedings of the Fifth Harvard University on Islamic Finance (Cambridge, MA: Centre for Middle Eastern Studies, Harvard University, 2003).

Islamic Finance: Innovation and Authenticity (Cambridge, MA: Harvard Law School, Islamic Finance Project, 2010).

Islamic Finance: Local Challenges, Global Opportunities: Proceedings of the Third Harvard University Forum on Islamic Finance (Cambridge, MA: Centre for Middle Eastern Studies, Harvard University, 2000).

Islamic Finance: The Task Ahead: Proceedings of the Fourth Harvard University Forum on Islamic Finance (Cambridge, MA: Centre for Middle Eastern Studies, Harvard University, 2002).

Islamic Finance into the 21st Century: Proceedings of the Second Harvard University Forum on Islamic Finance (Cambridge, MA: Centre for Middle Eastern Studies, Harvard University, 1999).

Shari'a-Compliant Microfinance (London: Routledge, 2011).

Vogel, F. E. and Hayes, S. L. (1998) *Islamic Law and Finance: Religion, Risk, and Return* (Boston, MA: Kluwer Law International).

Appendix B: List of theses accepted at Harvard

Binladen, A. M. (1992) 'Western banking practices and Shari'a law in Saudi Arabia', LLM thesis, Harvard Law School.

—— (2000) 'Negotiability of financial instruments in contemporary financial markets: An Islamic legal analysis', S.J.D. thesis, Harvard Law School.

Cisse, H. (1990) 'Leasing in Islamic banking and in the Unidroit Convention on International Financial Leasing: A comparative analysis', LLM thesis, Harvard Law School.

El-Torgoman, S. (1990) 'Islamic investment funds in Egypt', LLM thesis, Harvard Law School.

Guité, D. (2008) 'From radical Islam to "smoke and mirrors": The trajectory of Islamic finance and its effects on religious belief', BA thesis, Harvard College.

Khalife, M. (2004) 'Islamic banking in Lebanon: Remarks on the new law no. 575 dated February 11, 2004 on the establishment of Islamic banks', LLM thesis, Harvard Law School.

Khan, A. K. (2010) 'Essays on faith and finance', D.B.A. thesis, Harvard Business School.

Mian, K. M. A. (1997) 'Mudaraba, theory and practice: A case study of the Mudaraba institution in Pakistan', LLM Thesis, Harvard Law School.

Mohamed, A. H. (2001) 'Islamic finance as a tool of micro enterprise development in Sub-Saharan Africa', LLM thesis, Harvard Law School.

Montasser, H. E. E. D. (1997) 'Financial innovation in Islamic finance', A.B. thesis, Harvard College.

Musa, T. A. (2010) 'Islamic banking and the financial crisis: Shari'ah compliance and bank stability in the Arab Gulf', A.B. Hons thesis, Harvard College.

Othman, A. (2005) 'And Sulh is best: Amicable settlement and dispute resolution in Islamic law', Ph.D. thesis, Centre for Middle Eastern Studies, Faculty of Arts and Sciences.

Saffari, S. (1997) 'On the rollercoaster of development: Banking and economic growth in Iran under the Pahlavis and the Islamic republic', Ph.D. thesis, Faculty of Arts and Sciences.

Shakil, M. (2004) 'Islamic banking, risk analysis and the impact of Basel II on its future', LLM thesis, Harvard Law School.

Smith, K. (2004) 'Economic integration and cultural resistance: Islamic finance in the Arab Gulf', Ph.D. thesis, Faculty of Arts and Sciences.

Somane, M. (2011) 'Corporate governance in Islamic finance, promises and pit falls: An analysis of Islamic banking corporate governance vis a vis conventional banking', LLM Thesis, Harvard Law School.

Voliva, R. L. (2000) 'Al-Shari'a and monetary policy: Practices and results', A.B. Thesis, Harvard College.

Yasini, A. S. (2010) 'Mudaraba as a mode of Islamic finance: Challenges and opportunities', LLM thesis, Harvard Law School.

Yousef, T. M. (1997) 'Essays in 20th century Middle Eastern economic development', Ph.D. thesis, Faculty of Arts and Sciences.

Appendix C: Harvard Business School case studies

Esty, B. C. and Millett, M. M. (1999) 'International Investor: Islamic Finance and the Equate Project', Harvard Business School Case 200-012.

Esty, B. C. and Millett, M. M. (1999) 'International Investor: Islamic Finance and the Equate Project TN', Harvard Business School Teaching Note 200-013.

Esty, B. C., Millett, M. M. and Qureshi, F. (1999)'An Introduction to Islamic Finance', Harvard Business School Note 200-002.

Esty, B. C. and Sesia, A. (2004) 'Aluminium Bahrain (Alba): The Pot Line 5 Expansion Project', Harvard Business School Case 205-027.

Esty, B. C. and Sesia, A. (2004) 'Aluminium Bahrain (Alba): The Pot Line 5 Expansion Project (CW)', Harvard Business School Spreadsheet Supplement 205–708.

Esty, B. C. and Sesia, A. (2004) 'Aluminium Bahrain (Alba): The Pot Line 5 Expansion Project (TN)', Harvard Business School Teaching Note.

19
Islamic Finance in Sorbonne

Kader Merbouh and Pierre-Charles Pradier

Introduction

Sorbonne University was created in 1253 as a Theology faculty, and as early as 1270, Aquinas was lecturing about Ibn Roshd's philosophy. While the academic commitment to studying Muslim economic and moral philosophy may have fluctuated (especially during the early modern era) in line with the intellectual trends or the political agenda, there has been a steady interest over the last 40 years. During this late period, our research centres such as IRBIMMA (Research Institute for Byzantium, Islam and the Mediterranean during the Middle Ages) have hosted leading scholars in Islamic Studies. Not surprisingly, the perspective of developing Islamic Finance (IF) attracted much attention and sympathy with Paris 1 Panthéon-Sorbonne: together with our research federation (the PRES héSam), we are pursuing a prudent agenda aimed at structuring research and professional continuing education. This chapter features an overview of our first educational experience, our joint research strategy and future plans.

1253–2011: Nothing to declare?

Until 2011, there was no specific course of Islamic Finance (IF) at Paris 1 Panthéon-Sorbonne University. This is not to say that the students were not taught contents in IF, only that the topic was not given full visibility through the branding of an elective or core course. Contents could then be found in economic history (Master's in Medieval Mediterranean World, Professor Françoise Micheau), law (Master's in Law in Arabic Countries, Professor Ali Mezghani or Droit Financier with Professor Alain Couret), economics (Master's in Finance, Professor Christian de

229

Boissieu). All of these Master's programmes featured an introduction to IF in a more general course, hence the students with a specific interest in this matter could focus on it and write a term paper or a dissertation about it. Some even carried over for a Ph.D. Other higher education institutions from PRES héSam had the same policy; one notable exception was ESCP-Europe.

ESCP-Europe is one of the leading business schools in Europe and a founding member of PRES héSam. With a partner institution in Beirut (Lebanon) named Ecole Supérieure des Affaires (ESA), it set up a Master's in Finance in 1995 which has featured a strong IF component since 1997. Originally run by Franck Bancel, the programme was backed by Geneviève Causse-Broquet, one of the now leading French academics in IF. With the support of the Central Bank of Lebanon and the overall financial sector, the programme has proved very successful to date. The experience gained with this ESA Master's programme proved crucial in fine-tuning our overall strategy as it provided us with both the scientific expertise and a clear assessment of the market potential in Europe and the Middle East and North Africa region. It clearly became obvious that the potential of IF remains not fully realized in Europe: for this reason, Paris 1 Panthéon-Sorbonne University decided to focus first on research with worldwide visibility.

Since 2008 there has been a lot of media attention in France about IF. While the concept is receiving full support from the strong Muslim community, most French authorities do not dare to embody any new 'Islamic' institution. The topic thus appears as emotional and sensitive as in the United States of America, with a tacit rule that can be summarized as 'do whatever you like outside France'. The financial community has advocated that the development of IF could bring €100 billion and solve the crisis, but this has not been enough to convince the politicians to change their reserved stance. The consensus is still that no law should be passed to accommodate IF; all the legal compatibility issues should be resolved using 'tax instructions' which is the least kind of legal text. The same applies with French banks and insurance companies: they run Islamic subsidiaries (BNPParibas Najmah or Scor Retakaful in Labuan, Société Générale has even an Islamic subsidiary in Réunion Island, a French offshoot in the Indian Ocean) outside metropolitan areas to avoid 'image risk'.

Some pioneers nevertheless attempted to develop both educational and research programmes. Strasbourg (see Chapter 15 in this volume) and Dauphine Universities attracted fame and media coverage for their accomplishments. In the research arena, the Forums of Islamic

Finance (in 2008 and 2009) led to the creation of an Institut Français de Finance Islamique, which appears a stillborn. The 'Islamic finance axis' targeted academic research. This subgroup will be having is fifth workshop in October 2012 at Sorbonne University: research is now working steadily. Let us have a look at the consolidated balance sheet.

2012: Assessment

The strategy at Paris 1 Panthéon-Sorbonne University has been to focus on developing research until the IF sector or our own network become significant enough to provide jobs for our alumni. At the moment, we are addressing three different domains: IF is studied mostly from a professional and operational point of view, while Islamic Economics (IE) has strong connections with social economics and corporate social responsibility. There is also an interest in the socio-anthropology of the Muslim revival.

Operational Islamic Finance

Paris 1 Panthéon-Sorbonne has a strong record in finance: the Master's programme of Professor Christian de Boissieu is leading the pack in France, with Boissieu himself being a leading economist (he is president of the prime minister's Council for Economic Analysis, CAE) and a supervisor (member of the leading market authority ACP). This strong academic and institutional position of our leader enabled the creation in 2010, together with PRES héSam partners, of the Financial Regulation Laboratory, which was awarded by the ministry of research an excellence prize in April 2011. This LabEx ReFi now features an IF research group, teaming together academics from Conservatoire National des Arts et Metiers (CNAM) (Aldo Levy), ESCP-Europe (Michael Tröge) and Paris 1 Panthéon-Sorbonne (Pierre-Charles Pradier). As the website shows, there have been events about IF regulation organized by the Laboratoire d'Excellence sur la régulation financiére (financial regulation lab) (LabEx), such as a breakfast for industry professionals, a policy paper and a regular update via the LabEx Newsletter. The LabEx has strong links with the industry via Europlace, the representative NGO: we have been working since 2010 on the translation of the AAOIFI norms into French, as well as participating in the IF panel of the Paris Financial Industry.

At the same time, Paris 1 Panthéon-Sorbonne was having talks to create a joint research chair with King Abdulaziz University in

Jeddah. A memorandum of understanding was signed in January 2011. Since May 2011, seminars have been held every month every month through videoconferencing between Paris and Jeddah with both the Ladies Department and the Islamic Economics Institute. The chair was launched officially on 30 November 2011 and the year 2012 is showing significant results. On the one hand, the international network is expanding with IE Business School in Madrid and INCEIF in Kuala Lumpur joining the monthly video seminar. Partnership is expanding to include Durham and Reading Universities in the UK, Geneva Business School in Switzerland, the Université Libre de Bruxelles and the Law Faculty of the Université de Luxembourg, and partner universities in Tunisia (Sfax, Tunis), all featuring a strong interest in IF. On the other hand, the scientific activities are covering the full range of academic activities:

- Doctoral scholarships were offered via a call for projects released in May
- The first volume of a collection hosted by the Institut de Recherches Juridiques de la Sorbonne Editions will be published in early June
- The Chair is jointly organizing the Sfax Islamic Finance Forum in late June
- A workshop titled 'Frontiers of Finance' is organized together with the Centre National de la Recherche Scientifique in October
- A congress exploring alternate state financing is ready for November, featuring a regulator's club and industry forum.

The research in IF now clearly concentrates on legal aspects, with two dissertations already passed and some more under way (although they are still 'first-generation' dissertations comprising very general inquiries with a comprehensive approach). Two publications in ISI Journals were made, 1 in 2011 (HMS), 1 in 2012 (MCdF) under the chair's signature. It is expected that the two scholarships will fuel new publications and create more visibility.

The rising operational efficiency of the research group and the growing network gathered momentum for IF. Critical size as well as recognized expertise has been attained, hence one full Master's course will be offered next year as an elective available to all students of the Master's programme that feature some financial content. The course will be given by Sir Joseph Connolly, clinical professor at Fordham University, with leading experience in IF (as a founder of both Citi Islamic and Noriba banks, and a member of Institute of Islamic

Banking and Insurance (IIBI) in London). The aim of this collaboration is to help find jobs in the IF industry in either Switzerland (Noriba was a subsidiary of UBS), London or the Gulf, where there is a significant job market. The course has an unambiguous operational orientation that is backed by significant sessions with the monthly research seminar. This is the area where cooperation between mainstream researchers and Islamic scholars is the easiest as the contributions are symmetric.

Islamic Economics

IE is something difficult to grasp for French scholars, who mostly think secularity to be part of academic freedom. It is true that, for centuries, the Université de Paris being a clerical institution has exerted wild censorship on its 'deviant' members. Albeit these times are over, it is still uncomfortable for the French to mix up religion together with academia (one notable exception is Strasbourg, that was part of the German Reich when the 'separation law' was passed in 1905, hence Theology remains an academic discipline in the Alsatian city to this day). Solving that sort of misunderstanding is thus one of the aims of the joint chair for ethic and financial norms. One can judge how successfully this task was accomplished by reading the questions and answers of the seminar papers by Islahi and Houssem Eddine Bedoui. It is then clear that IE has a strong connection with moral and social economics in the West; more generally, it could be seen as 'heterodoxical' in that it openly criticizes the mainstream utility/profit maximization hypothesis as this is done by, for instance, the Mouvement anti utilitariste en sciences sociales or Anti-utilitarian Movement in the Social Sciences (MAUSS) in France.

Not all research in social economy has to be heterodoxical. Some papers by Gunther Capelle-Blancard, professor of Economics with Paris 1 Panthéon-Sorbonne, show how one can explore the foundations of socially responsible economics without venturing into uncharted territory. The Chair for ethic and financial norms is then patrolling the borders of conventional economics, not to hunt down clandestine immigrants, but to provide pioneers with support in their trailblazing research work: Eddine Houssem Bedoui went to Harvard with a grant from the Chair in March 2012, and Marie Claret presented a paper at an İktisadi Girişim ve İş Ahlakı Derneği (IGIAD) conference on corporate social responsibility in Istanbul in April. The same pioneering spirit can be found in socio-anthropology.

Socio-anthropology of the Islamic revival

The Islamic revival has attracted attention in France, both in the political arena and in the academic world. While the first area appears vested with prejudice, researchers are very interested in the possible resemblance between social phenomena appearing all over the Islamic world and the Reformation in early modern Europe. The cultural change, linking together rationalization of religious and business life, the emergence of new business ethics and the modernization of the overall society might be of the same sort as Max Weber's celebrated 'spirit of capitalism' (the meaning of this expression being that there is suddenly a spiritual dimension arising inside capitalism). Mehmet Asutay advocated this parallel in a recent paper, and this will be the subject of a seminar with the famous Ecole des Hautes Etudes en Sciences Sociales – a member of PRES héSam: Rémy Madinier together with Gwenaël Njoto-Feillard and Pierre-Charles Pradier will organize 12 research sessions during the academic year 2012–13 about 'The New Muslim 'Spirit of Capitalism': Anthropological, political and sociological approaches to Islamic Economics'. The work is aimed at describing the changes in Muslim countries, and assessing both the discourse about facts and facts themselves, as well as the interpretative framework of the actors of the Muslim revival.

The seminar will look not just at IF, but at the big picture, featuring globalization of thought, as well as 'religious commodification', asking whether the Muslim revival is just another instance of Max Weber's rationalization, or just another 'moral economy' in Edward Thompson's words. Several questions need to be asked: Is there any correlation between the sector of 'salvation goods', which can be identified in many social forms, and the more straightforward IF? Does this phenomenon relate to a collapse towards closed identity or a drive towards integration of the Muslim populations into a globalized world? Now that many Arabian countries are embarking on the road to democracy, can we say that this 'market Islam' will favour the emergence of a new civility, as Methodism did in nineteenth-century America? Is there any ideal or structural links between these new Muslim predicators and the protagonists of the 'Gospel of prosperity' of the Protestant revival? Does cultural embeddedness action theory give a satisfactory account for all these phenomena? The questions will be addressed by the seminar participants, featuring invited researchers from around the world, as well as a volume that should be published by the Chair for Ethics and Financial Norms as a sequel.

The seminars with the EHESS are an elective available to any Master's or Doctoral student of the PRES héSam research federation. This seminar will hence be the grand debut of a Master's course and Doctoral school in the sociology of IE. Although this is already precisely planned, it remains something in the future. What about the other plans?

Development agenda 2013+

For the academic year 2012–13, our assessment of the IF sector in Europe remains the same: it has not reached a critical size such that we could launch a dedicated Master's degree, and there is no corresponding academic discipline to vindicate a dedicated Doctoral programme. But for the first year we will have an operational hub to meet the students' expectations. During the first year of their Master's studies, they will get an initiation course with the option to write a term paper. In the second year, they will be able to choose an elective taught by a professional with a strong background and network so that they can land a job in a country where the IF sector is significantly developed. Then, there are some clear possibilities to carry on Doctoral studies with a focus on IF in one of the following domains: Anthropology, Economics, Finance, History, Law, Management, Philosophy and Sociology. Of course, the students will be first anthropologists, economists, etc. and the Doctoral programmes are still training them so they can work as experts in their field of knowledge or attain academic recognition. They will nevertheless show an undeniable expertise in IF as Paris 1 Panthéon-Sorbonne has developed a network where scientific authorities are within reach, whether they work in KAU, INCEIF or Durham.

Future development should go along the same way. At a national level, our partnership with the industry will likely lead to continuing education for financial sector executives interested in IF: although growing demand is conditional on the political agenda. The time for authorizing retail banking and *takaful* companies, issuing *sukuk*, endorsing *Shari'ah*-compliant private-public partnership (PPP) schemes etc. will come. While the ripe fruits are maturing, we are expanding our network thanks to our wonderful friends at King Abdulaziz University: they have already reached such far-flung places as Japan, New England and Australia. We should thicken the European network as well as develop it in the Americas and sub-Saharan Africa. The creation of a UNESCO Chair might be contemplated, with the benevolent help of Georges Haddad, honorary president of Paris 1 Panthéon-Sorbonne and head of Education Research and Foresight with UNESCO: 'Research and Foresight' should be our motto.

The creation of the Financial Regulation Lab as well as the Chair for Ethics and Financial Norms exemplified how quickly ideas can shape the world when the time is right. While there was a huge social demand for the regulation of finance and the restoration of ethics after 30 years of deregulation and financial crises, researchers were on their own until new institutions enabled a crystallization of creative dynamics. So far, papers are being published at a slow rate, but attendance at seminars is strong, responses to calls for papers are numerous, and sympathy among students as well as the general public is simply immense. We are careful not to confuse enthusiasm with business opportunities; hence our teaching strategy is very conservative. This does not mean we are not confident in the future of IF: conventional finance has to be developed into socially responsible and sustainable schemes, so that finance will serve human development throughout the world. IF is a crucial part of the big picture. For now, we are committed to training good professionals and good researchers in classic academic disciplines with an indubitable expertise in IF. Together with our partner institutions, we are ready for more.

20
Islamic Banking and Finance Teaching and Supervision at Westminster Business School

Abdelhafid Benamraoui

Introduction

The aim of this chapter is to reflect on my own experience of teaching Islamic Banking (IB) and Finance (IF) and on supervising undergraduate, postgraduate and Ph.D. students in this subject area. The first part of the chapter deals with the main issues associated with the delivery of lectures and tutorials in this field of study. This includes a discussion of the different sources of materials used in preparing the lectures and seminar sessions, the methods applied in organizing the syllabuses covered in the lecture notes, the type of questions and case studies used in seminar sessions, the assessment methods and the feedback given to students. The second part of the chapter covers the learning methods adopted in supervising undergraduate, postgraduate and Ph.D. students undertaking their research project in the field of IF. This entails an analysis of the approach followed in guiding the students through their dissertations, my role as a supervisor, the main problems which emerge with students on various aspects of their research projects and the solutions implemented when a problem arises with the students, who are considered to be the centre of the learning process. Finally, a critical statement is made on the implications of the personal experience presented in this chapter by outlining what I see as a way forward in teaching and supervising students in this field of study.

This reflective commentary has five sections including the Introduction. The one after this examines the concept of reflection and how it is implemented in our reflective exercise. Section 3 evaluates the main issues related to the teaching of IB and IF themes. In Section 4 I discuss the concerns relevant to the supervision of research projects in the field of IB and IF. Section 5 addresses the implications of the reflective exercise on my own personal developments and what I see as the way forward for teaching and supervision in this subject area. Section 6 concludes the reflective commentary.

Reflection as a learning tool

Many scholars endorse the view that reflection is part of individual growth, but it needs to be carried out within a specific context. Raelin (2001) notes that reflection enables individuals to challenge their own ideas and therefore find new ways of understanding what in the past were regarded as given facts. Marsick and Watkins (1990) argue that reflection cannot lead to the desired results without applying the concepts in a real working environment. Gray (2007: 496) states that 'reflection is an active and purposeful process of exploration and discovery often leading to unexpected outcomes'.

Self-reflection involves the individual examining the problems faced during the course of his actions and their effects on his own perceptions and beliefs (Gray, 2007). The person also needs to be courageous and free from such influence when making the assessment of his work, as stated by Boyce (1996). This leads to new assumptions and expectations over the norms adopted in the past and enhances consciousness within the individual. As a consequence, the person makes informed judgments over his actions and takes his own responsibility in relation to the change in the quality of the work undertaken.

Reflection results in immediate or future actions as noted by Høyrup (2004). The implementation of such action makes the person reflecting think further about the process used and outcomes achieved through the application of his thoughts and ideas. Weick (2002) argues that reflection, as a learning model, contributes to a person judging his own belief and assumptions over his previous actions, which were perceived to be true. This entails looking at the origins of the held assumptions and their implications. Likewise, reflection on the supervision process also entails challenging one's own notion of the most effective ways of providing the appropriate guidance and feedback to students.

Reflection makes the individual reconsider his experientially based learning (Gray, 2007). This is evidenced in my approach to teaching and supervision as the learning tools and actions are questioned, making me think about new ways of improving the delivery of lessons and supervision of the research students in terms of attitude and knowledge exchange. The position of the lecturer as a facilitator of the learning process makes him accountable in ensuring that the right atmosphere is in place for interactions and knowledge creation (Moss and Kubacki, 2007).

In line with Reynolds (1999), the supervisor also takes into consideration the political and social aspects surrounding the research process, including culture and power. Therefore, in the reflective exercise the social factors influencing both the students and myself as a supervisor have been considered. This has enabled me to capture the change in the practice of managing our relationships. A similar approach was adopted in evaluating my relationship with other supervisors in the case of group supervision.

It is noted in previous research investigations that using reflection as part of one's own personal development has its advantages and constraints (e.g. Gray, 2007). In terms of benefits, reflection helps the person to be a critical thinker and enhances his own self-awareness (Varner and Peck, 2003). The constraints of reflection are of two kinds: (a) the possibility of being highly descriptive due to limited analyses; and (b) the cultural discomposure of individuals who are brought into societies where a person's attitude towards his work is not disclosed. To achieve better results in our reflection exercise, all these factors have been taken into account.

Teaching in the field of Islamic banking and finance

Many books and articles have been written on teaching conventional finance (e.g. Gow and Kember, 1993; Kane, Sandretto and Heath, 2002). However, limited attention has been paid to the teaching of IB and IF, which has grown both in terms of size and scope. Therefore, shedding a light on how IB and IF is currently taught, having a clear awareness of the possible problems that can be encountered by the lecturer(s) in meeting students' needs in this field, and devising a better approach to the way students are educated on IF themes is imperative for the future educational development of this subject area.

As in other subject areas, the main focus of teaching IB and IF is to enhance students' learning and knowledge of this field by covering its theories and applications. Depending upon the level of delivery. the themes can be introductory, intermediate or advanced. Students are expected to have the correct progression between one level of study and another.

My role as a lecturer is to guide and direct students in their learning, and to enhance their intellectual capabilities in the field of IB and IF. As Skelton (2005) noted, the experience and context in which the subject area is delivered have direct influence on the form of intellectual input to the students' learning. This is attained by making sure that students are exposed to the key theories of the subject area and allowing the necessary connections to the real world of IF.

Students are provided with the necessary support to realize their potential in the discipline. This is exercised through better interactions with the students, appreciating their diverse needs, designing creative learning activities and increasing the level of dialogue with their representatives. Talking to other lecturers who are teaching in the field provides further insights on finding more effective tools in dealing, for example, with weak students and those who lack motivation and interpersonal skills.

The learning model is student-centred. To ensure that the approach is effectively implemented, a number of study activities are given to students before and after the lessons are delivered. These includes reading peer-reviewed research papers and articles published by well-established business-based newspapers and magazines, such as the *Financial Times*, the *Wall Street Journal*, the *Banker* and the *Economist*. Students are also asked to go through a number of case studies and to read the relevant chapters of the essential and recommended textbooks. Besides, students are encouraged to visit the websites of major global stock markets and gather information on companies adhering to Islamic trading rules.

A high emphasis is placed on improving students' competencies in the field of IB and IF. The technical as well as the ethical aspects of the subject area knowledge are covered. Real-life examples are given to reinforce students' understanding of the themes covered in each lesson. These examples are taken from the current practice of IF institutions, conventional banks with IF windows, the different regulatory boards setting rules for IF contracts, and the businesses using the Islamic form of financing.

The teaching/learning strategy applied in the delivery of IB and IF lessons has been designed so as to ensure that the programme-level learning outcomes have been acquired. The delivery of classes draws upon two main learning approaches: lectures and seminars (one-a-and-a-half hour lecture followed by a one-and-a-half hour seminar). The lectures provide students with key opportunities to develop their 'critical thinking' about the IB and IF themes, and to impart the subject-specific knowledge. Topics are covered in a structured way and lecture notes are made available via the Blackboard system (the university virtual learning tool). Seminars are used to reinforce students' understanding of concepts highlighted in the lecture by using a problem-based learning approach.

Problem solving and mini-case scenarios are done in groups and individually. The outlines for case studies are given out in advance to students and they are also made available on the module Blackboard site.

The students' learning experience focuses on four main areas: (a) acquiring knowledge of IB and IF; (b) critical evaluation of tools and concepts existing in this field; (c) application of the methods adopted in the subject area; and (d) reflection on the results obtained from real-case study scenarios, which lead to the acquisition of further knowledge and, then, start the process again (see Kolb, 1982). This learning model enables students to reflect on their knowledge and to judge their actions based on what they have learnt. The model also allows students to use their intellectual thinking and to challenge their own ideas and others' in their decision making. The result is a lifelong learning experience with positive effects on students' skills and later performance in the workplace.

The content of materials used in the delivery of the sessions takes into account the international context of the subject area and student diversity. There are extensive interactions taking place between the home and overseas students, which enable them to improve their self-confidence and to have a better appreciation of the socio-cultural dimensions underpinning this field. This is compatible with the 'universal teaching strategies' described by Sanderson (2011: 6), who emphasizes the need to incorporate internationalization into the curriculum. In another study, Terenzini, Theophilides and Lorang (1999) also argue that interaction among students as well as between students and faculty staff is the most important factor in furthering students' learning.

The teaching approach adopted in the study programme endorses the view of Mumford (1995) that learning takes place when students' knowledge of something has increased, or when they can do things that they were not able to do before. Therefore, the teaching style is set to accommodate different students' needs and to ensure that their learning objectives are fully met.

Students are encouraged to raise questions during the lectures and to discuss openly the theories of IB and IF. The lectures are organized in a way that provides students with the framework to guide them in their independent study and to reinforce their understanding of the subject area.

Students are asked to practise questions from the essential and recommended textbooks in order to test their understanding of the themes covered in the lectures and to deepen their intellectual thinking about the field of IB and IF. In the module outline. students are instructed to devote sufficient private study time in addition to the programme's formal lecture and seminar sessions. As a standard practice, students are asked to allocate a minimum of two hours of their private time for every one hour of face-to-face teaching. Students' effort and preparation are well documented in the current literature on higher education for their direct link with students' achievement and quality of education as they enhance their level of confidence and participation when it comes to group discussions (see Fassinger, 1995; Tinto, 1997; Weaver and Qi, 2005).

As part of encouraging students' self-learning management, the module outline booklet contains a section advising them to make full use of learning facilities available in the University including library, financial databases such as data stream, FAME and Bloomberg, and other online learning resources (i.e. e-journals, e-books). These learning facilities contain valuable information with direct relevance to the field of IB and IF. Students are also given the opportunity to seek clarifications on their further reading from online materials.

As many terms used in the field of IB and IF originate in the Arabic language, students are asked to familiarize themselves with each term and also to understand their equivalent names in English. Students are asked to use the glossary given in IF textbooks for non-English finance-related words and have a clear understanding of their definitions.

Students are made aware that the topics covered in the field of IB and IF are interrelated and should be used as an integrated part to make an informed decision. Therefore, it is essential that they have very good insights into each theme before proceeding to the next one. The topics are organized in the right sequence in order to ensure that the maximum learning benefits are attainted by students.

On a number of occasions, external speakers are invited to give presentations on the current issues and developments taking place in the field of IB and IF. These presentations provide an opportunity for students to ask questions to the industry experts and to acquire a better grasp of the subject area in terms of its unique characteristics and the challenges faced by the providers of IF solutions in the domestic and international markets.

Because the lessons on IB and IF are delivered as part of a Business degree, I take into account the programme skill matrix and ensure that this is fully incorporated into my teaching approach. Table 20.1 shows the skills developed in the lessons delivered in this subject area and their setting vis-à-vis Taught (T), Practised (P) and Assessed (A) benchmarks. It is evident from the table that teaching mainly focuses on the management of information and skills related to problem solving. Other skills are gained through the use of the University's other learning

Table 20.1 Cross-reference of skill indicators and subject benchmarks

Skill indicators	Taught (T), Practised (P) and Assessed (A) benchmarks
Self-evaluation	
– Self-awareness	P
– Self-motivation	P
– Critical analysis	TPA
– Challenge opinion	P
– Respond to feedback	P
– Reflect on own and others' functioning	P
Management of information	
– Information and data retrieval	TPA
– Creative and innovative thinking	PA
– Business awareness	TPA
– Research strategy	TPA
Autonomy	
– Ability to learn independently	P
– Management of own learning	P
– Time management	P
– Self-critical	P
Communication	
– Report writing	PA
– Oral communication	P
– Use of information technology	P
– Debating	P
– Consulting	TP
Problem solving	
– Application of methods/tools	TPA
– Identification of problem essentials	TPA
– Action planning	TPA
– Decision making	TPA

facilities, student interactions and self-evaluation, which are supported by the teaching guide for students.

In terms of the content covered in the lessons, the students are made aware of what makes IF different from conventional finance by introducing them to the concepts of *riba* (usury) and *gharar* (alea). This is supported by texts from the *Qur'an* and the sayings of the prophet Muhammad (peace-be-upon-him). Other issues such as the prohibition of *qimar* (gambling), *maysir* (game of chance) and investments in products such as tobacco, alcohol, pork, and conventional financial instruments are also discussed with the students.

Another important area that is viewed with the students is existing IF contracts including: *murabaha* (used for selling and buying of commodities); *mudarabah* (used in investment management); *musharakah* (Islamic form of partnership); *ijara* (equivalent of leasing under conventional finance); *sukuk* (Islamic form of bond); *takaful* (Islamic form of insurance); *Istisna* (contractual agreement allowing for the financing of manufacturing goods and commodities).

The teaching approach is fully informed by research as students are given articles in the field of IB and IF to read prior to lectures. Students are asked to summarize the key issues raised in each article and to synthesize and compare the interpretations given by different scholars based on their chosen research methods, philosophy and data.

Assessment methods and feedback

The main assessment methods used to test students' learning and knowledge of IB and IF are in the form of group coursework and end-of-module examination. The purpose of the group coursework assessment is to test the students' ability to interpret, analyse and evaluate relevant published financial information and intelligence on their chosen company and apply their knowledge of IF theory and applications. The purpose of the end-of-module examination is to assess students' individual ability to determine their wider knowledge of the field of IB and IF, including the ability to identify, interpret, critically analyse, evaluate and justify the arguments made on the themes covered in the assessment.

The method of feedback in the in-course assessment is a mixture of formative and summative feedback. Students receive comments on their ability to link theories of IB and IF to practice by applying what they have learnt and interpreting the financial data published by companies or financial institutions that follow Islamic business principles. Summative assessment feedback is used in the end of module examinations in which students are tested on their knowledge and understanding of the IB and IF themes covered in the module and given a score accordingly.

Reflection on Islamic banking and finance research projects supervision

There is consensus among researchers that the recent developments in higher education have shaped the way in which supervision of research projects is carried out (e.g. Conrad, 1999; Vilkinas, 2002). As a result, the pressure on supervisors has increased to comply with the changing research environment. This is no exception when supervising research projects or dissertations in the field of IB and IF. It is expected under the new academic milieu that supervisors have a clear understanding of their role in addressing the needs of their students at different stages of the research project (Acker, Hill and Black, 1994).

Beasley (1999) notes that supervisors need to possess good research knowledge as well as interpersonal and managerial skills in order to be effective in conducting the research process. Accordingly, the supervisors should be technical experts, innovators, resource generators, carers, and in some discipline team builders (Vilkinas, 2002). These qualities should be observed as required during each stage of the research project. Similarly, carrying out supervision in the IB and IF subject area requires specific theoretical and technical knowledge in order to be able to guide students through the various difficulties they face in setting their research questions, collecting the literature, devising the research methodology and analysing their study results. My experience shows that my role as a supervisor also extends to include examining and supporting the student(s) during their research investigation. However, there is clear variation in the extent of the role performed depending upon the need of the student being supervised.

Most students choose to apply qualitative research methods, such as interviews, due to lack of financial data on Islamic-based institutions and companies. Brew (2001) notes that the common view on research experience is based on the notion that research is driven by the nature of the discipline and methods used by the researchers. In line with this argument, Becher (1989) states that discipline is amongst the main factors that determine the research conceptions by supervisors as well as students.

Supervising a research project entails raising the level of awareness and interest of the students in the subject area. According to Sambrook, Stewart and Roberts (2008), the students' perceptions of research supervision are influenced by the research approach adopted by their supervisor(s). Applying a highly regulated or authoritarian approach makes students inclined to leave the research programme. Likewise, it is not advisable to implement a highly relaxed learning approach as this makes students receive less guidance from their supervisors (Phyältö, Stubb and Lonka, 2009). Therefore, an appropriate balance between the two approaches is required to create a better learning environment and reduce any dysfunctional behaviour by the research students.

The expectation gap between students and the supervisor

Understanding students' expectations is essential in every research discipline including IB and IF. Brew (2001: 276) identified four possible categories for how research is perceived: 'domino'; 'trading'; "layer"; and 'journey. There are clear differences in the ingredients that constitute each of these categories. In the domino model, research is viewed as a combination of several elements that can be combined in one form or another to test the research hypotheses or answer the research questions. The research strategy under this model entails subdividing the main research problem into a set of small related problems and applying a number of methods to resolve each of the sub-problems. Under the trading model, research is perceived as a social interaction between individuals who are involved in generating new ideas or carry out a number of research activities. In the layer model, researchers examine existing ideas and theories and make an attempt to add value into them. Corrections and explanations are made as necessary to the ideas in order to justify the research outcome. Therefore, new knowledge is not really discovered but rather based on an underlying understanding of such a phenomenon. Finally, in the journey model, the activities carried out by the researchers are considered to be directly impacting the way the research problems have been addressed. Hence, the fieldwork is considered to be highly significant under this model. In my experience of supervising students in the field of IB and IF, the domino and journey research models tend to dominate the way the research is carried out as the area is still not fully explored and the theoretical framework underpinning the discipline is also not well developed.

Studies investigating learning experience show that students' perceptions of learning vary from one set of circumstances to another (Ramsden, 1997, cited in Brew, 2001). The research supervisors and their students are also expected to behave differently when research circumstances change. Factors that would influence their behaviour include research culture, availability of facilities and support, teaching commitments and training programmes (Brew, 2001). These issues also apply to the supervision of IB and IF research projects. However, culture tends to be the most important factor with direct impact on students' perceptions when they undertake dissertations in the field of IB and IF, due to the influence of religion on students' perceptions of finance concepts and applications.

Kiley and Mullins's (2005: 254) survey shows three key parameters used by the majority of supervisors in identifying if the researcher is successful: (a) 'personal qualities'; (b) "research skills'; and (c) 'intellectual qualities'. These factors are equally important to students who choose their research topics in the field of IB and IF. However, the weighting of each factor varies from one student to another depending upon their educational background and whether the research methods applied to address the study aims and objectives are quantitative or qualitative.

Supervisors do share similar views on what students are lacking in order to become successful researchers including: working hard, stability, absence of the desired research skills, strong emotions and having wide interpretations of the ideas they are trying to explore or implement (Kiley and Mullins, 2005). To tackle these problems, supervisors interviewed by Kiley and Mullins note that they apply various strategies. Communication is amongst the preferred method used by supervisors to address the issues they have with their students. Examples of areas that supervisors would focus upon are students' commitment to their research, application of the appropriate standards and intellectual thinking to the research problems. Another technique used by some supervisors is asking students to work in groups with the aim that they share their own experiences. Some supervisors simply ask students to follow a specific research journey that they think makes the research project controllable and convenient. Leading by example is also used by a number of supervisors in helping the student acquire the desired research skills. This, usually, involves more time with the students as the supervisors react with extra care to the problems faced by the students. Other supervisors use the patterns occurring through the research project to identify the need of their students and provide the necessary support at each stage of the research programme. Some supervisors consider their strategy in line with the overall organization plan for the research courses. The approach I have followed myself with the students undertaking their research projects in the field of IB and IF entails offering the necessary support in terms of addressing students' questions and concerns, providing enough feedback on their drafts, and ensuring that they are progressing well with their research projects.

Wright, Murray and Geale (2007) adopt phenomenographic research methodology to explain how supervisors understand differently the role(s) of supervision. Their results reveal five groups of supervisors: (a) quality assurers; (b) supportive guiders; (c) research trainers; (d) mentors; and (e) knowledge enthusiasts. There is clear variation in the perceptions of each category of supervisors of what supervision means and the priorities they give during the research supervision process. Quality assurers concentrate on ensuring that the research project is completed on time and there are no major flaws in the thesis when submitted.

Therefore, they follow a structured approach focusing on giving proper guidelines to students at each stage of the research project. Students are expected to attend the scheduled meetings and provide justifications for every decision they make regarding their research methods and analyses. What is also vital for the quality assurers is that examiners are satisfied with the thesis, but publications can be produced later after the completion of the Ph.D. project. Supervisors who consider themselves as supportive guiders give more weight to the social aspects of their relationship with Doctoral students, such as communication, counselling and help. However, it is imperative for this group of supervisors that the students complete their Ph.D.s successfully. The third category of supervisors who regard themselves as research trainers see supervision as a means to develop students skills and research abilities to become qualified researchers. Thus, these supervisors focus more on giving extensive feedback and show students how to carry out a successful research investigation. For this group of supervisors, the student should have the right research qualities when the study programme is completed. Supervisors who are under the category of mentors see themselves as students' research partners and instructors. Hence they give more importance to learning, understanding and teamwork. There is also an emphasis on improving the morale of Ph.D. students by this group of supervisors. Finally, the knowledge-enthusiasts type of supervisor gives more value to furthering knowledge and initiating new insights within the area researched by the student. To achieve these outcomes, supervisors challenge students for their ideas, research tests and assumptions. However, it is evident from this group that pushing students hard for new insights may result in frustration by the students and therefore knowledge enthusiasts need to be selective about their students to avoid any disappointment during the research process.

The increase in the number of international students undertaking their Ph.D. programmes at Western universities, both inhouse or at a distance, has placed more responsibilities on supervisors who have to deal with students who come from cultures different to their own. On this concern, Pearson and Chatterjee (2004) note that the acceleration in higher-education commercialisation, which has led to a substantial increase in the number of international students applying for courses in the West, has resulted in more expectations from the individuals involved in the running of academic courses to meet the new demand for the higher education qualifications including Ph.D.s. The same phenomenon is experienced in the case of IB and IF research projects as most students who choose this field of study mainly originate overseas, coming from the Gulf region, Southeast Asia and North Africa.

Technological advances have their own effects on students' perceptions of the roles and responsibilities I undertake as a supervisor. For example, I always respond in a timely manner to students' queries using the mail system and other technological tools available via the University intranet site (i.e. Blackboard). This includes providing any necessary information, such as guidelines and notes, which students require to effectively carry out their research projects.

In terms of priorities given to the roles performed during the research supervision process I tend to give more attention to the role of knowledge creator as extensive feedback is provided on the theories and their implications for the research project undertaken by the student. Several interventions are made during each stage of the student's research project to address a number of issues related to student progress. For example, the students are asked to create propositions for the collected primary data and to outline the contribution made to the theoretical framework of the study.

I have realized that the tasks I carry out as part of my supervisory role are highly influenced by: (1) my own past experience, either as a Ph.D. student or as a supervisor; (2) my educational background; (3) and culture. The first factor seems to be the main driver for the way I supervise. On many occasions I have considered my ex-supervisor's approach in commenting on my thesis as a model to make suggestion on the drafts submitted by the students. Brew and Peseta (2004) presented similar views in their study on supervision practices in Australia.

The students' progress in their research projects appears to be substantially influenced by the views and recommendations I give to them during the face-to-face meetings. The students, however, responded better to suggestions given by the two supervisors on their drafts when the same line of thought or directions are given for example on how to improve the literature review, research methods or data analysis. To address this issue it has been decided that before the initial meeting with the Doctoral student, the first supervisor and myself discuss the comments in details and produce a joint report outlining the areas of strength and weaknesses for the submitted draft.

It is also learned that the extent and scope of the feedback given at each meeting has major implications for the students on how to address the various issues related to their research projects. Kolb (1982) agrees that feedback enhances the learning experience of the students, but it needs to be both useful and evocative. A more constructive feedback by the supervisor clearly helps the student better understand why a specific section of the dissertation is weak and what can be done to improve its content.

The students are given the chance to reflect on their own research investigation progress, to state their own views on the feedback received, and to ask questions on themes raised during the meeting. This proved to be appropriate at clarifying any issues that the students found difficult to understand in the first instance when reading my comments, or when they had misapprehended feedback provided on the work submitted. In line with this approach, Brown (2007) recommends that students should be allowed to reflect on their own work for the feedback to be more effective.

Interventions are also introduced to help students avoid duplications or unnecessary use of information in their research projects. This was particularly apparent in the literature review and primary data analyses sections. It was highly challenging for the students to address this issue in the first few drafts, but with more constructive feedback on how to include only relevant discussions and analyses the students usually make good progress in the later drafts.

Another area identified through personal reflection is the use of academic English in the students' early drafts. Advice is given to the students to read some of the textbooks outlining the approaches that should be followed in the writing of the literature review, methodology and data analyses. This proved to be useful as the students reflected on their own style of writing as well as correcting the structure, spelling and grammatical errors. The students also learned where to use the first and third person in their writing.

A further theme related to research projects' supervision is the level and shape of help that are given to students. Scholars agree that empowering the learner requires continuous encouragement from the educators (e.g. Maier and Warren, 2002). Students sometimes feel overwhelmed by the amount of work that needs to be done to address the comments made on their submitted drafts. Cheering up the students has been found to help them overcome these difficulties and become more independent and reflective, which are essential in the research training of individuals.

Another observation during my time as a supervisor has been that students are highly appreciative of the support received from myself and the supervisory team in the case of group supervision. On a number of occasions, students have admitted that external factors – such as family or health issues – have prevented them from accomplishing the revision of submitted drafts as scheduled. Good communication and counselling are therefore essential in making sure that students are not left alone when such problems occur. In line with this view, Sambrook, Stewart and Roberts (2008) stress creating a good environment for learning by supervisors.

Finally, it is found that students sometimes lose track of what needs to be achieved in relation to their research projects. To address this problem, students are asked to keep a record of all the comments received on their drafts and bring them to the subsequent meeting when further guidelines are given. The results obtained in the discussions held in each meeting enabled the students to critically evaluate their achievements against the targets set for them and to plan forward. This has also proved to be helpful at keeping students focused on their research projects.

Group Doctoral programme supervision

In this section the themes related to group supervision of Ph.D. programmes in the field of IB and IF are highlighted and examined. The first issue I have observed was the direct effect of my own and the first supervisor's length of experience in Ph.D. supervision on our views about matters arising in our meetings. Being a supervisor for a Doctoral student for the second time and working with a person who had many years of experience in Ph.D. programmes supervision led to rich discussions on how to direct the Doctoral student in his research project. I was mainly influenced by my past experience as a Ph.D. student and the supervision of my first Ph.D. student, but the first supervisor used his broad knowledge of dealing with many of previous Ph.D. students in addressing the various issues related to the student's progress.

Type of personality is the third concern with direct relevance to group supervision. Emilsson and Johnsson (2007) argue that supervision is influenced by the way supervisors relate to each other. It is apparent that my character and attitude as a person were different from those of the first supervisor. I have learned that I am more of a structured type of person and the first supervisor tends to place more criticism on the work of the student than myself. Looking into the implications of such style on the Doctoral student's progress, I came to realise, similarly to Gibbs's (1998) propositions, that an amalgamation of the two styles would be ideal when supervising Ph.D. research projects.

Additionally, I realised that the first supervisor was more inclined towards giving more time to the student in order to improve the content of the submitted drafts. This has made me reconsider my position in setting short deadlines for the student to carry out certain tasks, such as discussing the study results and improving the methodology section. In their research, Wright, Murray and Geale (2007) confirm the fact that supervisors have different views on the time needed for the students to accomplish their tasks, but all of them are geared towards the successful completion of the doctoral programme. In general, I came to conclude that on certain occasions it is better to give more time to the student to address the comments thoroughly.

My perceptions of what are acceptable in terms of research methods and analysis have also been reshaped as a result of the discussions held with the first supervisor. Being exposed to new thoughts in the research training courses has also inspired me to have a better understanding of what constitutes knowledge, which was implemented in my supervision of the doctoral student. On the same subject, Beasley (1999) notes that supervisors need to improve their research knowledge in order for them to meet the requirements of their doctoral students.

The method of making comments is similar between the first supervisor and myself. The remarks are electronically inserted into each draft submitted by the student. The doctoral student did not raise any issue on this matter as both supervisors gave an opportunity for the student to seek explanations on the comments made on his drafts during the face-to-face meetings. The student is also given room to ask questions on other matters related to his research project, such as data collection.

The final issue observed on group supervision is on the emails exchanged with the Ph.D. student. It is learned that sending comments by email has its own problems to the supervisory team as on a few occasions it resulted in students' misinterpretations of the supervisor's notes and suggested improvements made on the drafts. Therefore, it has been decided with the student that face-to-face meetings are to be used to address any unforeseen issues related to the information or comments sent to him by emails.

Implications of the reflective exercise on personal development

Many lessons have been learned from the reflective exercise, which directly influenced my understanding and approach to supervision. Challenging one's own ideas and practices makes the individual consider new learning tools and search for the most effective mechanisms of managing the supervision process. In the first instance, it is difficult to change the held assumptions and beliefs on what constitute the normal and right way of supervising students' research projects, but after careful evaluation of other methods of supervision and examination of their consequences new insights emerge.

An assessment of the incidents and issues arising prior, during and after each meeting with the students and other supervisors (in the case of the Ph.D. programme) has stimulated me as a supervisor to come up with solutions to matters being discussed. As a result, new information related to the observed problems is gathered and examined, leading to a better understanding of the tasks carried out by the supervisor and their limitations. Reflection has enhanced my interpersonal and communication skills due to becoming more receptive to criticism. Judging one's own thoughts and their implications makes the person give more attention to the quality of supervision offered to the students carrying out their research investigations in the field of IB and IF.

The reflective exercise allowed me to realize that my decisions as a supervisor are driven by various factors including: (a) own past experience as a Ph.D. student; (b) discussions with the students; (c) talks with other supervisors; (d) research interest and skills; (e) information gathered from academic sources; (f) skills attained during supervision of the research students' course; and (g) exchange of views with other scholars in the school and in the research events. However, the significance of influence varies depending upon the issue one aims at resolving with the students. In general, the first three factors tend to be the main facets impacting upon my approach to supervision.

Reflection has increased my awareness of learning from individuals with whom I am interacting during the supervision process. This is in line with Nuldén's (1997) constructivist model where the knowledge of others is considered to be valuable to the person's professional development. Looking for better options to carry out the supervision process effectively meant more active engagement with the students and the other supervisors in the case of group supervision. This has contributed to more trust between me as a supervisor, other supervisors and the students, which eventually has led to a better atmosphere for knowledge creation.

It is observed that my level of enthusiasm increased with reflection as new propositions to learning were tested. Trying to experiment with better ways to supervise the students during each stage of their research project has resulted in more discussions with them leading to better understanding of their research needs. However, due to time constraints, it has not always been possible to implement some of the ideas proposed in this reflective documentary, which proved to be obstructive.

Another point learned from the reflective exercise is the importance of considering social and cultural factors, particularly when dealing with international students. Emotions and attitudes towards heavy workload do play a part in how the students respond to the feedback received on their submitted drafts. In several meetings, the students showed high levels of stress due to an external pressure, such as having many commitments towards the family and work. Acker, Hill and Black (1994) agree with this observation and notes that supervising postgraduate projects is directly influenced by the change in attitude because of pressure to meet students' expectations.

At school and university level, the reflective exercise has enabled me to exchange my views and ideas with other supervisors, who have their research interest in the field of IB and IF, on what will be the best practice in the supervision of undergraduate, postgraduate and Ph.D. students. Besides, as noted in the third section previously, my beliefs and perceptions of the roles I am expected to carry out as a supervisor have been reshaped following the reflective exercise and the exchange of views with other course team members.

Conclusion

In this reflective commentary we have examined the key issues related to the teaching and supervision of research projects in the field of IB and IF. On the teaching side it is apparent that students are developing a number of skills in this subject area with some of them gained through face-to-face lessons and others through self-learning and evaluation. The teaching approach is student-centred and takes into account the different technologies available in the University, such as the Blackboard system.

On the supervision aspect, there is clear variation in the roles played during each stage of the students' research projects. Meeting students' expectations and needs is directly influenced by the type of research undertaken in the field of IB and IF, response to comments, and feedback given on students' drafts, discussions with the supervisory team in the case of group supervision, and external factors, such as those related to culture.

I suggest that further improvements be placed on students' engagement in their learning in relation to IB and IF themes. There is also a need for more materials to be made available by book publishers on this field of study. In terms of supervision, students are required to deepen their understanding of Islamic social and economic values and to avoid being immensely driven by culture. In general, the contribution to knowledge should be emphasised throughout the research project.

Acknowledgement

I would like to thank my colleague Bijan Hesni for his valuable comments on the early drafts of this chapter.

References

Acker, S., Hill, T. and Black, E. (1994) 'Thesis supervision in the social sciences: Managed or negotiated?' *Higher Education*, 28, 4, pp. 483–98.

Beasley, N. (1999) 'Staff development to support research supervision', in G. Wiskier and N. Sutcliffe (eds) *Good Practice in Postgraduate Supervision*, SEDA paper 106 (London: SEDA).

Becher, T. (1989) 'Academic tribes and territories: intellectual enquiry and the cultures of disciplines' (Buckingham: Open University Press).

Becher, T. (1994) *Academic Tribes and Territories* (Milton Keynes: SRHE and Open University Press).

Boyce, M. E. (1996) 'Organizational story and storytelling: A critical review', *Journal of Organizational Change Management*, 9, 5, pp. 5–26.

Brew, A. (2001) 'Conceptions of research: A phenomenographic study', *Studies in Higher Education*, 26, 3, pp. 271–85.

Brew, A. and Peseta, T. (2004) 'Changing postgraduate supervision practice: A programme to encourage learning through reflection and feedback', *Innovations in Education and Teaching International*, 41, 1, pp. 5–22.

Brown, J. (2007) 'Feedback: The student perspective', *Research in Post-Compulsory Education*, 12, 1, pp. 33–51.

Conrad, L. (1999) 'Contextualising postgraduate supervision to promote quality', in G. Wisker and N. Sutcliffe (eds) *Good Practice in Postgraduate Supervision* (London: SEDA), pp. 13–24.

Emilsson, U. M. and Johnsson, E. (2007) 'Supervision of supervisors: On developing supervision in postgraduate education', *Higher Education Research & Development*, 26, 2, pp. 163–79.

Fassinger, P. A. (1995) 'Professors' and students' perceptions of why students participate in class', *Teaching Sociology*, 24, 1, pp. 25–33.

Gibbs, G. (1998) 'What is the role of the supervisor of projects and dissertations?' (Chapter 5) in *Teaching in Higher Education: Theory and Evidence* (Milton Keynes: The Open University).

Gow, L. and Kember, D. (1993) 'Conceptions of teaching and their relationship to student learning', *British Journal of Educational Psychology*, 63, pp. 20–33.

Gray, D. E. (2007) 'Facilitating management learning: Developing critical reflection through reflective tools', *Management Learning*, 38, 5, pp. 495–517.

Høyrup, S. (2004) 'Reflection as a core process in organizational learning', *Journal of Workplace Learning*, 16, 8, pp. 442–54.

Kane R., Sandretto S. and Heath C. (2002) 'Telling Half the Story: A Critical Review of Research on the Teaching Beliefs and Practices of University Academics', *Review of Educational Research*, Summer 2002, 72, 2, pp. 177–228.

Kiley, M. and Mullins, G. (2005) 'Supervisors' conceptions of research: What are they?' *Scandinavian Journal of Educational Research*, 49, 3, pp. 245–62.

Kolb, D. A. (1982) *Experiential Learning: Experience as the Source of Learning and Development*, First edition (New Jersey: Prentice Hall).

Maier, P. and Warren, A. (2002) *Integrating Technology in Learning and Teaching: A Practical Guide for Educators* (London: Kogan Page).

Marsick, V. J. and Watkins, K. E. (1990) *Informal and Incidental Learning in the Workplace* (London: Routledge).

Moss, G. and Kubacki, K. (2007) 'Researchers in higher education: A neglected focus of study', *Journal of Further and Higher Education*, 31, 3, pp. 297–310.

Mumford, A. (1995) *Effective Learning* (London: Institute of Personnel and Development).

Nuldén, U. (1997) 'Designing environments for reflection and collaborative learning', The 9th Annual Convention and Conference of Australasian Association for Engineering Education, Ballarat, Australia, 14–17 December, pp. 325–9.

Pearson, C. A. L. and Chatterjee, S. R. (2004) 'Expectations and values of university students in transition: Evidence from an Australian classroom', *Journal of Management Education*, 28, 4, pp. 427–46.

Pyhältö, K., Stubb, J. and Lonka, K. (2009) 'Developing scholarly communities as learning environments for doctoral students', *International Journal for Academic Development*, 14, 3, pp. 221–32.

Raelin, J. A. (2001) 'Public reflection as the basis of learning', *Management Learning*, 32, 1, pp. 11–30.

Ramsden, P. (1997) 'The context of learning in academic departments', in F. Marton, D. Hounsell and N. Entwistle (eds) *The Experience of Learning: Implications for Teaching and Studying in Higher Education*, Second edition (Edinburgh: Scottish Academic Press), pp. 198–216.

Reynolds, M. (1999) 'Critical reflection and management education: Rehabilitating less hierarchical approaches', *Journal of Management Learning and Education*, 3, 4, pp. 27–47.

Sambrook, S., Stewart, J. and Roberts, C. (2008) 'Doctoral supervision ... a view from above, below and the middle!' *Journal of Further and Higher Education*, 32, 1, pp. 71–84.

Sanderson, G. (2011) 'Internationalisation and teaching in higher education, higher education research & development', 30, 5, pp. 661–76.

Skelton, A. (2005) *Understanding Teaching Excellence in Higher Education* (London: Routledge).

Terenzini, P. T., Theophilides, C. and Lorang, W. G. (1984) 'Influences on students' perceptions of their academic skill development during college', *Journal of Higher Education*, 55, 5, pp. 621–36.

Tinto, V. (1997) 'Classrooms as communities: Exploring the educational character of student persistence', *Journal of Higher Education*, 68, 6, pp. 599–623.

Varner, D. and Peck, S. P. (2003) 'Learning from learning journals: The benefits and challenges of using learning journal assignments', *Journal of Management Education*, 27, 1, pp. 52–77.

Vilkinas, T. (2002) 'The PhD Process: The Supervisor as Manager', *Education and Training*, 44, 3, pp. 129–37.

Weaver, R. R. and Qi, J. (2005) 'Classroom organization and participation: College students' perceptions', *The Journal of Higher Education*, 76, 5, pp. 570–601.

Weick, K. (2002) 'Puzzles in organizational learning: An exercise in disciplined imagination', *British Journal of Management*, 13, S2, pp. S7–S15.

Wright, A., Murray, J. P. and Geale, P. (2007) 'A phenomenographic study of what it means to supervise doctoral students', *Academy of Management Learning and Education*, 6, 4, pp. 458–74.

21
The Saudi-Spanish Centre for Islamic Economics and Finance at IE Business School

Ignacio de la Torre

In June 2011, the UK newspaper the *Financial Times* issued its first ranking of Master's in Finance programmes around the world. The IE Business School's (IEBS) Master's in Finance ranked second out of 30. A key element in this result was the professional progression of its students three years after graduation. Some of them did so because they had entered into the Islamic Finance (IF) industry.

Why have some IEBS students joined the IF world? We decided to include IF in our core curriculum by 2008. The reasons were various: (a) the astonishing progression of the *sukuk* market; (b) the need for qualified professionals in this field; (c) the connections between IF and ethical investment; (d) the sound results of Islamic Banks in value at risk metrics during the credit crisis; and (v) the need to explore alternative pools of liquidity. I was fortunate to have in our faculty Professor Celia de Anca, who was very knowledgeable about the IF industry, and she was also the mastermind for the creation of the Saudi-Spanish Centre for Islamic Economics and Finance (SCIEF). She was very supportive of the idea, and when I proposed it to the vice dean the first question I got was: What is IF about? Actually I have faced this question many times in my life, and to answer it is a key reason why IEBS and King Abdulaziz University (KAU) started conversations to create a joint centre for Islamic Economics (IE) and IF, namely SCIEF, with the purpose of disseminating academic content of IF around Europe, and to establish bridges between the academic and the professional worlds, with the ultimate purpose of facilitating chief financial officers (CFOs) with the necessary awareness so that they might consider using Islamic instruments as a financial tool.

In a financial crisis credit world, it is very relevant to understand the roots of financial instability. As we know, light regulation and easy credit standards are at the heart of such a crisis. We created a mandatory course on financial stability. I pointed out the good performance of Islamic banks compared to their Western peers during 2008–9. Ultimately I concluded that if as a bank you consider your investments as closer than necessary to equity than to debt then your risk policy would benefit. Total securitization (i.e. disposal or risk) through mortgage-backed securities, a key fact at the centre of the crisis, would never have occurred with Islamic banks. Tim Geithner, secretary of the US Treasury during the Obama Administration, proposed some rules to prevent a future credit crisis. One of these rules is to forbid banks from selling 100 per cent of a credit; the first 3 per cent loss must be retained, as a key element to establish a link between lender and borrower. This is a fundamental feature in banking, as credit comes from the Latin verb *credere*, which means 'to believe', and it is impossible to believe in a borrower if you have sold your credit to someone living in Korea. These rules implemented in the US make debt instruments much closer to equity, in a suggestive parallel to the Islamic Banking (IB) industry.

The role of derivatives is another intriguing paradox linking both banking worlds. Should derivatives be used to hedge or to invest? In a pre-crisis world, banks would favour the latter, and their proprietary trading desks took massive positions in the credit derivative segment. Hedge funds identified a systemic weakness in some of these positions, mainly on the junior tranches of collateralized debt obligations, and inflicted huge losses on many banks. Even in 2012, JP Morgan, with a value at risk of $67 million, incurred a loss of $2.2 billion in credit derivatives, showing that the risk control metrics remained flawed, and that even four years after the crisis credit derivatives could prove difficult in hedging some credit positions. Paul Volcker, former chairman of the Federal Reserve, in 2009 advocated forbidding US banks to take proprietary positions (the 'Volcker rule'). The argument is that if a government implicitly supports a bank due to its deposits and its systemic relevance, then there is no way for the bank to use this implicit guarantee to play highly leveraged investment bets. How this rule is applied in practice is difficult as some banks argue that they need to take positions to create liquidity in markets in order to execute clients' orders. Yet the debate on using derivatives as a hedge or as trade is also at the heart of the debate between Islamic banks and conventional ones. My view is that, through regulation, large commercial banks will be prevented from using derivatives as a trading tool, and, again, such a movement will make Western banks much closer to Islamic ones.

At the end of 2010 we were glad to see a large US corporation, GE, issuing a *sukuk*. This fact confirmed that we were moving in the right direction. Our Centre did some research and finally published a case study on this *sukuk*, one that is and will continue to be used by many of our Finance students, and will hopefully set the basis for a future generation of financiers knowledgeable about the emergence of this asset class.

King Abdulaziz University and IEBS took a brave decision to make SCIEF a reality. SCIEF aims to leverage the experience of KAU and IEBS, to enhance IF awareness and knowledge among Spanish and international businesses, state authorities and other interested parties, with the objective of becoming the leading IF centre in Europe. SCIEF rests upon four main pillars:

1. Education – courses in IF
2. Research – cases, theses, papers
3. Executive training – contemporary IF and regulatory issues
4. International awareness – think-tank in IF and sustainable finance.

SCIEF has been and continues to work on being 'electronically oriented' in most of its activities: online training, blogs, e-case studies etc., with a wide use of the online education platform of IEBS and KAU.

Hopefully, as we succeed in our tasks in the future, it will only be a minority of people who asks the question: What is IF?

22
Conclusion

Ahmed Belouafi, Abderrazak Belabes and Cristina Trullols

In the recent past, knowledge and skill have become important 'weapons' that many emerging and developed economies are relying upon to stretch the capabilities of their economies against those of their rivals in a very competitive and complex world. 'Highly skilled' and 'knowledge-based' economy are the catchphrases that summarize the depth of the 'fierce' competitive battle driving contenders in this rivalry. For instance, in the year 2004, 'the UK government commissioned Sandy Leitch to undertake an independent review of the UK's long term skills needs' to identify the UK's optimal skills mix for 2020 to maximize economic growth, productivity and social justice, set out the balance of responsibility for achieving that skills profile and consider the policy framework required to support it.[1]

Indeed knowledge and skills are being recognized as 'factors of production'. Knowledge economy is defined as 'production and services based on knowledge-intensive activities that contribute to an accelerated pace of technological and scientific advance as well as equally rapid obsolescence'.[2] This definition argues that the production or creation of new ideas helps create better goods and services and organizational practices. Increasingly, key sectors of today's economies rely on the generation of knowledge. It is important to point out that in order to create change through knowledge and further help develop emerging economies, improvement in the workplace needs to occur. 'The key link between workplace reform and the knowledge economy is that new flexible practices are most commonly found in firms that compete in international product markets, emphasize quality, or have a technology that requires highly skilled workers'.[3] Obviously, Islamic Finance Education (IFE), at its own level, contributes to this knowledge economy in different ways. Increasingly, the IF industry is expanding in international markets, with the challenge of adapting *Shari'ah*-compliant products and transactions in these organizations. However, the expansion and application of IF internationally has proved possible and continues to evolve. This trend may provide evidence that IF programmes have an added value in the creation of 'factors of production'.

Moreover, in having more institutions that offer training and education to those interested in pursuing a career in this sector, students and professionals may evolve into highly skilled personnel who will further help in the advancement of the industry in the long run.

But all these expectations depend on the rigour, adequacy and quality of the educational system that offers such programmes and degrees. A good educational system with carefully designed programmes provides the underpinning 'pillars' for any industry to progress and properly foster the correctly trained personnel with appropriate skills and in-depth knowledge in IF.

In this volume we have been able to provide a general survey of the features, trends and developments of IFE around the globe. Besides, insiders at various institutions and higher educational establishments in the West have been able to present their experience and insights into the evolution of this discipline at their respective organizations.

All institutions described in this book have identified a number of trends and features, as well as several challenges and prospects that IFE has within Western higher education.

Trends and features

We have seen via the different programmes described in this book that Europe is a leading power in the provision of IFE programmes in the West. Concretely, the UK, followed by France, account for the two leading countries in the region offering these programmes. While English is the main teaching language, there are other languages in which IF is taught.

We have also seen that each and every institution has approached IF from a different angle. Each institution has its own orientation: some focus mainly on research with a legal orientation; others concentrate more on finance, management and in some cases on regional development (e.g. the Italian case that emphasizes the Mediterranean dimension). These research programmes include both young academics and high-level professionals in the field. Others offer IF Master's courses within their academic programmes, as well as centres dedicated to developing IF research, increasing international awareness and executive training. These centres' objectives serve to create awareness, and encourage increasing interaction between theory and practice. In addition, these institutions want to foster the promotion and integration of IF within national jurisdictions.

The challenges

Although much progress has been made within IF in the academic world, there remains plenty of ground to cover. As emerged clearly in the description of each experience within these universities, some of the challenges included the lack of properly qualified tutors in the domain and relevant supporting material in teaching the courses. Both of these issues reinforce one another, given that the lack of proper textbooks limits the knowledge of a tutor and so his or her ability to perform competently. In addition, the link between research outputs and the programmes' contents remains a challenge given: (a) the lack of an adequate methodology to the epistemological bases of the Islamic worldview; (b) low implication and impact on IF development and concurrence of multiple structures and definitions of the Islamic economic model.

Lastly, another important challenge is the great diversity that exists within all these academic programmes, where many suggest that a standardization of practices would be favourable to address this issue.

The prospects

Will these programmes remain, persist and progress? Or will some of them drop out? The available data on employment opportunities, and the approach followed by the industry, indicate that there might not be a 'big' demand on the supply side of IF.[4] However, for those who are already working in the field, opportunities exist to obtain further specialization with certificates and Master's degrees in order to deepen and update their knowledge of the development of IF practices. Another argument may state that graduates of IF from Western institutions looking for employment in Muslim countries will compete with not only those professionals in conventional banking but with those graduates from Islamic universities. A third argument can be drawn from the description of the experience of these institutions that IF enhances the internationalization and pluralism aspects in the different programmes being offered. And this may add a special 'flavour' to the 'ingredients' of established conventional programmes provided by respective institutions. According to a special report on 'Executive Education – Islamic Finance in the British Isles', one of the reasons universities are offering modules in IF and associated fields is to differentiate themselves from other programmes due to 'MBA inflation'. They are too many schools offering MBAs and too many students entering the labour market with an MBA diploma; therefore there is a clear need for differentiation and specialization. One way that schools can differentiate themselves is by offering IF. According to Professor Stefan Szymanski, associate dean of MBA programmes at Cass Business School (part of the City University London), 'global business schools have to be aware of these issues. I'm pleased we can go so far as having specialist electives in Islamic finance, which is an example of the need to adapt'.[5]

In addition, IF may enhance the multidisciplinary approach in the teaching of Finance, relating Finance and Economics to their social-science and cultural roots.

This multidisciplinary approach may be reinforced by the calls and pleas that have appeared in the aftermath of the international financial crisis, demanding a revision of the way Finance is being taught at business schools and Finance departments. For instance, Robert Shiller, during his speech to the Finance Graduates, mentions: 'Your training in financial theory, economics, mathematics, and statistics will serve you well. But your lessons in history, philosophy and literature will be just as important, because it is vital not only that you have the right tools, but also that you never lose sight of the purposes and overriding social goals of finance'.[6]

Despite the importance of all that has been said about the progress and prospects of IFE programmes in Western higher education, it is important to bear in mind the complexity and interconnectivity of the factors that affect the reality of the development of these initiatives on the ground. In this regard, let us provide some imaginative but possible scenarios that may develop in future:

1. The growth in IF programmes and/or courses in existing conventional degrees remains significant. This scenario may be possible for the latter (i.e. introduction of courses), as has been indicated by the actions of the top ten business schools.
2. IFE experiences a modest rise with a small increase. This may be the case for 'academic' and sponsored initiatives, but not for executive degrees and certificates.
3. IFE is stagnant. Given the 'scarcity' of properly qualified staff in most institutions, establishing more degrees may come to a standstill.

The difficulty of starting some initiatives, as indicated further, may provide evidence for this scenario.

4. IFE witnesses a decline. This scenario is also plausible given the fact that most, if not all, degrees are executive. And the continuity of such initiatives depend upon the demand (i.e. of learners) side of the educational process. This case is not confined to IF, but affects also conventional finance as illustrated further.

In what follows, various incidents are recalled to provide the reader with more evidence relating to the previous scenarios:

1. Closure of the first postgraduate programme in Islamic Economics, Banking and Finance offered by Loughborough University, for five years (1996–2000), shows that the sustainability of a programme depends on several factors including the existence of a host higher education institution, reliable and adequate funding and an academic personality with a duty to ensure education continuity and progress. Moreover, some programmes, like the Master's in Mediterranean and Arab Finance and Banking of Sapienza – Università di Roma, have been announced for a while but have not yet been initiated due to lack of specialist tutors or learners' demand.

2. Lastly, the announcement by the University Paris Dauphine of the temporary closure, in 2009, of its famous Master's '203', specializing in quantitative analysis and trading, and launch, in the same year, of an executive Master's in Islamic Finance must be interpreted more as an invitation to the reflection on the evolution of financial education in an uncertain environment, and not as a 'victory' for IF over its conventional counterpart. This reflection could contribute towards a better understanding of the reasons for which some programmes continue and renew themselves, while others disappear or lose their force. The sustainability of a programme depends primarily on the capabilities of its financial, human and material resources, which implies a clear division of duties and responsibilities through a competitive information system and proactive risk management.

Finally, we must stress that while IF programmes have made significant progress in Western higher education over the last few years, that pace is unlikely to continue. In order to have sustainable programmes, attention should be given to collaborative initiatives between Western and Muslim institutions, or maybe for governments to establish well-grounded programmes in fundamental and applied research relating to alternative finance as the world continues to sink in the mess of turbulent financial episodes. 'Alternative' is used here to cover a broader spectrum of practices and is therefore not limited to IF. We believe that interaction between the various forms of alternative finance is vitally important to promote good practices and exchange ideas in an open intellectual exercise, not in a dogmatic or 'preaching' manner.

Notes

1. webarchive.nationalarchives.gov.uk
2. Powell, W. W. and Snellman, K. (2004) 'The knowledge economy', *Annual Review of Sociology*, 30, pp. 199–220.
3. Ibid.
4. Wilson R. (2009) 'Islamic Finance in Europe', *Banca D'Italai, Seminar on Islamic Finance*, Rome 11th November 2009, www.bancaditalia.it/ studiricerche/.../2009/islamic_finance/.../Wilson
5. 'Executive education – Islamic finance in the British Isles', http://www. executive-magazine.com/get article.php?article=10916
6. http://www.project-syndicate.org/commentary/my-speech-to-the-finance-graduates

Index

Printed and bound in the United States of America